Orphans and Destitute Children
in the Late Ottoman Empire

Gender, Culture, and Politics in the Middle East
miriam cooke, Simona Sharoni, *and* Suad Joseph,
Series Editors

Orphans *and* Destitute Children
in the
Late Ottoman Empire

NAZAN MAKSUDYAN

SYRACUSE UNIVERSITY PRESS

First Edition 2014

14 15 16 17 18 19   6 5 4 3 2 1

∞ The paper used in this publication meets the minimum requirements of the American National Standard for Information Sciences—Permanence of Paper for Printed Library Materials, ANSI Z39.48-1992.

For a listing of books published and distributed by Syracuse University Press, visit www.SyracuseUniversityPress.syr.edu.

ISBN: 978-0-8156-3318-1 (cloth)   978-0-8156-5297-7 (e-book)

Library of Congress Cataloging-in-Publication Data

Maksudyan, Nazan, 1977–
    Orphans and destitute children in the late Ottoman Empire / Nazan Maksudyan. — First edition.
        pages cm. — (Gender, culture, and politics in the Middle East)
    Includes bibliographical references and index.
    ISBN 978-0-8156-3318-1 (cloth : alkaline paper) — ISBN 978-0-8156-5297-7 (ebook)
1. Orphans—Turkey—History—19th century.   2. Poor children—Turkey—History—19th century.   3. Abandoned children—Turkey—History—19th century.   4. Foster children—Turkey—History—19th century.   5. Poor girls—Turkey—History—19th century.   6. Armenians—Turkey—Social conditions—19th century.   7. Orphanages—Turkey—History—19th century.   8. Social change—Turkey—History—19th century.   9. Turkey—Social conditions—19th century.   10. Turkey—Social policy.   I. Title.
    HV1276.7.M35 2014
    362.730956'09034—dc23   2014029935

Manufactured in the United States of America

To my Great-Grandmother Antaram,
who resisted wilting in a cruel world that orphaned her,
and who had the courage and strength to start life anew.

And to my son, Ara Fikret,
I hope he is enjoying a happy childhood.

Nazan Maksudyan is an assistant professor in the Department of Social Sciences at Istanbul Kemerburgaz University. Educated at Boğaziçi University and Sabanci University (Istanbul), where she earned her doctorate, Maksudyan was an Alexander von Humboldt Foundation Research Fellow for postdoctoral research between 2009 and 2012 at Zentrum Moderner Orient (ZMO), Berlin. She has published several articles on the social, cultural, and economic history of children and youth in the late Ottoman Empire, particularly on children with precarious means. Her essay "Foster-Daughter or Servant, Charity or Abuse: Beslemes in the Late Ottoman Empire" appeared in the *Journal of Historical Sociology* 21 in 2008; and her article "Orphans, Cities, and the State: Vocational Orphanages (Islahhanes) and 'Reform' in the Late Ottoman Urban Space" appeared in *IJMES* 43 in 2011.

Contents

Illustrations

Tables

Acknowledgments

ALTHOUGH I OWE MUCH to several scholars, former professors, friends, and colleagues, my first debt is to the members of my small, tight-knit family, where I found permanent encouragement, love, and patience. They made me the person that I am. Without them I would not have the strength, self-esteem, and hope to accomplish the writing of this book. My dearest parents, Vartan and Meri; my favorite and only sister, Sibel; and my beloved husband, Ali, always showed their continuous appreciation, belief, and support for my work. Their happiness is my greatest comfort.

Gratitude of another kind goes to those institutions that have supported my research and writing. I am thankful to Wissenschaftskolleg zu Berlin for the postdoctoral fellowship that I was granted in the 2009–2010 academic year as part of their program, "Europe in the Middle East—The Middle East in Europe (EUME)." Special thanks to Georges Khalil, not only for organizing a well-conducted seminar program but also for his efforts to integrate us fellows into German academia and local networks. I am also indebted to Zentrum Moderner Orient (ZMO) for hosting me during my research stay in Berlin. I profited greatly from the productive academic environment at the institute along with the insights and knowledge of my colleagues there, especially Ulrike Freitag, Nora Lafi, Florian Riedler, Dyala Hamzah, and Yasmeen Sabah Hanoosh. Thanks as well to the École des Hautes Études en Sciences Sociales (ÉHÉSS, Paris), for offering me a researcher position in the 2006–2007 academic year to pursue my researches in France, and also to François Georgeon, who, with his impressive and inspiring knowledge and direction, helped me find my way in a labyrinth of sources, archives, and libraries.

Several colleagues and friends agreed to read earlier versions of the book, in whole or part, and commented efficaciously on them. Several others generously shared their erudition and expertise at crucial times when I longed for advice and guidance. I particularly feel indebted to S. Akşin Somel, Iris Agmon, Beth Baron, Suraiya Faroqhi, Hakan Y. Erdem, Cemil Koçak, Nadir Özbek, Halil Berktay, Kathryn R. Libal, Méropi Anastassiadou-Dumont, Vangelis Kechriotis, Malte Fuhrmann, Fatma Müge Göçek, Julia Phillips Cohen, Ferhunde Özbay, Marjatta Rahikainen, Karen Sanchez-Eppler, Inger Marie Okkenhaug, Selim Deringil, Keith David Watenpaugh, Benjamin Fortna, Martin Stokes, Metin Kunt, Pablo Sánchez León, Fikret Adanır, Tülay Artan, Leyla Neyzi, Oktay Özel, H. Şükrü Ilıcak, Ekin Tuşalp Atiyas, Hülya Adak, Ayşe Gül Altınay, Edhem Eldem, Arzu Öztürkmen, Meltem Toksöz, Cengiz Kırlı, Zafer Yenal, Christoph Herzog, Anny Bakalian, Biriz Berksoy, Fulya Apaydın, and Erdal Kaynar.

I also thank my close circle of friends, who, during a long and lonely process, have helped me write this book in ways that even I am not aware of. I am especially grateful to Gökçe Akyürek, Seçil Alabucak, Başak Deniz Özdoğan, Susanne zur Nieden, and Maika Leffers.

Finally, my warmest compliments to the city of Berlin, where I worked with exceptional productivity and a true peace of mind.

A Note on Transliteration

THROUGHOUT THE BOOK I have used the anglicized versions of most Ottoman Turkish and Arabic words rather than writing them in italics or transliterating them, the criterion being inclusion in the *Merriam-Webster English Dictionary*. Hence, I use agha, bey, ghazi, mufti, pasha, sharia, ulema, vizier, wakf—but efendi instead of effendi and kadi instead of cadi. In place names I follow English spellings as well, except for place names that constitute part of the name of a book or a publisher in the footnotes; hence, Istanbul but İstanbul Üniversitesi.

Transliterations are based on a modified version of the system used in the *International Journal of Middle East Studies* (IJMES). Modern Turkish orthography has been used for the transliteration of Ottoman Turkish with certain modifications. In the main body of the text and in the identification of authors, I avoid all the diacritics associated with transliteration, namely underdots on consonants and macrons on vowels. The exception is the use of 'ayns and hamzas when they appear in the middle of a word, which I indicate with an apostrophe [']. Since modern Turkish no longer uses hatted vowels (â), I also omitted most of them from the text.

Transliterated Words and Phrases

besleme: foster daughter

beytülmal: public treasury

bint: the daughter of

çırak: apprentice

Darülaceze: poorhouse of Istanbul

Düstur: compilation of regulations

evlad-ı zina: illegitimate children

evlat: children (sometimes also used in singular)

evlatlık, ahiretlik, ahiret evladı, manevi evlat, evlad-ı maneviyye: foster child

eytam: orphan

eytamhane: orphanage

gayr-ı meşru: illegitimate

Hanefi: Islamic school of law

ibn: the son of

ırza: to breast-feed, to nurse

ırzahane: foundling home, nursing home

ıslah: reform

ıslahhane: vocational state orphanage (lit., "reform house")

istihdam: employment

kalfa: journeyman

kaymakam: head official of a district

kuruş: piaster

lakit, lakita (f.): foundling

lira: Ottoman gold coin

maaş: salary, wage

mekteb-i sanayi: vocational school

millet: officially recognized non-Muslim communities of the Ottoman Empire

muhacir: refugee, immigrant

muhtar: headman of district

mutasarrıf: local administrator

mütebenna: adoptive parents

mütebenni: adopted child

nafaka: maintenance, monthly alimony (of a child)

neseb: lineage, descent

nizamname: regulation

örf: customary law

piç: bastard (slang)

piçhane: bastard home

Salname: Ottoman yearbook

sicil: court case registration

tahrir: Ottoman census

Tanzimat: lit., reorganizations; an institutionalized process of

modernization that officially
began in 1839
tebenni: formal adoption
tellal: broker, middleman
veled: child
veli: guardian

Viladethane: birth/maternity clinic
vilayet: Ottoman province
yetim: orphan
zabtiye: police department, police
officer, ministry of police

Orphans and Destitute Children
in the Late Ottoman Empire

Introduction

Ottoman Children's "History from Below"

ACCORDING TO an orally transmitted family history, Haşim was born in the early 1890s somewhere in Rumelia.[1] Unlike many children in this book, his parents were still alive and his basic needs were met. Still, he ran away from home as a six- or seven-year-old lad because his parents were reluctant to send him to school, despite his eagerness and insistence. As a solution, Haşim found a boat going to Istanbul at the port and hid in one of the coalyards. According to the story, when the ship arrived, he immediately went to Yıldız Palace and told the soldier at the gate to take him to the sultan. He said: "I want to be educated, I beg you to enroll me in school." Curiously convinced, the soldier took the boy to the presence of his highness, Sultan Abdülhamid II. Showing a real interest in the boy, the sultan asked questions about his life and family. Haşim said that his great-great-grandfather, way back in his lineage, was Bayraktar Deli Hüseyin, who fought at the naval battle of Preveza in 1538. Then, he kept telling all he knew about the war—about Hayreddin Barbarossa, Andrea Doria, and so on. Charming the Ottoman sultan with his knowledge of glorious Ottoman history, Haşim was assured that he would be educated thanks to the benevolence of the sultan toward orphans and destitute children. Consequently, Abdülhamid opened a vocational school for destitute children, and Haşim was registered there to be trained as a foundryman.

A peculiarly similar story is also frequently repeated in a number of official documents in the Prime Ministry's Ottoman Archives. According to this account, one day the sultan was returning from *Hırka-ı Şerif*

1

Mosque in Fatih. On the Galata Bridge, and in other accounts simply on his way back to the palace, the sultan saw a number of vagrant boys idly strolling in the streets. Annoyed and depressed at the sight, he talked to a few of them and asked why they were wandering vainly. One little boy said that he was poor and destitute and lacked the necessary education and skills to lead him into a productive livelihood. Later, upon returning to his private chamber, the sultan decided to open an educational institution for needy children.[2] This story was mostly recounted as the origin myth of Abdülhamid II's Imperial Orphanage (*Dar'ülhayr-ı Ali*), which was opened in 1903 along the lines of a vocational school.

It is curious that the implementation of a serious imperial educational policy has been referred to the active agency of ordinary children in both an oral account and several archival documents. Historians, however, do not traditionally interpret Abdülhamid II's charity and welfare policies toward children as a "bottom-up" development or from the perspective of "history from below." Historical writing is often imprisoned by a rigid conception of what is important and what is not. For most historians, wars, statesmen, and treaties are considered important. While they fix their gaze toward the *significant*, what is regarded as *insignificant* remains in the background, with a capacity to change the world secretly and by surprise. The story of a destitute boy convincing the sultan to invest more on orphans' education points not only to the neglected role of children in the making (and writing) of history but also to their increased political significance in the period that is under analysis in this book.

Though its scope has been enlarged, historical writing is still notorious for its disregard and ignorance of a wide range of social groups. Even today children are almost invisible in historical writing, as women, working classes, blacks, or ethnic minorities were disregarded earlier. Children's history—their presence, experiences, and testimonies—is not considered to have historical significance, so children are left out of the narrative. Their viewpoint as actors shaping important processes, as partakers of significant events, and as witnesses of historic moments is simply overlooked. Historical and cultural studies tend to discount childhood as a significant site of analysis because children are primarily seen as passive receptors. They are rarely recognized as cultural presences.

Since childhood is legally and biologically understood as a period of dependency, it is usually easy to dismiss children as historical actors. The very belief in children's specialness—their vulnerability, innocence, and ignorance—also marks childhood as historically irrelevant. Children are often presented as inchoate and not yet fully human so that the figure of the child demarcates the boundaries of personhood, a limiting case for agency, voice, or enfranchisement.[3]

The crucial matter concerns the politics of age relations, which is instructed by adultism. In this view children are seen as naturally "less" than adults, insofar as they are in a state of becoming (adults), rather than being seen as complete and identifiable persons.[4] Consequently, in much of the published work to date, children have been denied both a voice and a rational standpoint (which is an essential feature of human identity).[5] Changes in the status of children have usually been considered with reference to what they indicate about shifts in social priorities—that is, changes in the desires and experiences of adults. Much of the insightful work on children has seen childhood essentially as a discourse among adults. The study of childhood is inevitably enmeshed in this politics. All accounts of childhood are structured by the impossibility of fully separating children from adult desires and control.[6]

Recently, children's studies became a separate field of inquiry, incorporating work in anthropology, education, history, literature, medicine, philosophy, popular culture, psychology, and sociology. New efforts to construct a proper historical identity for children, one that recognizes their "agency," are especially indebted to feminist historical scholarship. Historians of children and childhood learned a lot from their effort "to make women a focus of inquiry, a subject of the story, an agent in the narrative" and to construct them "as historical subjects."[7] Although sex and age differences cannot be seen as directly analogous, similarities between them suggest that studies based on age (or generations) suffer from the same sort of naturalist assumptions (in denial of socially constructed nature or relations), such that historical work predominantly reinforces and perpetuates the normalization of adult–child power inequalities. Therefore, the concepts of power, conflict, and contest are crucial in writing about children as social actors.

Children need to be viewed as capable of social action. Since person-hood is always associated with adulthood, children are excluded from the definition of rational capacity and thus denied agency. Yet, the agency of "ordinary people" has laid the foundations for a "new" social history. Recently scholars have tried to understand how children, and youth in particular, have exercised historical agency in the past. Within these per-spectives, children are viewed not merely as appendages to adult expe-riences but as individuals who participated in and helped to shape the history of their time. There is a greater degree of commitment to children as social beings in possession of their own standpoint.

This book, focusing on orphans and destitute children in the late Otto-man Empire, strives to go beyond the "rigid boundaries of importance" for Ottoman history and regard children as "significant"—as part of the history. The research behind attempts to see and listen to these habitually ignored and essentially invisible and voiceless actors. My work is based on the conviction that introducing a new angle of observation, that of children, into unexplored or even previously explored fields of study can expose and enlighten hidden or unseen parts of the phenomena. Voices of chil-dren in general—and, for purposes of this book, voices of orphan and des-titute children in particular—can be treated as newly discovered sources or belated testimonies for writing a nuanced and alternative history of the late Ottoman era.

In parallel with a growing interest in the meaning of childhood during earlier time periods, the last three decades have produced discrete histori-cal studies that provide richly detailed accounts of the lives of European and American children. Compared to many other fields of social history, the literature on the history of Ottoman children remains scanty. The researches on children and youth in the Ottoman Empire to date would not exceed a few articles and books.[8]

The growth of interest in the history of children and youth is, in part, due to the development of other related fields of research. Demography was one of the first domains that provided significant opportunities for the writing of a social history of childhood. Historical-demographic and micro-analyses based on such diverse issues as birth statistics, mortality rates, illegitimate births, and the prevalence of child labor offered opportunities of study. Statistical information and studies on the Ottoman Empire remain scarce, but urban centers like Istanbul have been studied in greater detail.[9] Monographs, including dissertations and books from an urban history perspective, which analyze the court records (*sicils*) of a single city for limited time periods, also provide numerical data on the number of children in households, the average age of orphans, and workshops in which children were employed as apprentices (*çırak*).[10] Legal historians and also those focusing on court records in general have productively studied seventeenth- and eighteenth-century Islamic legal rulings outlining norms for custody of children who had not reached puberty, acceptable practices for "child marriages," and the question of criminal liability for crimes committed by children who had not reached "the age of reason."[11]

Social historians working on gender and the family have provided the greatest insight into understanding childhood in Ottoman society during the period from the nineteenth to early twentieth centuries.[12] The more established field of family history has contributed to the development of literature on the history of childhood through common themes and interests. The study of family structures and of patterns underlying the organization and division of labor within the family raises numerous questions that have been studied from the perspective of history of childhood. The nature and actual time period of childhood and adolescence have also been subjects of considerable research. The efforts of feminist scholars to give voice to a traditionally repressed group paved the way for other previously unheard-from members of households to take the floor. The emergence and growth of scholarly work on "children as social actors" is theoretically indebted to this body of knowledge.

As an outcome of the development of neighboring disciplines, childhood studies became a part of Ottoman and Turkish Republican history as an independent area of research in the 1990s. Approaches that combined history with sociology, education, and social anthropology proved extremely fertile for the history of childhood. Bekir Onur, a specialist in educational sciences, published much of the scarce literature on the issue. He contributed to the development of the history of childhood as a research field through both compilations and original research.[13] Leaning upon a rich secondary literature from various disciplines, Onur's source material usually comes from the memoir genre. Mine Tan also works on the history of childhood in the Republican era.[14] Her studies are especially important in methodological terms since, in addition to published material, she relies on oral history. Tan argues that this method offers an opportunity to contact "common people" and their versions of history. Although both these scholars' primary concern is to write the history of Early Republican children, they provide remarkable information on Ottoman children.

Cüneyd Okay, on the other hand, focuses on the history of childhood in the nineteenth- and early-twentieth-century Ottoman Empire, largely on the Second Constitutional Period.[15] The issues he has dealt with are changes in the conception of childhood in the late Ottoman Empire and the instrumentalization of children for nationalistic aims. Though strongly underlining the significance of memoirs, Okay's works mostly rely on children's magazines of the period, which bring to light original primary material on the characterization of "ideal children" by contemporary political cadres and intellectuals. The bibliography of Ottoman Turkish (Arabic script) children's periodicals that he has compiled is an invaluable source for many researchers.

The approach and objectives of these detailed childhood studies can be summarized roughly under two categories. First, they are written with a developmentalist attitude, taking childhood as a period in the life-cycle of every human being. In that sense, childhood is narrated as a duration with different phases, such as infancy, weaning, circumcision, and going to school. Accordingly, these studies contain descriptive data on the growth of Ottoman/Turkish children from birth to puberty. Failing to consider children as historically active agents, these studies represent them as "becomings" who grow into adulthood (as transitional beings) and as objects who can be understood by simply activating images derived from developmental psychology and the sociology of socialization. Although this sort of information is valuable and rich in detail, enclosing the history of *childhood* within the frame of a life period actually limits the possibilities and richness that can be attained by studying *children*.

The second characteristic of studies on Ottoman/Turkish children and childhood is that they lean predominantly upon Philippe Ariès's *Centuries of Childhood* (1962). This school of historiography argues that there was no concept of childhood before "modernity." Before then, parents were distant and unapproachable beings and children were considered inferior, their demands and needs not sufficiently valuable to be met. Yet, a very serious transition took place in the modern era as the family became child-oriented and affectionate, with a permissive mode of child care and recognition of the uniqueness of each child.[16] Following Ariès, the abovementioned studies mainly focus on the transformation of the concept of childhood.[17] These studies argue that at any one time throughout society there is a dominant and overreaching notion of childhood, albeit one that encompasses a variety of perceptions. Scholars such as Onur, Tan, and Okay emphasize their and the field's indebtedness to Ariès and consequently focus on the concept of childhood rather than on the lives of children.

Theory on the "discovery of childhood" emphasizes the differences experienced in child-rearing practices, parent–child relations, forms of affection, and disciplining. A new generation of scholars, working with different materials and on different periods, have all in different ways rebutted the assertions of Ariès. They have gathered copious evidence to show that there was a concept of childhood in earlier centuries as well.[18] Taking either the *Tanzimat* or the Republican era as the crucial breakpoint, childhood studies in Turkey still rely on the "discovery" theory. It has been argued that the social meaning of childhood among Ottoman urban elites was undergoing a significant transformation. Childhood was sentimentalized and idealized. The middle classes from various backgrounds started to realize the existence of different products for children, including foods, clothing, toys, books, and other goods. Publications that primarily targeted parents emphasized "modern" child-rearing practices and through consumer advertising communicated new ideals of health and robustness in children.[19]

Works on the "discovery of childhood" dismiss another strong historiographical school emphasizing the worsening of conditions for children in modern times. Relying on the theoretical legacy of Michel Foucault, scholars such as Robert Jütte, Erving Goffman, David J. Rothman, and Jacques Donzelot emphasize the institutionalization of children under the inhumane disciplinary conditions of boarding schools, orphanages, and reformatories.[20] They argue that children were not objects of care in modern societies; on the contrary, they were kept under surveillance, disciplined, and indoctrinated.

In sum, the general weakness of Ottoman/Turkish childhood studies is their neglect of the historical activity of children as a part of social, economic, and political processes, while concentrating on the conception and cycle of childhood. Childhood is not only an idea in adult minds, nor is it solely a cultural construction. As people, children are active historical figures who deserve a history of their own. Children are social actors and informants in their own right. The experiences and viewpoints of children have an unexploited potential to open new horizons on many significant processes of the late Ottoman period, such as urbanization, industrialization, nationalism, and state-formation. Those fields of research have the potential to *liberate children from their childhood*.

The intricate relationships among children, nationalism, sports, and Boy Scouts in the late Ottoman and Early Republican periods constitute an important field in which children partially appear as actors.[21] In parallel with this field, some scholars have underlined the obsession of the founders of the Republic on the physical strength and health of Turkish children and youth who became symbols of the new nation.[22]

Another established and still growing area is the education, indoctrination, and socialization of children, who came to be conceived as future citizen-subjects deserving of special treatment.[23] Factors such as modern educational reforms and opportunities, which resulted to a large extent from the emerging rival nationalist movements threatening the integrity of the Ottoman lands, together with the rapidly growing number of missionary-sponsored schools, are analyzed in a detailed manner.[24] Other studies underlined the role of nationalist ideology, religious doctrine, gender roles and models, and militaristic/paternalistic idealizations in the formation of childhood identity.[25]

The growth of research on philanthropy, charity, and welfare is especially important for this book.[26] These studies provide invaluable perspectives on the significance of children for nineteenth-century phi-lanthropists—religious men, state officials, and missionaries. Imperial concern for portraying an image of benevolence and care for the popula-tion led the Ottoman authorities to create new ceremonies, institutions, and regulations that addressed child poverty, orphanhood, and mortal-ity in addition to other educational opportunities for children. From the perspective of philanthropy, children became more visible actors on the historical stage.

Numerous tenets of the social history of childhood in the Ottoman Empire are still waiting to be written. More research is needed to uncover the lives of children in rural areas, juvenile delinquency, class variations in urban environments, and continuities and differences between confes-sional and ethnic communities. The gendering of childhood in each of these realms also merits much greater attention. Within this still-under-developed field of the history of children and youth, marginalized chil-dren, working-class children, foundlings, orphans, and destitute children have attracted even less attention.

This book gives voice to destitute and orphaned children and lets them narrate their own versions of history. It directs attention toward previ-ously unnoticed yet essential aspects of the late Ottoman era and mod-ernization, since children were assigned significant roles in this period. Specifically, during the nineteenth century child-related concerns entered the agenda of the Ottoman intelligentsia and policymakers. In the mod-ern era, the ineluctable issues of children and childhood and how they functioned as relevant actors began to haunt adults. Child anxiety came to constitute a general trend of modernity, and by the 1870s it spread to all societies that perceived of themselves as part of that "modern and civiliz-ing world."[27] While levels of industrialization, literacy, urbanization, and other measures of modernization varied considerably from place to place, accompanying social values spread more rapidly and with greater chron-ological coincidence. Therefore, despite the discrepancies in economic or demographic indices with regards to France or Britain, Ottoman reform-ers and intellectuals developed similar concerns toward children insofar as they constructed their legitimacy from within the larger Western modernizing discourse of the period.

In addition to "concerned" discourses, newly emerging tools of governmentality were also directed at regulating the population and citizenry in a different way.[28] Late Ottoman modernization and centralization projects elicited the disciplinary implications of a modern state apparatus, which made use of microtechnologies of power in everyday social life. Forsaken members of the population, including poor and needy children, all of a sudden became important. Destitute children and orphans had incremental value, as questions of citizenship and identity construction redefined the "control" over children as a modernist project. However, they were not only objects of social control and discipline. Kent Schull's conceptualization of late Ottoman prisons as "laboratories of modernity" is a plausible perspective for understanding the elevated concern regarding children and youth.[29] Many of the pressing questions of modernity, such as administrative efficiency and centralization; economic reform and industrialization; new gender regimes; management of time and space; ethnic, religious, and national identities; and philanthropic state engagements were all reflected in discourses and policies regarding children in need.

The latter half of the nineteenth century witnessed the partial transformation of a communally segregated Ottoman society into a centrally administered polity. The multinational and decentralized empire was approximating to a centralized modern state. The attempts to "modernize" established regulations concerning population control with new administrative designs of governmentality challenged the customary autonomy of communal authorities. The central state could now penetrate into communal affairs and have a presence in its workings. Non-Muslim religious authorities felt threatened, for they were losing their right to self-governance.

Different interested parties, the state, non-Muslim communities, missionaries, and the bourgeois public started to see orphaned and destitute children through different lenses. The motivation and discourse, on the one hand, was based on the desire to save unfortunate children from the dangers to which they were prey. These dangers included losing or being alienated from one's ethnoreligious identity, being sold into slavery, sexual abuse and exploitation, juvenile criminality, prostitution, health problems, death, conversion, and apostasy. And it was not only children who were at risk. These unwanted phenomena would create new classes of children who would pose themselves as threats to the public in the future. The collection or "kidnapping" of abandoned children; the forced or inveigled emigration of little girls to urban centers or abroad; vagrant, idle, and begging children; juvenile crime in the cities; and missionaries' ambitions over massacre orphans were all dangers that several interested parties fought against, either with defensive or offensive strategies. The image of orphans and destitute children was that they were, first, endangered by the modernizing world they were being raised in; and, second, that they themselves were new dangers engendered by that world.

Still, a threat can always be turned into an opportunity. Dangerous children—foundlings, street children, refugees, or "unchaste" maidservants—can always be refashioned as laborious workers, loyal citizens, or staunch religious believers. In the case of abandoned children, the protagonists of chapter 1, there were both sanitary concerns—infants were either found dead in public places or they had enormously high mortality rates—and political stakes. The religious and civil status of foundlings became a realm of rivalry for the state, non-Muslim communities, municipal authorities, the police department, and missionaries at the same time. The policies or strategies created toward foundlings were not only about saving abandoned babies from perishing in the streets but also about strengthening communities, constructing a modern image through new institutions, or raising religious or political adherents.

Standard interpretations of the Ottoman reform era do not include less obvious actors, such as women, peasants, or children, as part of the historical account. The focus is on the state and statesmen—in other words, to adult men—while the rest of the society is simply discounted on the assumption that they are extrapolitical, namely insignificant, invisible non-actors. Contrary to the neglect of present-day historians, nineteenth-century adult opinion became well aware of the significance of children and reassessed their role within adult male politics. This was especially due to the new meanings and identities children acquired in their relations with provincial and municipal authorities, foreign missionaries,

religious and civil leaders of communities, and the state. As child philanthropy and child saving was embraced by large sections of the society, destitute children became a part of the political, economic, and social
agenda, both in material and discursive terms. They were no longer outside the historical scene. On the contrary, children gained channels for
being visible and loud. They assumed significant roles, which left traces in
the records. More than a hundred years later, it is possible to perceive how
their part was crucial in enforcing, challenging, or rewriting history. This
book suggests an alternative vista of Ottoman modernization from within
the viewpoint of orphans. Different aspects of Ottoman modernization,
such as industrialization, urbanization, economic development, welfare
policies, educational centralization, and strengthening of nationalist ide-
ologies, are analyzed through children's lead.

The book is divided into four different categories of threatening
(and also promising) children. Each chapter brings a different group of
destitute children to the forefront as the protagonist and discerns their
subjectivity in the picture. A generalized concept such as "children in
need" would suppress the agency of separate categories of children into
a homogenized, ponderous, and dehumanized childhood. Each chapter delineates distinct inner dynamics and differing actors. Yet, all those
individual accounts are parts of the same history. Whether portrayed as
victims or perpetrators, children became the main targets of both modernization and reform agendas.

The first chapter dwells upon the foundlings, specifically the issue
of child abandonment and provisions for them, while also addressing
national identity, citizenship, and demographic politics. The nineteenth-
century developments on foundling care demarcate certain significant
traits of the political agenda. In the late Ottoman Empire, multilingual and
multireligious urban centers shared certain aspects of a cosmopolitan life-
style. In addition, there was a rather politicized and sensitive concern for
strengthening the solidarity and integrity of communities that felt threatened about losing their members' identity, language, and religion. The sen-
timent of dissolution was triggered by reforms for the modernization and
centralization of the state. These gave way to many tendencies of a nation-
state and threatened the relative autonomy of communities. Under these

circumstances, questions of religion, nationality, and citizenship of abandoned children became contested terrain, over which arduous efforts were spent by local authorities, missionaries, non-Muslim communities, and the central state. In an unexpected manner, these infants became the main characters in a politics of demography, conversion, and national rivalry.

The leading role of the second chapter belongs to *besleme*s, foster daughters, taken into households in the form of domestic servants. In this part of the book, different facets of urbanization, child labor, and youth sexuality are elaborated from the perspectives of gender and class. Deprived of the relatively protective environment of their own families, orphaned, destitute, and poor girls were under three orders of subordination and disadvantage. First, they were materially exploited and sexually abused by their masters, who neither paid them a fair wage nor showed respect for their bodily integrity. Second, they were put into a disadvantaged position by the patriarchal order of the society, which subordinated them as young women and specifically discriminated against them as working women. Third, they were left powerless in courtrooms as the sexist rulings of Islamic jurors and judges routinely favored their masters, relying on the well-established status of the latter in society as opposed to these usually rootless, destitute orphans. However, this is not to say that young *besleme*s were completely suppressed and silenced in the nightmarish environment that surrounded them. The research points to the fact that they were able to find strategies of resistance and ways of taking agency. The existence of escape stories, attempted suicides, and accusations in the court records is a clear sign of the assumed agency on the part of these girls, who took an active part in determining their life-course and writing their own history.

Moving out of the private setting of late Ottoman households, the third chapter provides a detailed account of the emergence and expansion of a large network of vocational orphanages for orphans, street children, vagrants, beggars, and children of the poor and/or refugee parents in urban centers of the Empire throughout the second half of the nineteenth century. This episode underlines how children became both targets and actors of a politics of urbanity. As technicians and workers, they participated in the realization of aspirations for economic development and industrialization. The chapter also provides a novel and nuanced understanding of the Ottoman reform era. The birth of orphanages was linked to such immediate considerations as establishing order and security in urban spaces and rejuvenating local industries. The project was intrinsically linked to new definitions of vagabondage, vagrancy, and begging. New urban structures of provincial governments, municipalities, and the police were determined to solve these "problems." The orphanages would help discipline the "outer space." The emergence of a protectionist economic discourse, proceeding hand-in-hand with the heightened importance attached to industrial productivity of domestic producers, constituted the second layer motivating the opening of orphanages. Centrally planned vocational education would revive declining guild structures. The institution was also a part of the larger context of the "Ottoman Reform" and the dissemination of Ottomanist ideals.

The final chapter deals with Armenian orphans of the Hamidian massacres of 1894–1896 and how they became a matter of international dispute between different religious denominations and self-interested philanthropy. Discussion in this part centers on conversion, international rivalry, and Ottoman attempts to prevent foreign intervention. The involvement of foreign missionaries and the Ottoman state in the relief of massacre victims suggests that crisis situations, such as wars, massacres, and armed conflicts, "invite" only certain parties to take philanthropic measures to help out some of the "needy."

In the aftermath of these events, different actors fought for legitimacy, power, prestige, and hegemony over the seemingly philanthropic field of the opening of orphanages. Orphans, whose lives were under threat and who were torn apart from their families and their social environment, were represented perfect opportunities for religious and nationalistic aims. In this picture, all sides—the Ottoman state, foreign missionaries, and the Armenian Patriarchate—were disturbed by the effectiveness of their rivals and attempted to compete with, block, or supersede each other. The fact that all actors had regarded the others as accomplices, despite their deeply felt animosities in general, also symbolizes the significance of diffidence, doubt, and rivalry in a seemingly philanthropic realm.

The history of childhood brings the historian into contact with many different disciplines, theoretical backgrounds, approaches, sources, and methods. Each chapter of this book is in close dialogue with other major fields. The first chapter, for that matter, communicates with demographic studies, state welfare policies, and heightened concern toward health issues, such as hygiene, and infant and child mortality. The second part could be read as a chapter of Ottoman feminist history, family/household studies, domestic labor, or sexuality. The third chapter communicates with perspectives of labor studies, economic history, the reverberation of Ottoman reform in the provinces, the institutionalization of modern forms of order, security, and surveillance, or the centralization of educational policies. The last chapter constitutes a significant part of nineteenth-century diplomatic history, with its emphasis on the extent of the missionary presence in the Empire, the discontent of the Sublime Porte, and the construction of modern ethnoreligious identities and/or states.

From the perspective of the private/public divide, the chapters flow from the most inner/intimate sphere to the most global/international. The first chapter is on pregnancy, birth, and infants. The second revolves around family and household structures. The third chapter focuses on domestic politics, provincial governments, municipalities, and "Ottoman reform." Finally, the fourth chapter deals with diplomacy and international politics. The structure of the book, as a whole, is reminiscent of the nesting of Russian dolls but in reverse. Moving from the most intimate sphere of infant foundlings to the larger international context of missionary orphanages, the book offers a rich and engaging history—not only through disciplined passion but also through meticulous research reproduced from one chapter to the next.

Sources

Admittedly, unearthing source material on children and youth from the past is problematic. Although different sorts of sources might be referred to, the evidence is not evenly distributed for all subject areas. Certain aspects of childhood, such as education, employment, and health, are better preserved in official sources. Other aspects, which did not arouse official or philanthropic interest at the time, are more difficult to trace. The inner lives of families, the extent and meaning of violence (including sexual abuse), and children's own views on their life experiences, work, school, play, and their own childhood are not easy to discover.[30] Children themselves leave few records, and artifacts designed for them, such as books and toys, have a poor survival rate. Literary texts, polemics, biographies, diaries, letters, advice books, paintings, and historical demography were the bedrock upon which the "early founders" of childhood history developed the classical ideas that still loom over the discipline. With regards to the Ottoman Empire, autobiographical material proves to be elusive and rare. Examples of the genre usually afford very small space to the childhood of the author. Furthermore, with regards to historical demography, sources for the Ottoman Empire are extremely limited. Most of the researchers were compelled to rely on children's periodicals.

Due to the range of topics and actors covered in the present study, the primary sources used for the book were multiple within and between the chapters. The overall research of the book was undertaken in the Prime Ministry's Ottoman Archives (BOA), the American Board Archives (ABA),[31] the Archives of Papers of the American Board of Commissioners for Foreign Missions (ABC),[32] and the French Foreign Ministry Archives (Archives du Ministère des Affaires Étrangères, AMAE).[33] In addition, the Capucin Archives (Archives des Capucins, AC)[34] and Lazarist Archives (Archives Historiques de la Congrégation de la Mission, AHCM)[35] were also part of the research agenda.

Several missionary periodicals were also among the primary sources consulted in this research. These weekly or monthly publications contained original letters and reports of the missionaries. For the American Board of Commissioners for Foreign Missions (ABCFM), the monthly periodical *The Missionary Herald* was analyzed from the 1850s onward.[36] Another periodical of the ABCFM was a weekly, *The Orient*, which was published from 1910 to 1922 by the Bible House of Istanbul. In addition, annual reports of the society were also studied for recapitulation of the yearly activities.[37] In opposition to the relative monopoly of the ABCFM over Protestant missionaries, Catholic missionaries in the Ottoman Empire consisted of several more or less equally powerful groups. For that reason, three different periodicals were analyzed. First, the bimonthly periodical *Bulletin des Oeuvres des Écoles d'Orient* published a wide range of reports from various missionary groups, dispersed into different areas of the Orient.[38] The weekly periodical *Les Missions Catholiques* was also very significant since it was closely related to the papacy and the Jesuits.[39] Third, the periodical of the Lazaristes, *Annales de la Congrégation de la Mission*, was studied due to the significance of this missionary group, especially in the port cities of the Empire.[40]

The original attempt to hear the voices of the children themselves enforced the usage of different source material, since children have been customarily underrepresented in records, archives, and documents. The first two chapters on abandoned children and foster daughters in households rely on both literary and legal data in addition to archival sources. The third chapter benefits mainly from sources in the Ottoman archives along with yearbooks (*Salname*), compilations of regulations (*Düstur*), local periodicals, and memoirs. The fourth chapter is built upon archival material and periodical collections as well as a large body of missionary memoirs from the nineteenth century.

A historian's methodological stance definitely shapes the framing of questions and also the identification of sources, as well as their subsequent interpretation. Scholars who deny that children have a voice, and see them only as passive figures, would not ask relevant questions relating to their presence and instead would render them as being outside of history. As a result, many sources should be read with a cautious eye vis-à-vis the intentions and prejudices of their authors, since in all probability they reflect an adultist outlook.

Though traditionally disregarded and ignored, the history of children cannot be separated from political, social, economic, and cultural processes that were conceived as essentially pertaining to the lives of adults. This book is written with the conviction that historically relevant developments and discourses of the nineteenth century, such as urbanization, welfare policies, the growth of urban workshops/factories, along with domestic labor, imagined statehood, and nationhood, can be reconceptualized, rewritten, and better comprehended if children are rescued from oblivion.

1

The Politics of Child Abandonment

ONE NIGHT IN MAY 1902, Konstantin *veled-i* (son of) Foti, an Ottoman Greek from Langa (Aksaray, Istanbul), found an abandoned baby in front of his door. There was a little note on the baby's swaddling clothes bearing information on his short life story. The baby's name was Todori, and he belonged to the Greek Orthodox community. The mother had to abandon him due to poverty and disgrace. When Konstantin notified the police, the officers took him to the newly opened foundling department of the poor-house of Istanbul, *Darülaceze*. Soon after, the Greek Orthodox Patriarchate filed a complaint claiming that the child had been taken on an improper basis, as *Hanefi* Islamic legislation ordered that foundlings should be raised by their own coreligionists. After an investigation by the Ministry of Justice and Sects and the Ministry of Interior, Todori was returned to the local church, where he was immediately baptized. Consequently, he was entrusted to a Greek household for his breast-feeding. Tragically, the boy lived only a few months, one of many victims of the high infant mortality rate of the period.[1]

Todori's is a very typical child abandonment case, which offers information on the basic state of affairs in the late Ottoman Empire. First, child abandonment was a common practice in Ottoman society. Illegitimate births, poverty, migration, and the difficulties of wartime were the most stated reasons. Second, institutional care was introduced only in the beginning of the twentieth century, and most foundlings were looked after in private care with the help of wet nurses. Whether in homes or institutions, most of these foundlings ended up as infant mortality statistics due to malnutrition and unsanitary conditions. Finally, ambiguity over the religious and/or ethnic identities of abandoned children created serious disputes toward the end of the nineteenth century, when a multireligious, multiethnic society began to develop concerns about increasing centralist tendencies of the state and the weakening of their communities.

From an institutional perspective, state provisions for abandoned children became depersonalized, institutionalized, and modernized in the nineteenth century. Following religious teachings, the Ottoman state customarily provided stipends for abandoned babies of the Muslim community when caretakers submitted a formal application. These allowances were meticulously registered and centrally controlled, pointing to the established and bureaucratized nature of support. During the second half of the nineteenth century, the state gradually changed the direction of support from foundlings to wet nurses. With this policy change, wet nurses acted as intermediaries between the state and infants. As a third stage in modernization, a foundling unit was opened in the poorhouse of Istanbul (*Darülaceze*), in which abandoned children were now taken care of by institutional, bureaucratized systems. Each new regulation inflated the number of intermediaries, assigning significant roles to police departments, birth registry offices, and municipalities.

The institutional picture looks promising thanks to concepts like "centralization" and "modernization." Deconstructing the same era from a "history from below" perspective, which takes into account the experiences of infants, abandoning mothers, and wet nurses, proves that centralization of relief mechanisms lengthened the distance between the relief provider and the needy. This shift resulted in deprivation, suffering, and higher mortality rates for the foundlings. State-subsidized wet nurses contributed to the poor health of the foundlings, since many of them were extremely poor and usually had to breast-feed more than one nursling. Required birth registration made foundlings suffer in filthy police departments. The opening of *Darülaceze* meant they also had to suffer from hospitalism in crowded wards. Modernized administration and institutional progress ironically caused deprivation and had mortal impacts on Ottoman foundlings.

The ethno-religious communities (*millets*) were also badly affected by these "modern" regulations. The state had a new obsession of properly

registering new-born infants in line with the new Regulation on Population Registration. This administrative reform increased the power of various governmental bureaus, police departments, municipalities, and the
foundling unit of the *Darülaceze*. It was an obvious challenge to the authority and autonomy of non-Muslim communities, especially when it came to
the nationality and citizenship of abandoned children. Communal leadership resisted these practices through dozens of official complaints in order
to retain their traditionally established rights and privileges over children
of non-Muslim descent. At the same time, they tried to join the competition by opening and/or strengthening their own foundling facilities. The
imminent danger was losing precious prospective members of imagined
communities. The crisis was implicative of the paroxysms of transforming a communally divided multi-national empire into a centrally administered modern state.

Unprotected children and foundlings were no longer invisible, insignificant, or nonpolitical. Their political significance was elevated as they
became actors in political rivalries regarding demographic politics, the
politics of conversion, and nationalism. The state, foreign missionaries,
and religious and civil leaders of the communities were increasingly
involved in determining the identity of these once-invisible members
of society. While child abandonment was an ancient practice, political
competition over abandoned children was a new phenomenon in the late
Ottoman Empire. The processes of modernization and centralization,
through newly emerging tools of governmentality, were directed at regulating the population and citizenry in a different way. The disciplinary
implications of the modern state apparatus, which employs microtechnologies of power in everyday social life, generated concerns and aspirations on the part of non-Muslim religious authorities for a more tightly
knit community life.[2] Therefore, disputes over foundlings were intrinsically linked to characteristics of nineteenth- and early-twentieth-century
urbanity and the new Ottoman public sphere, which was no longer segregated into religious communities, but founded upon interaction and the
permeation of individual and collective subjectivities. Emerging forms
of governmentality and questions of community identity construction
redefined "control" over abandoned children as a modernist project. The

manifest objective of saving abandoned children from perishing in the streets was actually a means of strengthening (or weakening) communities. For the Ottoman administration, the establishment of new foundling institutions for raising future citizens was part of the effort to construct a modern state image.

Transforming Patterns of Ottoman Child Abandonment

Child abandonment has been thoroughly analyzed from many perspectives in European historiography, benefiting from the rich documentation of foundling asylums and hospitals as well as parish registers.[3] The research field in the Ottoman context covers only a few connected processes and conditions—such as orphanhood *in the Ottoman and former Ottoman* regions, the work of missionaries, and the extent of social welfare policies.[4] The exclusive investigation of the phenomenon is still rare.[5]

The term "child abandonment" refers to the anonymous desertion of infants in the courtyards of places of worship, on streets, outside houses, or at convents and hospitals. The circumstances of extreme poverty or birth outside of marriage are the most obvious reasons. In Mouradgea d'Ohsson's famous legalistic account of the Ottoman Empire, *Tableau Général* (1787), abandoned children (*lakit*)[6] were defined as "unfortunate fruits of crime or of misery."[7] The "crime" in that context is having an illegitimate relationship and an extramarital child, while "misery" bespeaks conditions of destitution and poverty.

Poverty, desertion, and widowhood were all powerful reasons. Child abandonment was a primary means for regulating family size under conditions of poverty. Infants were frequently deserted in the hope that they would be found and adopted by a wealthier person and would enjoy a better life.[8] In her article on the Greek foundlings of Beyoğlu, Méropi Anastassiadou's analysis of the little notes pinned to the swaddling clothes underlines the importance of financial difficulties. In one such note, there is a direct reference to the regulation of the family size: "My sweet mother . . . we are five brothers and sisters and we do not have the means for livelihood, so they have sent me to you."[9] According to a newspaper article, a few-weeks-old healthy female infant was abandoned at the doorstep of Henry Felix Woods Pasha's house in February 1893. The note attached to her clothes explained that the mother had five other children and had no means of providing for this one.[10]

Abandonment was also frequently used as a device for disposing of illegitimate children. At times the contemporary terminology became confused, and the terms "foundling" and "bastard" became interchangeable. Unwed mothers' fear of dishonor and rejection forced them to abandon their babies shortly after giving birth, while poverty or widowhood meant variation in the ages of the foundlings.[11] In the nineteenth-century Ottoman Empire, most of the abandoned infants were only a few days old, "abandoned to streets right after their birth" (ba'de-t tevellüd sokaklara bırakılan).[12] Several documents define foundlings openly as "illegitimates" (gayr-ı meşru).[13] Anastassiadou also underlines the overwhelming role of illegitimacy among child foundlings.[14] Ahmet Midhat, famous novelist of the nineteenth century, depicted child abandonment as a practice of unwed mothers.[15] Abandonment was a direct result of the sexual unions of unmarried women, who became mothers when they were still regarded as girls (fille mères).

The quantitative prevalence of child abandonment is difficult to know, since it is by definition a clandestine act. Still, secrecy and anonymity could be hard to achieve in late Ottoman society. Thorough research in various collections of the Prime Ministry's Ottoman Archives (BOA) brought about a pretty crowded group of almost 150 foundlings. Supported with legal regulations, religious teachings, and literary representation, this much evidence is sufficient to construct a table of trends, patterns, and repetitious themes. Child abandonment in the Ottoman Empire had an urban character. Archival evidence points to activity in relatively big cities and towns, including Istanbul (59.72%), Salonika (11.11%), Mosul (5.56%), Rize (3.47%), Beirut (2.78%), and Bursa (2.08%). The association of illegitimacy with urbanization has often been noted. Child abandonment was never a major problem in small cities and villages in the way it was in big cities. There were informal but organized networks of child care at the parochial level.[16] It is also true that unmarried pregnant women from the countryside came to the city to deliver their babies for reasons of fear and secrecy.[17]

Previous studies underline that there was not a discernible pattern of gender distinction in the overall gender distribution of foundlings in

TABLE 1. Frequency of Child Abandonment in Different Cities

City	Frequency	%
Istanbul	86	59.72
Salonika	16	11.11
Mosul	8	5.56
Rize	5	3.47
Beirut	4	2.78
Bursa	3	2.08
Ankara	2	1.39
Trabzon	2	1.39
Edirne	2	1.39
Bosna	1	0.69
Çanakkale	1	0.69
Diyarbekir	1	0.69
Eski Zağra	1	0.69
Heraklion	1	0.69
Kastamonu	1	0.69
Malatya	1	0.69
Monastir	1	0.69
Muş	1	0.69
Plovdiv	1	0.69
Mardin	1	0.69
Sana	1	0.69
Serres	1	0.69
Tekirdağ	1	0.69
Yozgat	1	0.69
Unknown	1	0.69
Total	**144**	**100**

The data in this table was prepared from records of almost 150 child abandonment cases gathered from the Ottoman archives. The dates of the cases range from 1811 to 1911.

cases of illegitimacy or poverty. The child was forsaken regardless of gender.[18] My data however suggests that abandoned girls were slightly more numerous (55%) than abandoned boys. Abandoned girls also were higher in number among the Greek community of Beyoğlu.[19] The difference was even more marked for Greeks of Izmir: in 1899 twenty-four girls and only seven boys were entrusted to the foundling asylum; in 1901 there were twenty-two boys, as opposed to thirty-four girls.[20] This gender imbalance

suggests a slight preference for boys. Households placed a greater emphasis on producing male heirs for their lineage, so it might have been more
acceptable to retain illegitimate boys rather than illegitimate girls.

According to Islamic law, the legitimacy of children is conveyed
through descent (neseb), which is only conferred through marriage or by
an admission of paternity in a court of law.[21] Accordingly, all abandoned
babies are considered illegitimate and without attachment to a lineage or
a genealogy. The determination of the religious status of the foundlings
has always been undertaken according to the traditional Hanefi (Sunni)
school of Islamic jurisprudence. Foundlings were Muslim and free, since
all orphans belonged to the state.[22] However, if the foundling was discovered in a quarter specifically inhabited by non-Muslims or in the courtyard of a church or synagogue, the child was presumed to belong to one
of those non-Muslim communities.[23]

The milieu of abandonment played a strong role in determining the
religious status of foundlings, and this differed between Muslims and
non-Muslims. For Muslim babies, mosques were the most frequent places
for abandonment (48.15%). Those who abandoned their babies hoped to
benefit from the piety of the believers of Islam, since legal doctrine recom-
mends taking care of abandoned children.[24] After the mosques, streets
were the most usual places for leaving infants (25.93%). The entrances of

TABLE 2. Gender Distribution of the Foundlings

Gender	Frequency	Percentage
Boys	41	28.47
Girls	49	34.03
Unspecified	54	37.50
Total	144	100
Gender	Frequency	Percentage
Boys	41	45.56
Girls	49	54.44
Total	90	100

The data in this table was prepared from records of almost 150 child abandonment
cases gathered from the Ottoman archives. The dates of the cases range from 1811 to 1911.

public baths were also used for the same purpose (7.41%). These locations were chosen when it was intended that the baby be found, rescued, and adopted. Yet, in cases of latent infanticide, the babies were left in secret places hidden from passersby.[25] They were left in invisible corners of streets, cemeteries, cellars, or abandoned buildings (*virâne*).[26]

For non-Muslims, the most prevalent place of abandonment was the door of a house (49.21%), usually one belonging to a relatively known and affluent person.[27] Despairing parents understandably looked for the best alternatives, which often were the wealthiest households, for their babies. The second choice was to leave infants on the streets (20.63%). It is interesting that only a few babies were abandoned at churches (11.11%) (this low figure may result from a research bias, due to underreporting by the church to the police). Non-Muslim *millet*s had their own communal relief mechanisms. When an infant was left at a church, religious authorities made the necessary arrangements to entrust the foundling either with a family or a wet nurse. Women who took them were for the most part needy immigrants, living in quite poor districts and in unpleasant dwellings.[28]

TABLE 3. Frequency of Child Abandonment in Different Milieus

Milieu	Muslims		Non-Muslims		Total	
	Frequency	%	Frequency	%	Frequency	%
Brothel			1	1.59	1	0.69
Cellar	1	1.23	1	1.59	2	1.39
Coffee house			2	3.17	2	1.39
Cemetery	4	4.94			4	2.78
Church			7	11.11	7	4.86
Door	1	1.23	31	49.21	32	22.22
Mosque	39	48.15			39	27.08
Public Bath	6	7.41			6	4.17
Street	21	25.93	13	20.63	34	23.61
Maternity			1	1.59	1	0.69
Empty Plot			1	1.59	1	0.69
Unspecified	9	11.11	6	9.52	15	10.42
Total	81	100	63	100	144	100

The data in this table was prepared from records of almost 150 child abandonment cases gathered from the Ottoman archives. The dates of the cases range from 1811 to 1911.

TABLE 4. Religious Affiliation of the Foundlings

Religious Affiliation	Frequency	%
Muslim	81	56.25
Non-Muslim	63	43.75
Total	144	100

The data in this table was prepared from records of almost 150 child abandonment cases gathered from the Ottoman archives. The dates of the cases range from 1811 to 1911.

So the church could not promise these children better lives than those of their parents. If left to private households, they could have a chance to lead a more prosperous life.

Most of the abandoned children died a very short while before or after they were discovered. Some others managed to survive thanks to the combined efforts of private families, *millet* authorities, municipalities, and governorships. These efforts took the form of private adoption by families, state allowances for foundlings, state stipends for wet nurses, and the opening of foundling asylums.

Private Efforts

John Boswell argues that in the absence of institutions for foundlings, a child could only survive thanks to the "kindness of strangers." Society needed "virtuous people" who accepted abandoned children into their households. The majority of examples from the Ottoman Empire fit into this category. Foundlings were provided for and sheltered in private houses out of a sense of charity and benevolence. "Adopters" were advised to bring the baby to the kadi so that his or her status could be registered. The registration ensured the basic necessities, such as maintenance and upbringing, which were assigned by the public authority to a member of the community, usually the finder.[29] It was common for affluent families to take orphans and destitute children into the household, usually in the form of domestic servants. The next chapter discusses in detail how adoptive children (*evlatlık, ahiret evladı,* or *besleme*) were "adopted" only in name. In reality they were servants. The head of the household pledged to supply the child with his or her basic needs, and in return the child would serve in the house in the future.[30] The hosting family was considered to be performing a charity by taking custody of a destitute child. For that reason these children's labor was unpaid. Thus, the motivation behind welcoming foundlings into a household was more concrete than a vague "kindness." It was a form of recruitment through which cheap or even free labor was secured.

A British diplomat noted in 1853 that many rich Turkish ladies carried on a practice of collecting and training orphan girls, foundlings, or daughters of the poor in their "Nurseries of Wives and Mothers."[31] This effort did not merely result from kindness but actually accrued certain gains when these women acted as intermediaries for the employment or marriage of prospective maids or wives. Men of status also adopted orphans and foundlings to develop their households and courts. Koca Hüsrev Paşa, grand vizier of Sultan Abdülmecid, did not have children of his own, yet he had innumerable foster children in his household.[32] There were teachers in residence as tutors for quite large groups of children. Most of these children rose to important administrative and military positions. The grand vizier İbrahim Edhem Paşa (1818–1893), for instance, was taken to Koca Hüsrev's household as a one-year-old orphan after the Chios massacre of 1822.[33]

Literary sources are also filled with characters taking in foundlings without hesitation. In Ahmet Midhat Efendi's *Dürdane Hanım* (Ms. Dürdane, 1882), Dürdane secretly gives birth to an illegitimate boy. The lady of the mansion next door, Ulviye, arranges this clandestine birth and then her servants leave the infant on her quay, as if he was anonymously abandoned. Ulviye accepts the boy as her *"ahiret evladı"* (adopted child).[34] In *Müşahedat* (Observations, 1891), a widowed woman's illicit affair with a Tunisian sailor ends up in pregnancy and an illegitimate baby. Afraid of the judgment of society toward both herself as an unwed mother and her child, she abandons the girl at the door of an Assyrian church. The sexton finds the swaddled baby and takes her to the house of a merchant whose wife has recently given birth. The family welcomes the baby sincerely.[35]

State Provisions

While it was a common practice for affluent people, it was not easy to accept a new member into a household of modest means. In order to facilitate the survival of foundlings in such cases, the Ottoman state assumed an active role. D'Ohsson states that "an abandoned child belongs to the state, and it is the state who has to nourish and raise it."[36] The authorities repeatedly acknowledged their responsibilities regarding abandoned children. The maintenance of their health, their right to breast-feeding, and their provisions were all the state's duty.[37] The Public Treasury (*beytülmal*) took responsibility for foundlings' maintenance and upbringing by granting monthly allowances (*nafaka*) to them.[38] Muslim households who took responsibility for foundlings could benefit from this financial support that the state offered. Within the period 1811–1911, the stipends ranged from 10 to 55 kuruş.[39]

In parallel with certain regulations of the *millet* system, provisions for abandoned children differed between Muslims and non-Muslims. Only Muslim foundlings sheltered in Muslim households were offered state benefits. In order to receive support from the state, adopting families had to prove that the child in question was Muslim. In February 1817 in Koca Mustafa Paşa, an unknown woman came to the house of Sulti *bint* Dimitri, a Christian woman, with a forty-day-old baby. The woman told her that the baby was the daughter of her son, a recent convert to Islam. The man was missing at the moment and the wife was incapable of providing for the baby. Sulti applied to the Islamic court and tried to prove that the baby was Muslim in order to get some form of allowance from the treasury. The court concluded that the testimony of Sulti could not determine the genealogical line of the baby. The infant was a foundling (*lakit*) with no descent, so she was free and a subject of Islam. As a result, the court ruled that Sulti, as a non-Muslim, did not have the right to take a Muslim foundling into her household.[40]

The maintenance and upbringing of foundlings was specified as a duty of the Public Treasury in legal texts. Despite its preeminence, the financial source of the allowance also came from local administrative and municipal revenues. In 1811 a stipend for a foundling was assigned from the Istanbul customs revenues (*gümrük*).[41] In a later period, in 1853, a wet nurse was hired with a stipend of 25 kuruş, paid from the prison revenues (*tomruklar hasılatı*)[42] collected by a local police department (*zabtiye*).[43] Changes in the provincial administration of the Empire redefined the

rights and responsibilities of local governments and affected foundlings as well. Municipalities were established from the 1870s onward
and spread to the provinces after the 1880s. Certain duties of the center
were delegated to these municipalities, as the state was increasingly shar-
ing authority with provincial governments. Relief for the poor and destitute was also part of the municipalities' mandate.[44] In June 1886 a girl
was found in a mosque in Kuvaroz, a town in Trabzon. She was given
to Çolakoğlu Osman Çavuş, and a stipend was granted to her from the
budget of the municipality.[45] There are numerous examples during the
1880s from other provinces, such as Mardin, Rize, Salonika, and Beirut.[46]
The assistance of the municipalities enabled those households that did not
volunteer for adoption to accept foundlings for material gain.[47]

The duration of the support was variable, and the authorities assumed
changing positions in different contexts. In most of the cases, foundlings
were granted temporary (*muvakkaten*) allowances.[48] This was applicable
only for the breast-feeding period, since suckling is the primary and
inalienable right of a newborn. In 1852 the Supreme Council of Judicial
Ordinances ruled that granting a monthly allowance after the breast-feeding period ended was contrary to "some precedents."[49] But there were also
"other precedents" of granting allowances for longer periods, especially
when the foundlings were abandoned to mosques (*cevami-i şerif*). Those
boys were entitled to a monthly stipend until they could earn their livelihood (*kar u kesbe muktedir* or *istiğna hasıl edinceye kadar*).[50] And girls received
a stipend until their marriage (*hin-i tezvic; izdivacında kat' olunmak üzere*).[51]

Long-term allowances were a huge financial burden for the state. In
order to limit the duration and economize, financial support was transferred to the wet nurses. The state played a direct role in entrusting the
babies to women volunteers as a form of employment.[52] Financial registers in the Ottoman archives contain long lists of stipend assignments
to wet nurses.[53] The state as the employer was in a position to determine
wages in a centralized manner. In 1864 a decision of the Council of State
increased monthly stipends for wet nurses in Istanbul from 25 to 50 kuruş
after many of these women returned foundlings entrusted to them. They
argued that their income was insufficient to support themselves and the
infant at the same time.[54] The council admitted that women applying for

the job were usually "deprived and destitute" (*bikes ve bivaye*) and that they hoped the allowances would serve as their own "means of livelihood" (*medar-ı maişetleri*). In 1888 the council approved the decision of the Governorship of Salonika to increase the stipends of wet nurses from 25 to 55 kuruş, which remained insufficient in the face of increased cost of living.[55]

Most of the wet nurses were widowed and needed the stipend to take care of themselves and their families. The monthly allowances were only moderate, yet taking in abandoned infants was an important form of female wage labor. These women made their "work agreements" as individuals without relying on a male figure.[56] A married wet nurse could contribute to the household income as much as approximately one-quarter to one-third of the wage of her husband (if he was an unskilled worker).[57] In 1908 İzzet Ağa's wife Fatma Hanım was granted a stipend from the municipality's budget for breast-feeding Saniye, a baby girl.[58] The opening of *Darülaceze*, the well-known poorhouse founded in 1896 as a modern welfare institution during the Hamidian era, would change the employment terms of wet nurses, especially when it came to monetary compensation. Based on concerns for infants' health and the prestige of the institution, these women were offered much higher stipends than a regular female worker. In 1909 wet nurses were recruited with a monthly stipend of 250 kuruş.[59] This was actually five to ten times more than what they traditionally had been paid.

The passage of stipends from foundlings to wet nurses gradually made these women act as quasi-institutional solutions for the issue of child abandonment. Parallel to the emergence of different sorts of bureaucratic structures and intermediary mechanisms to deal with the ever-increasing concerns of a modernizing state, wet nurses acquired a new identity in their relations with the central state. The state, instead of taking care of each foundling as a single individual, relied on wet nurses who decreased the state's burden and expanded its access to wider areas. Wet nurses immediately found themselves as state employees and became subjects of direct state interference and discipline. Their political significance was elevated when the authorities realized that losing track of foundlings, who were entrusted to wet nurses, had unhealthy and dangerous results for the former.[60]

State Institutions

The Ottoman society was quite late in creating institutions for foundlings. Apart from the homes opened by Catholic missionaries, semi-formalized solutions such as wet-nurses and foster families were more common. In the latter half of the nineteenth century, abandoned children were sheltered in larger institutions, such as hospitals or orphanages. The Armenian Surp Prgiç Hospital in Yedikule, Istanbul, had such a foundling department. The Greek Orphanage of Izmir, founded in 1870, also admitted foundlings until the opening of a separate foundling asylum in 1898.[61]

The terms "foundling asylum" and "bastard home" were frequently used interchangeably in nineteenth-century parlance. Hayrullah Efendi, in his *Avrupa Seyahatnamesi* (Travels in Europe) from the years 1863–1864, refers to "bastard dwellings" while giving information on a number of educational institutions in Paris.[62] Catholic foundling asylums in the Empire were also labeled as such. In Izmir, the Nazareth de St. Roch complex, housing a convent, a school, an infirmary, and a crèche for abandoned children, was opened in 1870–1871. According to Charles John Murray, this was a proper Foundling Hospital "for all nationalities and religions."[63] Yet, in the contemporary language, the institution and the building was referred to as *piçhane* (bastard home).[64] The same terminology was also employed by Ahmet Midhat in his 1882 novel *Acayib-i Alem* (Wonders of the World). He referred to the foundling asylum of Moscow as a bastard home for illegitimate children (*evlad-ı zina*).[65]

Ottomans were interested in learning more about these institutions. William Deans, in his book on the history of the Ottoman Empire, writes, "Nothing excites the horror of the *Osmanlis* so much as the details of the foundling hospitals, and fearful multitude of natural children in Vienna and Paris. They cannot conceive how society can exist under such an accumulation of evils."[66] Ottoman intellectuals were appalled, yet a little gleeful, at the immense numbers of abandoned children in Europe. They were glad to be able to cite the statistics as a way to refute Europeans' self-righteous criticisms of Ottoman society and the general European standpoint of moral superiority. Their callous use of terms like *piçhane* was cultural payback for Christians who harped on the immorality of harems. For Ahmet Midhat, the absence of certain Islamic traditions and practices, such as concubinage and polygamy, increased adultery, prostitution, illegitimacy, and child abandonment in European society. The link between foundlings and morality was part of the period's culture wars.[67]

The term "bastard home" was also used in a derogatory sense for the first birth clinic in Istanbul (*Viladethane*), which was opened by Besim Ömer Paşa, the famous Paris-educated pediatrician of the late Ottoman Empire.[68] Contemporary social norms dictated that pregnant women gave birth in their own beds, in their own homes. The ones who had to do it elsewhere were those who had to hide their pregnancies. These were unwed mothers, those who had illegitimate affairs, and prostitutes.[69] These prejudiced assumptions were not far from truth. The maternity hospital was opened to secure healthy births, but the babies born in *Viladethane* were mostly illegitimate.[70] For instance, in February 1908 a young Jewish woman gave birth to a baby girl. Arguing that the father of the baby was dead and that "she was sick and poor and incapable of breastfeeding her child" (*alil ve fakir ve çocuğunu ırzaa gayr-ı muktedir*), she abandoned her at the maternity hospital. After the investigation of the records of the hospital, it turned out that her name was Fortüne *bint* Baruh and that she was "from among the wealthy families" (erbab-ı yesardan) of Balat. The reason for abandonment was not her poverty but her "illegitimate affair" (*münasebet-i gayr-ı meşru*).[71]

The first Ottoman institution accepting foundlings was the Hospital for Women in Haseki. The hospital was founded in 1869, and in the 1890s the municipality of Istanbul started to send foundlings to the institution. They were collected from the streets and taken to police departments. When local residents did not volunteer to adopt them, their lives were in danger. In 1893 police officers found a boy in the courtyard of Şehzadebaşı Mosque, prepared his identity card (*tezkire-yi Osmaniyye*), and send him to the Haseki hospital.[72] Around the same time, a boy was found in a street in Pangaltı and was taken to the hospital after birth registration.[73]

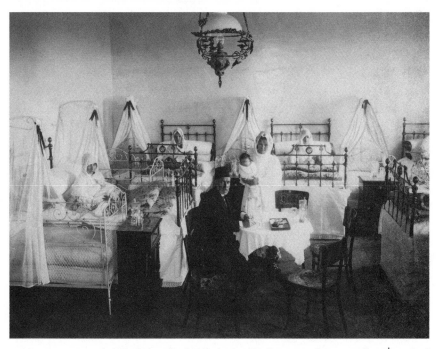

1. Maternity ward (*Viladethane*) of *Darülaceze*. Unknown photographer, İstanbul Üniversitesi Kütüphane ve Dokümantasyon Daire Başkanlığı, *Fotoğraf Albümleri Dizini*, 779-39-0023.

The hospital did not have special facilities for foundlings, but authorities counted on the positive impact of the medical staff and female patients.

The first genuine state foundling home, *Darülaceze Irzahanesi*,[74] was opened under the roof of the poorhouse. It was one of the prestigious institutions of the Hamidian era. Like the children's hospital (Hamidiye Etfal Hastahane-i Alisi) and *Dar'ül-hayr-ı Ali*, it underlined the power and legitimacy of the sultan.[75] The Poorhouse Regulation prescribed that abandoned children (*lakitler*) would be among the inmates of the institution.[76] The foundling department started to accept infants in 1899, although the official opening was in April 1903.[77] The department took care of infants younger than four, and older ones were under the responsibility of the orphanage. The institution admitted foundlings and orphaned babies only. Infants with both parents living were refused. In 1907, Ramazan Ağa

2. Group of foundlings in the *Darülaceze Irzahanesi* (Crèche). Unknown photographer, İstanbul Üniversitesi Kütüphane ve Dokümantasyon Daire Başkanlığı, *Fotoğraf Albümleri Dizini*, 90602-0017.

3. Outside view of the *Darülaceze Irzahanesi* (Crèche) and a group of foundlings. Unknown photographer, İstanbul Üniversitesi Kütüphane ve Dokümantasyon Daire Başkanlığı, *Fotoğraf Albümleri Dizini*, 90620-0001.

4. Group of orphans in the orphanage of *Darülaceze*. Unknown photographer, İstanbul Üniversitesi Kütüphane ve Dokümantasyon Daire Başkanlığı, *Fotoğraf Albümleri Dizini*, 90602-0024.

was rejected as a divorced father when he applied to the institution for the suckling of his son.[78]

The foundling facility was initiated in 1899 with 17 foundlings.[79] The number increased to 38 in 1905. The department was still minuscule compared to a total of 863 inmates in the institution as a whole. In 1907 the foundling population reached 75. The foundling home actually admitted around 200 infants each year. This number sadly eroded due to high mortality rates. In 1916, 180 foundlings were admitted and 111 of them died. In 1917, only 50 of 251 foundlings survived.

The regulation of the Poorhouse underlined that neither religion nor nationality would be a hindrance for admittance into the institution. Yet, the foundlings in the institution were predominantly Muslims. In March 1911 the foundling hospital housed thirty Muslims, as opposed to one Greek, one Armenian Catholic, and two Jews.[80] This uneven distribution was related to both the privileging of Muslim foundlings by the Ottoman

TABLE 5. Yearly Distribution of Foundlings in the *Darülaceze* Foundling Asylum

Years	Admitted	Left	Died	Transferred to the Orphanage	Resulting Population
1903–1915[1]	932	300	572	18	42
1916	180	42	111	12	57
1917	251	48	201	22	37
1918	250	29	216	9	33
1919	218	32	184	3	32
1920	175	37	146	0	39
Total (1903–1920)	2,016	488	1,426	64	

BOA, DH.UMVM., 113/58, 01/Ra/1339 (12.11.1920).

1. The registers of these 12 years were not kept in a yearly manner and the figures for children were given as a total covering the whole period.

welfare system and the reluctance of non-Muslim communities to send their foundlings to the hospital.

The foundling home was designed to follow the lines of institutional care. Several wet nurses were recruited to stay on the premises and care for the infants. In 1904 the Ministry of the Interior tried to make sure that the ratio of the wet nurses to foundlings would be one to two.[81] In the early 1920s, the administration was forced to foster out some foundlings to limit the ever-increasing costs of the institution. Infants were entrusted one after the other to needy women who applied for wet nursing. These women were examined to ensure that they had no health problems.[82] Still, the system of foster care raised recurrent doubts about infants' nutrition and health.[83] These women were living in remote districts of the city under very poor conditions of hygiene and cleanliness, and their economic resources were extremely limited. As a result, a monitoring system was introduced in the early 1920s, under which the doctors of *Darülaceze* would provide medical examination to the infants and control wet nurses with regular visits to their houses.

Modernization of Foundling Care

Even though the journey from monthly stipends to wet nurse assignments to the opening of a foundling asylum was praised as part of the expansion and modernization of welfare policies of the Ottoman state, from the perspective of the foundlings, "modern" meant deprivation, mortality, and suffering. With these changes in welfare policy it became less likely that abandoned children would live within a family environment, have access to sufficient nutrients, and be the object of real affection without having to compete with other infants waiting for the same sort of attention.

The opening of the foundling unit was directly related to the state's new concern to expand control over forsaken prospective members of the population. Formerly anonymous and scattered babies were now gathered under one central roof. The mechanisms and logic of how Ottoman governmentality operated on the ground, and what the modernization of foundling care meant for the babies, can be better analyzed with reference to infant mortality, which was a huge problem in Ottoman society. Including the royal family, only a third or fewer of born children survived. During the course of the nineteenth century, infant mortality and its causes became important research matters. The foundling population and asylums were examples picked up for further analysis, due to enormous mortality rates. In the asylum of the *Filles de la Charité* in Jerusalem, the mortality rate for the years 1886–1890 was 42.5 percent.[84] In the report of 1901, it was stated that, during the past fifteen years, 486 infants were received and two-thirds of them had died.[85] The mortality rate in the foundling asylum of the church of the Franciscan missionaries, Sainte-Marie Draperis of Beyoğlu, was around 50 percent for the thirteen years between 1860 and 1873.[86] For the period between 1840 and 1880, Anastassiadou calculates the mortality rate for abandoned Greek children as 60 percent. The overall picture was not much better for the foundling asylum of the Greek community in Izmir. Every year, only one-third of the babies brought to the institution survived. As a worse example, in 1901, of the eighteen babies admitted, fourteen passed away.[87] The "foundling factor" definitely played a role within the general picture of infant mortality, since infants born out of wedlock had significantly higher mortality in the first year of life than their legitimate peers.[88]

The main reason for higher mortality among the foundlings was undernourishment. Until the late 1920s, physicians attributed the vast majority of infant deaths to a lack of mother's milk. Due to the high death rate among artificially fed infants, the medical community preferred wet

nurses to bottles well into the twentieth century.[89] Yet due to the permanent dearth of wet nurses, foundling asylums established their own dair-
ies, and in order to keep the animal milk fresh and use it in a healthy
way they purchased devices for sterilization and pasteurization. The
foundling unit of *Darülaceze* was remarkably well-equipped with modern
technology and an educated staff. The head of the foundling unit was a
French woman, and there were Austrian nurses under her.[90] An incubator
for premature infants was purchased shortly after the foundling unit's
opening.[91] From 1903 onward the department had a dairy of its own.[92] In
1906 the Ministry of the Interior approved the purchase of a special device
for sterilizing animal milk.[93] Also in 1906, classes were provided to the
nurses by an obstetrician so that the children were properly taken care of
"under rules of hygiene and sanitation" (*hıfz-ı sıhhaya uygun olarak*).[94]

All these improvements were propagated as signs of a capable and
modernizing state. The press advertised the institution as a solution to the
problem of infant mortality since it was abiding by the rules of hygiene
and sterility. On 13 February 1899, the daily newspaper *Sabah* (Morning)
published the striking story of a young unmarried mother who had to
hand over her baby to the *Darülaceze* foundling unit. It was argued that
she wanted to retrieve her child after finding a job as a domestic servant,
yet when she saw how well the child was being cared for, she decided that
it was best for the baby to stay. The author of the article claimed that "the
compassion of the sultan was even stronger than maternal instinct."[95] The
story was probably a fabrication, since a newly hired domestic servant
had very little chance to bring her illegitimate baby to her workplace. Due
to their working conditions, domestic servants actually predominated
among the mothers who abandoned their children.[96]

A poem was hung in the lobby of the asylum to praise Sultan Abdülhamid II's philanthropy for the foundlings (*ırzadar*).[97] The journalist and
writer Ahmet Rasim (1865–1932) visited the foundling home in 1907 and
described an extremely positive picture exalting the sultan. He described
in detail the facilities of the institution (a device for the sterilization of
milk, a scale, a bathing room, a quarantine room, a bedroom for the older
ones, a playroom, and a variety of toys) and praised the capabilities of the

French head. He noted that all the children were beautiful and they were cleanly dressed.[98]

Despite these modernized facilities and positive propaganda, mortality rates were alarming. In order to comprehend the contradiction of applauded technical superiority with high mortality rates, it is necessary to take into account the limits of public criticism and the unbridgeable gap between the state-centered presentation of the institution and the experiences of the infants. Technological improvement proved insufficient in the face of maternal malnutrition, unassisted childbirth, childhood diseases and epidemics that circulated in the general population, and the dynamics of infection within the enclosed environment of the asylum.

From 1903 to 1915, 932 children were accepted into the institution and 572 of them died (61 percent). In early 1915 the mortality rates of abandoned children in *Darülaceze* was already a concern for the government. The administration of the institution was asked to give an explanation. The director complained that the procedure that followed from the moment an infant was found to the time he or she was taken to the foundling asylum was too long and painful. Infants had to remain a long time in police departments while their identities were investigated.[99] The accusations against the police were rather grave. The pediatrician of the *Darülaceze* claimed that the infants were put into baskets (*zenbil*) and hung on the walls during the night. A piece of bread was put into a dirty cloth and

TABLE **6.** Number of Foundlings Admitted to the *Darülaceze* Foundling Asylum (1903–1920)

Age	1903–1915	1916	1917	1918	1919	1920	1903–1920
1 month–6 months old	672	153	180	221	166	143	1,535
6 months–1 year old	171	17	34	21	42	49	334
1–3 years old	89	11	37	8	10	28	183
Total	932	181	251	250	218	220	2,052

BOA, DH.UMVM., 114/44, 13/Ra/1340 (14.11.1921).

TABLE 7. Number of Foundlings Who Died in the *Darülaceze* Foundling Asylum (1903–1920)

Age	1903–1915	1916	1917	1918	1919	1920	1903–1920
1 month– 6 months old	500	100	171	200	155	110	1,236
6 months– 1 year old	62	10	20	14	27	37	170
1–3 years old	10	1	10	2	2	14	39
Total	572	111	201	216	184	161	1,445

BOA, DH.UMVM., 114/44, 13/Ra/1340 (14.11.1921).

stuck into their mouths to stop their cries.[100] Poor infants were deprived of necessary care and nutrition during such a vital period and thus arrived at the institution "in a half-dead condition" (*nim-murde bir halde*). In the end, all efforts spent for their survival "remained futile" (*semeredar olamadığı*). The police were ordered to deliver the foundlings "directly and with fast means of transport" to the most appropriate caregivers, based on the initial guess about their ethnoreligious identity. In order not to risk the lives of the babies, they should carry out the investigation afterward.[101]

Throughout the decade the infant mortality rate at the foundling home remained embarrassing. The pediatrician of the institution, Ali Şükrü, reported that it was 80 percent in 1917, 86 percent in 1918, 84 percent in 1919, and 73 percent in 1920.[102] In total, from 1903 to 1921, 70 percent of all children accepted into the institution died. Most of them passed away when they were less than six months old; the risk for those above one year old was much smaller. The doctor argued that the "foundling home's current pitiful and miserable state" (*ırzahanenin bugünkü acınacak hal-i perişaniyesi*) could be explained neither by the insufficiencies of its building nor by the negligence or weakness of its doctors. What these poor infants essentially lacked was a "mother-like compassion and affection" (*merhamet ve şefkat-i maderane*), which was not provided by their wet nurses. These women, the doctor argued, were recruited without much scrutiny, and it was obvious that their interest in the job had little to do

TABLE 8. Mortality Rates of All the Children in the *Darülaceze* Foundling Asylum (1903–1920)

Years	Admitted	Died	Mortality Rate(%)
1903–1915	932	572	61
1916	181	111	61
1917	251	201	80
1918	250	216	86
1919	218	184	84
1920	220	161	73
1925	325	120	37
Total (1903–1920)	**2,052**	**1,445**	**70**
Total (1903–1930)	**4,685**	**2,360**	**50**
Total (1920–1930)	**2,633**	**915**	**35**

BOA, DH.UMVM., 114/44, 13/Ra/1340 (14.11.1921); Yıldırım, *İstanbul Darülaceze Müessesesi Tarihi*, 165.

with the "joy of raising children" (*çocuk büyütme zevki*). Rather, they were preoccupied with gaining their livelihood and escaping from starvation. To reinforce the women's motivation, the poorhouse administration asked the Ministry of the Interior to give rewards to wet nurses.[103]

The Ministry of Health reported in September 1921 that the mortality rate was still disastrous.[104] In parallel to the pediatrician's claims, this report underlined the poor conditions of care. According to the male gaze of the administrators, these infants were victims of ignorant, superstitious, and lazy wet nurses.[105] After an eight-month-long governmental investigation, civil inspector (*mülkiye müfettişi*) Hikmet Bey argued in January 1922 that since wet nurses were entrusted with more than two infants in addition to their own babies, the supply of milk for each was insufficient. He suggested keeping the ratio of wet nurses to infants at one to two. The foundling asylum could only be rehabilitated with the recruitment of a full-time pediatrician and five more wet nurses.[106] From 1903 to 1930, 4,685 children were accepted into the institution and 2,360 of them died.[107] The inability of the institution to lower the mortality rate led to a discussion of relocating it to the city center.[108] However, the mortality rate fell to as low as 37 percent in 1925. The average rate for the decade between 1920 and

TABLE 9. Mortality Rates of Infants between 1 and 6 Months Old in the *Darülaceze* Foundling Asylum (1903–1920)

Years	Admitted	Died	Mortality Rate (%)
1903–1915	672	500	74
1916	153	100	65
1917	180	171	95
1918	220	200	90
1919	166	155	93
1920	143	110	77
Total (1903–1920)	1,535	1,236	80

BOA, DH.UMVM., 114/44, 13/Ra/1340 (14.11.1921).

TABLE 10. Mortality Rates of 1- to 3-Year-Olds in the *Darülaceze* Foundling Asylum (1903–1920)

Years	Admitted	Died	Mortality Rate (%)
1903–1915	89	10	11
1916	11	1	9
1917	37	10	27
1918	8	2	25
1919	10	2	20
1920	28	14	50
Total (1903–1920)	183	39	21

BOA, DH.UMVM., 114/44, 13/Ra/1340 (14.11.1921).

1930 was 35 percent. Fostering-out mechanisms were decisive in producing this result. Babies were better off outside the institution, even with "ignorant" and "lazy" wet nurses.

It is interesting that the ministries, administrators, and doctors ignored the fatal results of institutionalization itself. The most advanced hygienic and medical regimen did not make these babies any healthier. They were victims of "hospitalism," as forsaken members of families who were deprived of maternal attention during their first year of life.[109] Independent of the conditions of feeding and nourishment, the foundlings taken care of in homes had a much lower mortality rate, both because they did not suffer hospitalism and also because the danger of infection

TABLE 11. Number of Children under the Care of the *Darülaceze* Foundling Asylum (1903–1920)

Year	Infant Population
1903	17
1905	38
1907	75
1911	34
1914	50
1916	57
1917	37
1918	33
1919	32
1920	39

BOA, DH.UMVM., 114/44, 13/Ra/1340 (14.11.1921); BOA, DH.UMVM., 113/58, 01/Ra/1339 (12.11.1920); Yıldırım, *İstanbul Darülaceze Müessesesi Tarihi*, 145; Özbek, *Osmanlı İmparatorluğu'nda Sosyal Devlet*, 210; Yarman, *Osmanlı Sağlık Hizmetlerinde Ermeniler*, 364.

was much lower compared to that in institutions. It is not unusual that hospitals, nurseries, maternities, or foundling asylums were themselves "killing fields," since sometimes buildings as a whole got infected.[110] The administrators of the late Ottoman Empire were obsessed with a particular interpretation of modernization and centralization, such that they ignored the harmful effects of modern forms of care for the infants.

Children's Civil Status and Nationality

In 1904, Hacı Osman bin Islam took in a foundling girl (*lakita*) he had discovered in the European quarter (*Frenk mahallesi*) of Salonica, named her Kamile, and wrote a petition to the municipality for a stipend to have her breast-fed. When she died within a short time, Osman took in a second girl from the street and gave her the same name. His chances of discovering foundlings were high, since he was a night guard strolling through the empty streets at night.[111] In this case, two foundlings from a non-Muslim quarter were entrusted to a Muslim, despite the well-established regulation on the determination of the religious status of foundlings. The traditional Hanefi regulation ruled that all foundlings were Muslim and free. Yet if they were discovered in a quarter inhabited by non-Muslims, or in a house of worship, they were presumed to belong to one of the People of the Book (dhimmi) communities.[112]

In parallel to the regulations of the *millet* system, provisions for abandoned or destitute children had a religiously compartmentalized nature. Muslim children received state stipends while non-Muslim *millet*s had their own communal mechanisms to take care of the foundlings. The customary function of the state was to transfer them to the relevant religious authorities of their communities. The new foundling unit of the *Darül-aceze*, on the other hand, targeted all Ottomans regardless of religious denomination as part of the state's new policies of regulating the citizenry and population. Modernization of foundling care meant the expansion of state welfare toward non-Muslim foundlings. This caused serious communal disputes throughout the 1900s.

The Ottoman Nationality Regulation recognized the principle of *jus sanguinis*, the "right of blood," as the principal form of obtaining nationality. It also accepted under certain circumstances the principle of *jus soli*, the "right of soil" or "right of territory," as a way of obtaining nationality.[113] The civil status of foundlings was determined under the concept of *jus soli*. They were entitled to an Ottoman nationality because they were born on Ottoman territory. This was a standard legal procedure applied to foundlings in general. For all communities of the Ottoman Empire, foundlings were considered separate entities. Having no familial descent, they were attached primarily to the state or the church. The Ottoman identity cards (*tezkire-i osmaniye*) of the foundlings verified their lineage in relation to religious authority. Greek foundlings, for instance, were registered as born of unknown parents (*namalum, meçhul*) and belonging to the Christian religion (*Hıristiyan*), and their abode (*mesken*) was invariably the church (e.g., *Beyoğlu'nda Rum Panayia* [Panaghia] *Kilisesi*). None of these infants were living in the church; yet, the church was the only address that the Ottoman authorities recognized, since they belonged to the family of abandoned children associated with a given religious community.[114]

The procedure was similar for abandoned children of the Armenian community. The foundlings abandoned at the doors of Armenian churches were immediately baptized. According to medieval Armenian legislation, children "of unknown parentage or resulting from fornication" left "at the doors of churches or elsewhere" could be reared by those who gave the child milk, since feeding a foundling gave the right to rear it to the caregiver's discretion.[115] Infants whose mothers and fathers were unknown were registered in Armenian baptism records as "the child of the church" (*Yegeghetsvo zavag*). Individual Armenian churches have kept records of such entries in their registers.[116] The children were usually named Asdvadzadur or Asadur, meaning "given by God." The same procedure also applied to illegitimate children. When mothers were left alone with their illegitimate children, they applied to the church, and the infant was baptized as a child of the church.[117]

For the Jewish communities of the Ottoman Empire, regulations concerning illegitimate children were confounded with those concerning abandoned ones. Among the Jews of Ottoman Tripoli (Libya), there were specific regulations regarding illegitimate children. If the father of a boy was unknown, either because he was a foundling or because only the mother was known, it was customary for him to be named "Israel" during his circumcision and afterward considered a full-fledged Jew.[118]

With the introduction of modern tools of population control (such as birth registry) and the more extensive involvement of state authorities in diverse communal affairs, many of the previous regulations covering the administration of non-Muslim foundlings were challenged or altered. The newly introduced practice of registering foundlings into official population records became a matter of strife between state and community authorities regarding the future of the abandoned infants. In the 1900s, non-Muslim authorities applied to the government numerous times with the grievance that, despite the traditional arrangements concerning the identity of foundlings, policemen disregarded indicators of religious affiliation and frequently registered all abandoned babies as Muslim, despite contrary evidence at hand.[119] Babies carrying notes or labels attached to their clothing with a written declaration or sign (*yafta*) indicating the child's Christian origin, along with those who were abandoned in front of churches or non-Muslim households, were taken into either Muslim households or the foundling unit of the *Darülaceze* and registered as Muslims.[120]

In 1903 a girl was abandoned at the door of a Greek household. attached to her swaddling clothes, there was "a note in Greek" (*Rûmî ilmühaber*) explaining that she had not been baptized. She also carried "a tin cross" (*sarı tenekeden bir ıstavroz*). Even in the presence of such indicators she was sent to the *Darülaceze* and registered as Muslim.[121] In another instance, in July 1904, the Patriarchate complained that two Greek boys were taken to the institution before an investigation of their identities. When they passed away in a short while, they were buried as Muslims.[122] Similarly, in August 1904 a newborn baby was left in front of a Jewish house in Beyoğlu, with a piece of paper attached to his diapers that said in Greek that he was "not baptized." The infant was brought to the Church of Hristos in Galata by a police officer. The priest immediately baptized the baby, "so that he was not sent to the Ottoman *brefokomeio* (hospice for foundlings)."[123] Here the concern seems exaggerated; yet, it stands as evidence to a well-established controversy between non-Muslim communities and the state.[124]

The complaints of communal authorities regarding non-Muslim babies being registered on census records as Muslims were also confirmed by the authorities. The director of the *Darülaceze* reported in 1902 that the police and municipality officers had brought to them all the abandoned babies regardless of the streets or neighborhoods where they were found.[125] The Municipality of Istanbul (*Şehremaneti*) admitted that after the opening of the *Darülaceze* there had been a change in the traditional policy on determining the identity of foundlings.[126] Now the municipality had to "investigate the religious denomination" (*tahkik-i milletleri*) of the foundlings with the help of the police department. The established procedure was outdated, and the number of abandoned children found in all sorts of places was much greater. A baby left in front of a church or synagogue did not have to be a member of that community. "Necessities of secrecy and urgency" (*mecburiyet-i ihtifa ve istical*) usually forced mothers or fathers to leave their babies "anywhere they came across" (*rast geldikleri yere*). The municipality had to make a thorough inquiry for each case to prevent controversy between different communities and to properly register the infants to the Ottoman census (*sicill-i nüfus*) and issue their identity cards.[127] During the inquiry, babies had to remain in the care of the *Darülaceze.*

The proper registration of citizens, including newborns, was a new concern of the modernizing state.[128] It was during this time that an article on foundlings was added to the Regulation on Population Registration of 1881 (*Sicill-i Nüfus Nizamnamesi*).[129] All abandoned children would be registered as Muslim unless they carried on them any other religious sign. The finder of an abandoned infant was obliged to report to the Council of Elders in the villages and to the police department in towns or cities as to where, how, and when the baby was found. Finders were also required to bring the original clothes and belongings of the infant to the authorities. The responsible body, in return, would prepare a record of the baby's estimated age, sex, assigned name, and religion. This document would be used for registering the baby in the census and for issuing his identity card. The authorities of non-Muslim places of worship were not allowed to take in babies directly, even if they were forsaken at their door. They had to deliver the baby to the relevant authority.

From the other end of the dispute, there were complaints against the non-Muslim authorities. They were not cooperative in following the new regulation. The priests constantly resisted sending foundlings to the headman of their district (*mahalle muhtarı*). For example, in 1905, a woman abandoned her illegitimate child in the Greek neighborhood of Keşan in Edirne. The local church took the baby, baptized him with the name Todori, and entrusted him to a Greek household to be breast-fed. The governorship opposed this and claimed that the child was Muslim. The baby's swaddling clothes indicated that he came from the refugee (*muhacir*) neighborhood, which was very close to the Greek one. After a thorough investigation in the district, the mother of the baby, actually a Muslim refugee, was found. According to the records, she confessed "her crime" and admitted that she had abandoned her baby in the Greek neighborhood. The government then accused the Greek clerics of proselytizing and asked them to return the baby. Arguing that there was no evident sign of religious or national origin on the baby, the church authorities refused to do so. The Ministry of Justice and Sects, the Greek Patriarchate, and the Ministry of Interior all became involved in the case to determine the baby's fate. The conflict tragically ended when the infant died before he was three months old.[130]

Also in October 1903, a boy was found at the door of a house in Boğazkesen, Galata. The piece of paper attached to his diaper indicated that he was seven days old, unbaptized, and born of Orthodox parents. The Greek Patriarchate resisted delivering the boy, arguing that he was definitely Greek.[131] In another example from November 1904, the *mutasarrıf* (local administrator) of Beyoğlu demanded that a baby girl abandoned at the door of the house of Kostaki, an employee of the Consulate of Greece, be delivered to state authorities. But the Patriarchate refused, claiming that the foundling belonged to the Greek community according to traditional regulations.[132] These and countless other cases reveal that abandoned children were the subject of a growing debate and confrontation between communal authorities and the Municipality of Istanbul. The *millet* representatives "demanded the preservation of old regulation" (*usul-ı kadimesinin muhafazası talebi*), while the municipality underlined the new needs and requirements of the administration.

After ceaseless petitions and complaints, the Council of State ruled in February 1905 that abandoned children found in front of non-Muslim religious institutions and quarters would be delivered to the authorities of that community, and not to the *Darülaceze*. Infants found in front of mosques and in Muslim quarters would be registered as Muslims.[133] The municipality objected to this once more with its report in June 1905 arguing that new urban spatial relations necessitated the inquiry.[134] The city was no longer strictly segregated into quarters. Almost every neighborhood was inhabited by diverse religious and ethnic communities. In the end, the Council of Ministers ruled in June 1906 that regardless of where a baby was abandoned, police investigation was necessary to establish his identity.[135] Every abandoned baby should be taken immediately and directly to the police department. Their swaddling clothes should be opened in the presence of a committee made up of the local police, municipality officers, and the *muhtar*.[136] Based on evident marks and signs, such as a written note (*varaka*) bearing information on the baby's identity or little pieces of information such as the nature of the cloth and the swaddle, the investigators attempted to establish the identity of the baby. Only after that process would the foundling be transferred to the relevant religious authority. The demands of non-Muslim ecclesiastics to be present during this investigation were rejected. This would only lengthen the process, they were told, and endanger the life of the foundling.

In the early twentieth century, non-Muslim *millet*s regarded foundlings as inalienable members of their imagined community. Forsaken members of their own lineage, these babies ironically became the main actors of a serious political and religious rivalry. A new vision of governmentality became materialized with the introduction of standard birth certificates and established census records. These changes not only implied proper registration of the new-born but also challenged the customary autonomy of the communal authorities with a new administrative design. The boundaries of a communally segregated society were being redrawn to a homogeneously administered polity. A multi-national and decentralized empire was approximating a centralized modern state. These changes created an acute dispute over the citizenship status of foundlings.

Gradual changes in state provisions for abandoned babies imply the appearance of a structured, bureaucratized, and relatively centralized administrative apparatus that introduced new governance techniques, matching the regulations of a modern state. Unexpectedly, reformed regulations and institutions risked foundlings' chances for survival. The publicly assisted wet-nursing service was detrimental to the standards of living of the foundlings, since usually they shared the nurse's milk with other nurslings and they were no longer targets of particular care. The bureaucratization of relief exploded the volume of correspondence between the police, municipality officials, religious authorities, and the poorhouse. Elevated concern for birth registration and the opening of the *Darülaceze* turned foundlings into anonymous babies in dirty police stations or packed hospital wards, where there were permanent queues to receive attention.

Non-Muslim communal authorities were also discontented. They perceived centralized and uniform regulations as a challenge to their

relative autonomy over administering community affairs. This created
sensitivity and a politicized concern for strengthening the solidarity and
integrity of communities who felt threatened at losing their youngest
members' identity, language, and religion. They resisted administrative
reform by submitting official appeals to the government and by introducing or strenghthening their own foundling facilities. Modernized governmental structure triggered the emergence of its mirror image on the
communal level.

In this new settlement, the foundling started to figure as a main character in demographic politics, conversion and national rivalry, infant and
child mortality, state philanthropy and welfare, and hygiene and health
policies. The lives (and deaths) of abandoned children became a contested
terrain. The state, local authorities, foreign missionaries, non-Muslim communities, municipalities, the police, all fought for a piece of it. Campaigns
to rescue abandoned children hardly derived from an elevated concern
for children's well-being, or a new awareness about childhood, or a sen-
timent of pity and disinterested charity. Rather, children were valuable
with reference to their future role as citizens and subjects—as members
of an imagined community.

I just called them the "main characters," but actually abandoned children are the subaltern of the subaltern. Not only are they poor, destitute,
or without a lineage but also they are babies, who are generally nonverbal
creatures. "Not having a voice" cannot be better depicted than in their
early life experiences. The narrative of the modernizing state, and the cal-
culus of mothers deciding to abandon their children or of wet nurses try-
ing to support their own families, could partially be constructed. In order
to recover only fragments of foundlings' silenced voices, focusing on their
experiences from a doorstep to the police station, from a church to *Darülaceze*, was the method I followed. Their cries, their dead bodies, but also
their rescue stories were more than enough to write a nuanced version of
Ottoman modernization.

What were the life prospects ahead of abandoned children? Although
in the imaginative literature foundlings are almost always promised

happiness, then majority of them experienced moderate living conditions. Chapter 2 might offer a little bit more on the lives of at least some of the foundlings, particularly girls, who were taken into private homes for fostering. In the pages to come, the reader will have a chance to read more on the Ottoman version of "kindness of strangers" and the intricate relations between adoption and domestic child labor.

2

Private Negotiation of Child Fosterage

MARUŞA ANASTASI APOSTOL lost both her parents and *was a complete orphan* when she was entrusted by her uncle as a *besleme*, foster daughter, to the household of Süleyman Efendi, head of the Court of Appeals in Janina. Her life was full of hardship. She assumed household chores and looked after the children with no payment at all. She also had to endure sexual harassment. In 1903, Süleyman raped and deflowered the girl,[1] and as a result she got pregnant. When her condition became visible, she was sent to her native village to give birth discreetly and was forced to abandon the baby at her sister's house. In order to buy her silence, Süleyman promised several times to give her a proper dowry and arrange a marriage.[2] He did not remain loyal to his pledge, and Maruşa started to threaten that she would denounce him and no longer maintain her discretion about the incident. Eventually, she was expelled from the house in 1905. She then applied to the Court of Appeals with her accusations about the incident. Given his status in the society, Süleyman Efendi easily denied all the accusations, saying he was an honorable man who would never do such a thing. The case was then dropped.[3]

*Besleme*s were foster daughters who were adopted (though not legally) into relatively rich households at a very young age and brought up as servants. The practice was a form of child circulation, which encompassed a diverse constellation of practices involving minors who were sent out to be reared by unrelated caretakers. Often these girls were illegitimate, orphaned, and abandoned. The practice usually involved the daughters of the poor. They were often nursed, reared, and "rented out" for service in the households of others. The employers paid no wages, relying on the assumption that taking custody of a child was a form of charity—a benevolent act that did not result in an employer–employee relationship. The children performed household chores and the employers, in return, pledged to supply the children's basic needs—shelter, food, and clothing. The "job description" of *besleme*s also included a de facto form of unregulated concubinage, since their dependent and vulnerable position made them easy prey for the molestations of their masters.

The Ottoman Empire, like Prussia and Tsarist Russia, experienced a process of authoritarian-state modernization from the top-down that attempted to bring about new forms of centralization, control, and discipline. With the proclamation of the Reform Edict of *Tanzimat* (reorganizations) in 1839, an institutionalized process of modernization officially began in the Empire. Basic institutions were reformed to deal with social, political, and economic challenges. The reforms primarily targeted reorganization of the state apparatus in legal, financial, administrative, and military terms. However, wider social implications were inevitable and the realms of gender, family, marriage, morality, and sexuality could not remain untouched.[4] Under nineteenth-century legislation and regulations, the sexuality of women-citizens was covered by the jurisdiction of the state, as opposed to Islamic law, which considered conjugal issues to be in the inviolable private realm. Women's sexuality, together with intrafamily affairs, gender, procreation, morality, and hygiene, became issues of increasing public concern as the Ottoman state modernized. Adultery was redefined as an attack on public morality; abortion was seen as an attack on the nation. So, women faced rigorous state regulation of their sexuality.[5] In this turbulent context, the position of foster daughters, actually quite an old and widespread practice in Ottoman society, came to be noticed along with novel critical discourses on sexuality, decency, and morality.

European historiography on servant sexuality is rich.[6] The abuse of dependents by the house lords, however, is a largely unaddressed theme in Ottoman historiography.[7] Similar to other European practices, foster daughters were in no sense treated like real daughters but were used as helpers in the households. Masters'/fathers' sexual relation with them, as a social case of incest and sexual harassment, was an expected, if not natural, part of the agreement. The perception of nineteenth-century contemporaries, however, rarely involved pity for "sexually abused children." On the contrary, late Ottoman society had a tendency to define foster daughters in terms of sexual insaturation, unchastity, promiscuity, and indecency, or as "coquettes." The fact that they were sexually active children and adolescents was not considered as deviance. Disturbance, in reality, was a result of their unmarried status and seduction potential in and outside the household. The modern bourgeois discourse on sexuality prescribed the distribution and education of desire only in the familial space.[8] When they performed as maids, foster daughters were no longer regarded as children, irrespective of their age. As an essential part of the normalizing regime of this discourse, they were subject to surveillance and control due to the seduction potential attributed to them.[9] Both child labor and child sexuality were legitimized by Ottoman courts and judges, who consistently resisted declaring the masters guilty of either material exploitation or sexual harassment. The childhood of *besleme*s, therefore, was subsumed under their servant position.

The vulnerability of foster daughters in the Ottoman legal and social setting is obvious. Still, these young girls were not silenced, compliant, or passive characters. They played an active role in negotiating or refusing abuse and in determining their fates. They took initiative in many diverse ways, such as escape, official complaint, or, as a final resort, suicide, and through these means made their voices heard. They left so much evidence about themselves, either in court records or the Ottoman archives' petition registers, that their lives are discernible. This chapter delineates the intricacies of fostering girls as domestic servants in the late Ottoman Empire. The practice blurred the lines between servants and concubines, between incest and taboo, and between charity and abuse.

Orphans, Foundlings, and Children of the Poor

In etymological terms, *besleme* means "feeding." The word is derived from the verb *beslemek*, to feed. According to the nineteenth-century Turkish-English dictionary compiled by James W. Redhouse, which is famous for portraying designations by contemporaries and a social understanding of concepts, a *besleme* is "a maid or woman servant, a child fed in the house for charity."[10] There is an apparent ambivalence in this definition: child labor is intertwined with child raising. The same confusion can also be found in official documents. In 1910, the police department referred to a certain "Hadice" both as a *besleme* and as a servant (*Ahmed Muhtar Bey'in beslemesi Adanalı hizmetçi*).[11]

These girls could also be defined by other terms that, while not exactly synonyms, have closer meanings. *Evlatlık* was one of the most-used terms for foster children. It differs, however, from the term *besleme* in the sense that it encompasses boys as well. A foster boy was usually called a *yanaşma*, which literally means "the one who snuggled." Other gender-blind formulations of a fostered child include *ahiretlik, ahiret evladı, manevi evlat*, or *evlad-ı maneviyye*. In general, terminological formulations for foster children usually comprised the appellation "child" (*veled, evlad*). Sadly, being the daughter of one's foster family did not imply incorporation as a valued daughter and heir of the household. Rather, it actually implied a servant's filial subordination to a father-master or mother-mistress, situated in a rhetoric of kinship that naturalized relations of dependence.

Many orphans were taken in as *beslemes*. When one or both parents of a girl died, she could be adopted as a servant into the households of distant relatives, neighbors, or unrelated foreigners. Archival evidence provides many such examples. In 1846, when the parents of a girl named "Emine" passed away, an affluent lady took her in as a *besleme*, arguing that she was in danger of falling into the hands of slave-dealers.[12] In another case in 1903, eight-year-old Vesile was completely destitute, having neither living parents nor an uncle or brother.[13] She was taken into the household of a *mutasarrıf* (provincial administrator) of Yozgad, İsmail Hakkı Efendi, as a foster daughter.

The number of *beslemes* increased notably during times of serious crisis, multiplying the number of orphans. The influx of refugees from the Caucasus and the Balkans after World War I created such circumstances of emergency. Other examples include the aftermath of the 1894-1896 Armenian massacres when the Catholic Armenian Patriarchate called on believers to take orphan girls in their homes as "charitable work."[14] The orphanages played a part in this picture. Most of the "graduates" of girls' orphanages were entrusted to reliable families to become their daughters and to serve as their servants. The prospects in front of Ottoman orphan girls—irrespective of their ethnic-religious identity—were limited. Most of them remained as unmarried servants throughout their lives.

The curricula of girls' orphanages, whether in institutions run by non-Muslim communities, Catholic and Protestant missionaries, or the Ottoman state, stressed the inculcation of "duties" of a housewife and/or servant. The girls were trained to become proficient in cooking, cleaning, and washing. They acted as actual helpers/servants of the orphanages as part of their "applied training," and graduates were destined to serve in households. For instance, girls in the orphanage of Alliance Israélite in Izmir were placed as maids in the households of Jews.[15] Marriage could be another option for the girls, but it was a weaker one. The position of a wife depended largely on the strength of her family and the means she brought into the marriage (dowry). Orphans were deprived of both family and dowry. Their natural refuge was a position as a domestic in a friendly household.

Monsieur Galland, the superior of the "Dominican mission in Meso-potamia, Kurdistan, and Armenia," writes in 1904 that a great number of girls in the orphanage of the Sisters became servants in good families of the city.[16] American missionaries also "put children in Christian fami-lies" in Mardin, though without success. As the missionary in the field explains, the relatives of the children were ready to "give" the children to missionaries, but they did not agree to entrust them to families.[17] The locals considered being an orphan in an institution preferable to becom-ing a foster child in a non-kin household. They knew about the difficul-ties and suffering of orphan girls as servants in private households. The director of the Bursa Orphanage of the American missionaries also placed some orphan girls in families in the city circa 1902. But before long, the director regretted this practice and refused a number of applicants. He claimed that it was for "the best interest of the girls" to remain at the orphanage and that they should be "more discriminating in selecting positions for them."[18] The report latently describes that the girls at homes were unhappy. There were probably complaints about hard work and/ or abuse. One way or another, the American missionary discovered the hardships an orphan girl might face while working as a domestic servant.

Ottoman reformers defined the objective of girls' orphanages as training the girls to become domestic servants. In 1886 the Council of State (*Şura-yı Devlet*) decided that grown-up orphan girls at state institutions would be given to households as domestic servants.[19] Children in the *Darülaceze* orphanage and foundling asylum were entrusted to volunteering households from 1909 onward.[20] The 1912 Regulation of the institution specified that older girls would be either given to the applying parties as foster daughters (*evlatlık*) or married to suitors. The Regulation of 1914 even removes the age limit and states that "little or grown-up orphan girls will be given as foster children to the applicants in return for a deed (*senet*)." In 1921, the requirements became stricter. Applicants needed to have sufficient financial resources, a guarantor, and a clean judicial record.[21] In order to prevent maltreatment and abuse, there were inspections of the households twice a year.[22] However, the official rulings were often in contrast with a dismal reality. The authorities were often negligent both in making necessary investigations before entrusting girls to households and in paying regular visits to the families.[23]

Abandoned children were also brought up in the households to become servants. Leslie Peirce notes in her study on sixteenth-century Aintab that the foundlings taken into houses were destined to become *besleme*s.[24] The adoption of a girl foundling was often done only in name. The real aim of those who adopted a foundling was to find a girl to do the house chores. In 1888, a committee of Greek doctors investigated patterns of foster care in Beyoğlu and noted that, from among a mixed group of abandoned children, only girls were adopted. This meant that these adoptions were "nothing but a disguised form of domestic employment."[25]

Many destitute girls were raised to become maidservants in non-kin households. But most of the *besleme*s had at least one parent, if not two, who were still alive. Poor families and despairing parents, unable to support their children, sent their daughters to serve as servants in wealthy households so that they would be brought up and supported while carrying out their duties. The practice can be traced back to the sixteenth century and was common among various ethno-religious communities all around the Empire.[26] In nineteenth-century everyday vocabulary, the term *besleme* was used for the "circulated children" of the lower classes. An important women's magazine of the Second Constitutional Period, *Kadınlar Dünyası* (World of Women), discussed the issue of *besleme*s and defined these girls as daughters of the poor who were entrusted to wealthier families.[27]

Court records contain numerous legal contracts through which poor parents handed over their daughters to persons of high status, such as government officials, well-to do artisans, and merchants or their wives. In a case from 1748, a father handed over his daughter Havva, while she was still a minor, to serve at Ümmetullah's house. In return, he assumed his daughter would receive food and clothes in lieu of a fair wage. She worked there for fifteen years, until her sudden and unexplained death.[28] In Bursa, Şerife Zeynep entrusted her five-year-old daughter to Hatice in 1865 for her "moral improvement and education" (*tehzib ve taallüm-i adab ve maarif*). In the contract, it was underlined that she was only temporarily given (*iare*) and would be returned to her mother.[29]

Although educational purposes were stressed in many court records (*liecli't-tebenni ve't-terbiye* or *li't-tebenni ve't-terbiye ve'l-iyale*), the contracts were of an economic nature for both sides. The guardians of girls were given some money in return for the girl's nonpaid service in the household. In 1902, Cumali Mehmed bin Kazım, resident of Salonika, gave custody (*bilvelaye*) of his daughter, Şükriye, to the wife of Muzhir Kamil Efendi, chemist at the hospital of Salonika. He said he was "incapable of providing for her" (*infaka gayr-i kadir*) and the little girl was in dire need of alimony and clothing.[30]

Unpaid Maidservants

Adoption in the legal sense was unknown in Ottoman society. Formal adoption (*tebenni*), which existed in pre-Islamic Arabic societies, was prohibited after the embracing of Islam, with the sura of Ahzab (33), verses 4 and 5.[31] According to legal experts, adoption was impossible in Islamic law, since it was not in accordance with the Islamic understanding of lineage (*neseb*). The jurists assumed that adoption would cause confusion about lineage and lead to approval of various forbidden acts concerning the rights of legal inheritors and the borders of intimacy (*mahrem*) in households. As adopted daughters lived with the family, the rules of veiling (*tesettür*) and intimacy were usually disregarded or loosened. However, persons whose marriage was religiously permissible were to always abide by these laws.[32]

The absence of a legal regulation for adoption did not prevent Ottomans to have foster children. La Baronne Durand De Fontmagne, who lived in Istanbul during and after the Crimean War, writes that "Turks adore children and when they do not have their own, they willingly adopt." According to her account, adoptive children, "enfants de l'ame," were common in Ottoman society and transactions to adopt were handled by a court in the presence of witnesses.[33] In most instances, the agreement was an oral one, but the prevalence of child transfers (*tebenni*) in court records also verify the legalized nature of fostering.[34] These transactions did not produce the expected legal consequences of proper adoption, such as creating lineage, inheritance rights, and sexual taboos. Rather they were prepared to regularize the monthly alimony (*nafaka*) spent for the child. In some cases, adopting families demanded a judicial certificate so as to enumerate the girls' duties in households and the families' authority over them. Thanks to such a document (*hüccet-i şeriyye*), İsmail Hakkı Efendi, the *mutasarrıf* of Yozgad, could avoid having third parties take away his *besleme*.[35]

In everyday language, the term *besleme* was synonymous with maidservant. In the novel of Refi Cevat Ulunay *Eski İstanbul Yosmaları* (Old Cocottes of Istanbul, 1959), the protagonist of the book, Rânâ, does not want to marry a neighbor boy. His family, she says, does not employ enough helpers in the household and "they are actually looking for a servant, not a bride." Her father responds in anger, "so they don't have servants, they don't have a cook, and you will become a *besleme* over there. . . . Of course, you will."[36] The story of a *besleme* in Henry Otis Dwight's *Constantinople and Its Problems* (1901) is also a perfect summary of the intricate relationship between fostering a child and recruiting a servant. These children were euphemistically defined as "like a daughter," although they did hard work, such as carrying wood and water.

> The candle-maker Ahmed Ağa *bought* the little girl [of six or seven years] from her mother for fifty pounds. . . . He took little Sabiye home to his

poor little house in Sarı Güzel and handed her to his wife. . . . She was treated like a daughter. The child helped the woman in the kitchen, she brought the wood and carried water, she ran errands."[37]

Foster daughters were unpaid domestics, and they had to serve in the household for an unspecified length of time. Although sharia requires a fair wage in any work contract, in the case of adopted servants, these legal requirements were set aside and the hiring period and wage were not stipulated. The courts displayed no objections to this kind of employment, referring to these minor servants as "those who were employed without any salary contract."[38] In Ottoman documents, the relationship was portrayed by parents of the girls as "working without payment, and only for one's keep."[39]

A small and insignificant amount of money was given when masters decided to dismiss their *besleme*s after years of service. Girls also asked for compensation when they got fired or when their adopters died. Hadice *bint* Hüseyin applied to the court of Salonika in 1749 to receive a fair wage for the ten years she had served in her master's house. She admitted to declaring previously in court that she had exonerated him from any responsibility for her, but she argued that she had done so because she was beaten and forced to relinquish her rights against her will.[40] Maslina, an inhabitant of Monastir (Bitola), worked for thirteen years as a *besleme* in the household of a non-Muslim, Tevahir ibn Malko. When she was sent away in 1783, she submitted a petition to the court claiming the equivalent of wages.[41]

Adopters resisted payment, relying on the assumption that taking custody of a pauper child was a charity.[42] Rabia went to the court of Salonika in 1725 with a claim of payment for working as a *besleme*. Her mistress, in response, said she had taken Rabia when she was only seven years old and provided for all her needs while she was too young to perform any work. It was inevitable that she should take upon herself some of the household tasks. The court found the mistress to be right.[43] In Istanbul, Nazife was taken as a foster child in 1812 to the household of Mesud Efendi and served for his wife Ayşe Hatun. When her mistress died in 1817, the girl went to court to demand the money she deserved (*ecr-i mislimi*). Mesud Efendi argued that she was given 100 kuruş, together with some clothing and bedding, which could be proved from another court record. Nazife denied that she received any of these items; yet, the court trusted the master.[44] In that sense, fostering a girl was a profitable charity by which a servant could be secured at little or no expense.

The *besleme*s' vulnerability is clear from their failure to receive favorable verdicts. The girls relinquished their claims to receive a fair wage in return for an insignificant sum of money. These reconciliations attest that unpaid child labor, in return for raising the child, was acceptable and common in Ottoman society. The judges usually legitimized reconciliation and never positioned themselves next to maidservants. The subordination of female servants is demonstrated likewise in their late application to the court. In most cases, the *besleme*s' claims were submitted after their dismissal and sometimes years later. As benefactors enjoyed a much higher social and economic position, young girls were dependent on their goodwill and forced to accept their conditions. In many cases, tacit approval of this mode of employment and unequal relationships resulted in the marginalization of pauper girls to such an extent that they became veritable slaves.

Working conditions of foster daughters were hard, with unceasing demands, almost no private space for themselves, and no days off. They were dependent on the decisions of household heads or mistresses about their lives. A *besleme*'s leave from the house frequently created serious problems, based on the assumption made by the adopters that "their investment"—their upbringing expenditures, spent when the child was very little—only were paid back when the *besleme* grew up and became an able servant.[45] In some cases, the parents were asked to pay the accumulated expenses of the child.[46] If the *besleme* left the house earlier, the "investment" became "unprofitable." This is what Davidoff calls "the extent of control over the lifespan of the subordinate."[47] The maidservants were attached to their masters for unspecified periods. Often the former wished to believe that the attachment was permanent, as if they had *bought* these *daughters* and it was their right to keep them as long as they wanted.

Some parents attempted to call their daughters back. They said that the family was going to live elsewhere, or that the girl was no longer a child to stay in a non-kin house, or the girl would get married. Azime's mother, who had previously sent her daughter as a *besleme* from Erzurum to Istanbul, put forward religious and moral concerns in her plea for the return of her daughter. She argued that now that the girl had turned seventeen, it would be improper for her to act as a servant in a foreign house.[48] In 1905, a certain Talaslıoğlu Hasan requested the release of Vesile, a ten-year-old *besleme* working in Yozgad, for they were going to get married. Her master refused, arguing that she was an orphan with no legal guardian and that her age was not appropriate for marriage.[49] Hasan was able to convince the authorities in June 1908 that she "reached the age of puberty" (*sin-i büluğa vasıl*).[50]

The parents of the *besleme*s also faced some practical difficulties. Many of the girls were entrusted with government officials or members of the military class. They frequently moved from one place to another and hence the girl's family lost trace of the adoptive family. In 1916, Mustafa, the brother of seven-year-old Şükriye, took her from Sapanca to Istanbul to be adopted into an affluent household. After three years, Mustafa lost track of her and applied to the General Police Department for the investigation of his sister's life.[51] In another case, Cemile's master, *mutasarrıf* of Bolu, took her with a promise to her father that he would send her back if he was assigned to another post. After two months, the father realized that *mutasarrıf* had already left for Istanbul, soon to move to his new duty in Debre. The poor man then had to sell whatever he had, including a black beef cattle (*kara sığır ineği*), to travel to Istanbul in a twenty-eight-day journey by boat.[52] He not only had to make such a long trip but also had to file depressing applications at various bureaus in hope of taking back his daughter.

Taking a foster girl into a house was a charity only in name. The household heads were interested in a return on their investment. Foster parents seldom permitted the girls to go to school, which would have cost money, and marriage was another problematic area. There were agreements made in kadi courts regarding marriage for foster daughters. At the beginning of the service of a *besleme,* it may have been agreed on as to whether her parents or the family for which she worked were to select her husband. In most cases, the adoptive family insisted that they had full authority on the decision of marriage.[53] In a short story by Memduh Şevket Esendal, when a *besleme* of the house wants to get married, the mistress refuses in a revealing way: "Take a poor naked girl, clean her louses, and the moment she starts to become useful, she leaves the hell out of here. . . . Who told you that I am a soup kitchen?"[54]

Sexually Abused

As vividly described in Fatma Aliye's 1892 novel *Muhadarat* (Virtuous Women), there were three major types of female slaves in Ottoman households: the menial domestic (*cihaz halayığı*), the concubine (*odalık*), and the girl brought up in the household and later married off and set up in life (*besleme*).[55] Although *besleme*s were free persons in legal terms, they were frequently confused with young female slaves in harems, who were trained for patronage and the prestige of the lady. Considering their position and duties in the household, *besleme*s had similarities with female slaves. Their job description embraced the traits of both menial domestics (doing housework or similar services) and concubines (leading a husband–wife relationship with their masters). The fact that adopted children had no rights of inheritance and that they were excluded from the parameters of incest reduced their position so that they were closer to being slaves.

From the perspective of morality and sexuality, the practice of fostering *besleme*s was harshly criticized by nineteenth-century reformers and intellectuals, based on concerns of chastity and indecency. The sexuality of young female servants provoked uneasiness and suspicion, for they were unmarried, unprotected minors yet were "possessed" by their masters. Frequently the blame was put on the girls for being immoral and prone to unchaste sexual behavior. Since they were known to be economically and sexually vulnerable, even the most chaste and respectable maidservants were suspected. The stress was not on the sexual activeness of young girls but was centered on the fact that they were having out-of-wedlock relationships, which obstructed their prospective marriages. The real taboo, for that reason, was not the sexuality of young girls, but unregulated female sexuality.

In contemporary literature and in women's magazines, foster daughters were depicted as morally degenerate. The novelist Ahmet Midhat argued that employing foster daughters as servants was an evil practice, killing the girls' chances for marriage and having a family since they led a low and unchaste life in households and were pushed into prostitution.[56] In his novel, *She is Seventeen Yet* (1882), he describes the life prospects of a *besleme*.

> And those girls who work as *besleme*s in Christian households? Well, they are absolutely and entirely prospects for brothels. A poor girl enters into a household as a *besleme*. She finds a number of boys there. She starts having sex with them. Then, the affair is sensed. The girl is fired. Since she has a bad reputation now, other households do not accept the poor thing. And her parents are poor! Yet, she has seen nice clothes and jewelries. Her desire is awakened. As a consequence, she can only go to a brothel.[57]

Midhat's conscious intent to exempt Muslim households distorts historical reality. The research clearly reveals that this practice was common among Muslims and non-Muslims alike.[58] The only difference was that non-Muslim households could only foster non-Muslim *besleme*s, since it was against sharia law for a Muslim minor to live with a non-Muslim, while Muslims were free to take in both Muslims and non-Muslims.[59] In 1898, the governorship of Konya reported that many Muslim girls were employed in non-Muslim houses as *besleme*s.[60] The government ruled that the practice was against religious teachings and should not be allowed.[61] Most of the lower-class Christian girls and women were employed in rug making in home-based workshops. For the authorities, this was a chaster form of employment and the governorship proposed taking the necessary steps to open weaving workshops for Muslim girls. In another such example from 1847, two-year-old Fatma was entrusted as an *evlatlık* to a recent convert, Mustafa, formerly a Gregorian Armenian named Artin.[62] After twelve years, it turned out that Artin never left Christianity and raised the girl accordingly. The court ordered that she should be taken away from Artin and given to a "true Muslim."

Ahmet Midhat's description, despite its exaggeration, reflects the moral concerns of the day. The girls' status was ambiguous and they had a particular kind of vulnerability. They were subject to annoyingly persistent demands from their employers as well as a measure of social disgrace.[63] Upper-class mistresses underlined the worry that the girls might "seduce their husbands." In an article published in *Hanımlara Mahsus Gazete* (Newspaper for Ladies) in 1893, it was suggested that maids should always be kept busy and burdened with more work, since spare time led them into having affairs with men.[64] In 1911, another magazine, *Kadın* (Woman), raised the same concern regarding the sexual degeneration of *besleme*s. The author claimed that these girls entered into houses to seduce either the household head or the son. They used all their charm and tricks so as to become equal to the mistress and destroy the happiness of the family.[65] Likewise, many foster girls of the Greek community were returned back to the Orthodox churches they were taken from amid accusations that they had a "bad character" and inclination toward prostitution.[66]

The upper and middle classes consciously blamed foster daughters for unregulated and illicit sexual relations. Yet, it was embarrassingly often that *besleme*s became targets of sexual harassment and rape from their upper-class fictive kin. This duality, from a methodological perspective, points to the difference between the sources from below and those from above. Based on stories in court cases, the girls were subordinated and exploited, as opposed to the stories told by their all-powerful and *reputable* household heads. In literature and newspaper opinion pieces, however, the upper classes depicted an atmosphere of threat caused by these "unchaste creatures." Foster daughters were both sexually exploited and monitored under the suspicious gaze of the upper classes. So, *besleme*s experienced a paradoxical social status because they challenged and disturbed discourses of adolescent sexuality, sexual agency, and matrimonial morality in late Ottoman society.

Even if their status implied a form of lineage, according to Islamic jurisprudence, foster daughters were not considered a part of the taboo of incest, and in terms of kin relations, they were regarded as "outsiders," "others" of the household, like slaves and servants. It was religiously permitted to have sexual relations with them or to marry them. As a result, *besleme*s were not seen by the male members of the household as daughters or sisters. In that sense, keeping their bodily integrity against them was a permanent concern. They were often sexually exploited by their masters, as if they were concubines. In early 1895, the former Telegram Inspector of Biga, Hilmi Bey, raped and deflowered (*izale-yi bikr*) his foster daughter, and yet the office of public interrogation (*daire-yi istintak*) decided to debar his trial.[67] In 1895, two Circassian refugees, Mahmud and İbrahim, found out that *mutasarrıf* of Latakia, Reşad Bey, raped their virgin sister Fatma, the *besleme* of the household. They immediately asked for her release.[68]

Foster daughters were also targets of other men outside the house. The prerogative of heads could be extended to other members of the master class—to sons, brothers, relatives, friends, and visitors. A fourteen-year-old *besleme* of Ayşe Fitnat Hanım, Sadiye, was raped by one of the neighboring tradesmen, Kazım the coppersmith, in 1915.[69] This was also the case with the *besleme* of Major Agah Bey in 1910. Agah's adjutant visited his mansion. Finding the girl alone and unprotected in the house, he raped the virgin girl.[70] In addition to sexual violence, the foster daughters also suffered from other forms of physical violence. The *kaymakam* of Eğin had four *besleme*s in his house, all below ten years old and taken from poor peasant families. One night in 1894, he got very drunk and started to beat the girls severely. A seven-year-old girl was killed.[71]

*Besleme*s easily became victims of sexual assault and abuse, because they were separated from the structures that would normally look out for their honor. Many of them entered service upon losing their parents, and a vast majority had left their community of origin. Those who harassed them were aware of these factors. Men of high social standing could also convince or coerce servants by means of extravagant promises, small gifts, threats of dismissal, or brutal force. Undoubtedly, many such liaisons were never recorded. Masters concealed pregnancies, bought the girls' silence, or terrorized them into lying to the officials. Such measures were not always necessary, thanks to the overpermissive attitude of the juridical authorities. The judges were prone to grant de facto rights of concubinage to masters over their servants. Many legalized such acts by not convicting the men.

Intermediaries of Child Circulation

Girls seeking a position as a *besleme* needed intermediaries to be accepted into households. As minors, they had no credentials to apply by themselves. These intermediaries could be poor parents or relatives, as well as professionals known as *tellal*s (brokers, middlemen). It is interesting that the same term was used for those working in the slave markets and in brothels. *Tellal*s could be neighborhood-based or engaged in larger-scale businesses. They went to villages and smaller towns to collect girls from poor families and then brought them to large cities, especially Istanbul, to become *besleme*s in wealthier households. The reason for recruiting rural girls for urban households was related to expectations of chastity and honesty.[72] In 1890, Fatma Hatun went to Safranbolu to collect some orphaned and poor girls. She convinced the guardians of three "virgin little girls" (*bakir kız çocuğu*) to make them *besleme*s in Istanbul. Since none of the girls had a travel permit, Fatma arranged for them to secretly get on a British boat.[73] In another example, in 1910, Cemile *bint* Abdullah came from Bandırma to Istanbul with the intermediation of a *tellal*, a certain Mehmed, who told her that there was a good household there where she could serve as a *besleme*. He took her to the city and left her at the mansion. Yet, after only a month the master told her that they no longer needed a servant. Having no family or relatives in the city, she applied to the police department to receive help to go back to Bandırma.[74]

In the mid-nineteenth century, the practice of carrying girls away from their hometowns disturbed political authorities due to its similarities to the slave trade. The practice of fostering girls was as old as slavery in the Ottoman lands, and the two existed for long periods side by side. Recruiting foster children as domestic servants was not a nineteenth-century invention related to attempts to suppress slavery.[75] But the practice gained momentum with the shrinking of the market for slaves. Russian domination in Eastern Europe and annexation of the Crimea in 1783 had ended the profitable trade of the Tatars. The Russian control of Caucasian lands, circa 1801–1828, also meant that the last remaining source of white slaves for the Ottoman world was reduced and soon after this trade stopped.[76]

Another new factor was the attitude of Ottoman elites, who adopted a negative stance toward slavery and gradually disengaged from it on moral grounds. Slavery was gradually replaced with free forms of service and patronage, such as raising freeborn young girls in the household.[77]

Alan Duben and Cem Behar, in their book *Istanbul Households*, based on an analysis of the empire-wide censuses of 1885 and 1907, argue that servants in the Muslim households of Istanbul were predominantly young and female. In 1885 85 percent of those discernible as servants were females, and in 1907 the figure was 80 percent. According to both censuses, almost 24 percent of these women were under the age of fifteen.[78] In the census of 1885, the frequency of the entry "foster child" (*evlatlık*) was much smaller compared to entries like "slave" or "servant." However, Ferhunde Özbay's analysis based on the 5 percent sampling of Istanbul muslim households in the 1885 and 1907 census rosters shows that the number of *evlatlık*s tripled.[79]

Child circulation was also criticized due to the possible outcomes of sexual maltreatment and abuse. There was general European concern about the kidnapping of girls for prostitution. Several "child-saving campaigns" raised awareness about the sexual abuse of girls, especially when they left the protection of their family to seek employment.[80] The Ottoman state was concerned with the preservation of public morality and the prevention of prostitution. Children's sexuality as such was not a real issue; it was extramarital sex that should be controlled and suppressed.

In 1887 the Ministry of Interior was informed that certain men deceived destitute girls or poor and weak parents with promises of placing the girls as *besleme*s in wealthy households. The girls were continuously sold from one master to the next. In the end, they were engulfed by misery and prostitution. The Council of State sent circulars to the provinces to stop these "corrupt men" (*hamiyetsiz eşhas*) from practicing their "mischief" (*mefsedetleri*).[81] In 1899 the government started another investigation in Bahçecik, İzmid, on the issue of the "sale of little girls" by their parents as *besleme*s. The inquiry ascertained the middlemen and the purchasing households.[82] Then, in 1900, there was a scandal in Bulgaria on the same subject. The authorities came to the realization that poor girls were promised employment as *besleme*s and sold into prostitution.[83]

The girls sent from the islands of Lemnos and Imbros became the main actors of a similar dispute in March 1904. The Ottoman authorities realized that some persons, calling themselves *consignee* (*emanetçi*, or depository), were going to the islands and pretending to be the intermediaries of middle-class families. They said they were there to collect young Greek girls for fostering positions, but the girls were then kidnapped to Alexandria. From there they were embarked on ships to Europe or America, where they would "be dragged into prostitution" (*fuhuşata süluk*).[84] In order to end the practice, the government asked the metropolitan bishop of the islands to prohibit the girls from leaving the islands. The religious man said the practice was an inevitable result of extreme poverty (*fakr u zaruret*). There was nothing he could do about it. The provincial government still demanded an official document from the bishop attesting that these girls "would gain their livelihood via legitimate jobs."[85]

In the summer of the same year, a similar controversy was again staged. Upper-middle-class families, who came to the islands for their summer vacation, were taking in little girls as seasonal *besleme*s. But then some of them were eager to take the girls with them when they left the islands.[86] The Ottoman authorities criticized the practice of detaching vulnerable girls from their families or legal guardians. Unaccompanied young girls going away, or abroad, could especially face sexual dangers. In order to prevent them from abuse, the Ministry of the Interior asked the adopting families to sign a covenant upon departing the islands. These were to guarantee that they would not "lead these girls into naughty paths."[87]

Efforts to prevent child circulation resulted from increasing criticism against slavery and active intervention of the state into the domain of sexuality and public morality. The official discourse criticized organized fostering practices and the presence of intermediaries for such arrangements and also voiced paternalistic and disciplinary concerns for public morality. The upper class reproduced the discourse of matrimonial family values. These "unchaste and sexually active" adolescent girls were to be repressed and disciplined. They accused the *besleme*s of deteriorating the public morals rather than criticizing the built-in ambiguities of fostering.

Glimpse of Agency among Foster Daughters

*Besleme*s were dependents who were both sexually suspect and exploited. Even so, they were free agents who fought back through the courts and other state mechanisms as well as through more micro ways. The court cases are a powerful reflection of *beslemes'* vulnerability as well as their level of access to the public sphere. Reconstructing their stories requires not only listening to voices of oppression, exploitation, and discrimination but also acknowledging agency, resistance, and empowerment. Working conditions and the job itself finalized a *besleme's* subordination. But she became a self-conscious identity and an agent through the same means.[88] The possibility of resistance to norms is also located within the structure of power itself.

Networks of relations and "relational determinations" based on gender should also be taken into account.[89] These young girls' agency was constantly shaped by societal norms—by their relationship to fathers, uncles, mothers, brothers, neighbors, masters, and mistresses as well as how they were viewed by rulers, lawmakers, or judges. These networks of relations tolerated only certain prescribed modes of agency. Not all modes brought about resistance to relations of domination, but they at least ensured a certain capacity for action. *Beslemes'* agency, however, did not always imply progressive change; most often it only gave them the capacity to endure and suffer.[90]

Young women's defiance of law or custom, including such crimes as robbery, arson, escape, unapproved marriage, and even prostitution, can be interpreted as a form of resistance in some cases and an indication of deprivation and despair in others.[91] They disobeyed orders, acted defiantly, or took advantage when running errands to visit friends or family. Some of these "crimes" were committed against the state powers, while others, perhaps the majority, were aimed at a source of oppression much closer to home—the family and work with its specific rules for women. Either as a form of resistance or due to despair, quite a few foster daughters robbed their master's homes, set their houses on fire, or acted negligently. In 1857, the *besleme* of Hacı Resmi set his house on fire "in an instance of anger and despair."[92] In 1904, Dane the grocer in İştip (Štip) reported to the authorities that his *besleme*, Bezoş, had robbed his house and run away.[93]

Few of these girls engaged in premarital sex because they were promiscuous or romantically inclined. Most of them yielded to the men who harassed them because they were forced by sheer brutality or gave in to seduction hoping that it would be a step toward securing a marriage partner.[94] The historical record also leaves space for the possibility of variation, opportunity, and pleasure in their lives.[95] *Beslemes* had an active role in negotiating or refusing abuse and in determining their fates. They were not totally suppressed, compliant, and mute. Sometimes they took the initiative and made their voices heard, specifically by running away, applying to the court, or, as a more desperate solution, by attempting or committing suicide.[96]

One of the viable options for maltreated and abused girls was escape. When they could, they tried to go back home. In 1911 Captain Hüseyin Bey reported to the Istanbul police that his ten-year-old *besleme*, Zehra, was lost. In a short while, she was found in her hometown, Değirmendere, in the house of her uncle. She said she escaped to evade the difficulties of her life.[97] Some girls found refuge in other households. *Beslemes* applied to their nicer neighbors for employment or to other people they encountered while they were running errands in the district. There was no guarantee that they would be luckier with their new masters, but they probably assumed it could not be worse. In 1910 Hadice, the *besleme* of Ahmed Muhtar Bey, assistant of the Minister of Foreign Affairs, escaped and found shelter in a neighboring house, that of Abdullah. When her master demanded Hadice's return, she firmly rejected him and said she would commit suicide if further demands were made. The threat was convincing for both household heads, and Abdullah wrote a petition to admit Hadice into his household.[98]

When there were institutions for destitute girls in the neighborhood, the girls also tried their chances there. In 1858 the *besleme* of a merchant, Hacı Ahmed Efendi, escaped from his house and found shelter in the nearby school of the Catholic Sisters (*Sœurs de la Charité*). Despite the demands of her master, the Sisters refused to send her back.[99]

Some *beslemes* managed to marry with persons they met while working. In 1894 the Ministry of Interior received a complaint that a Bulgarian *besleme*, Petra Theodorova, was abducted from her master's house in Ortaköy (Istanbul) by an Armenian Catholic, Petri, and that the Armenian Catholic Patriarchate married them ignoring both her age (fourteen) and the consent of her parents.[100] Her master, Nicola Lazaroff, demanded the punishment of Petri and also asked for monetary compensation from the Patriarchate for his losses. According to the following police investigation, she had not been kidnapped; her escape was voluntary. Petra was an orphan, adopted into Lazaroff's house as a foster daughter three years before. Her life was difficult: she not only had to perform household chores and look after her master's five kids by herself, with no payment at all, but also endured sexual harassment. Running away with Petri, who owned a haberdashery near the house, was her escape. Petra declared that they were acquainted for a while and that they planned the escape and marriage "with motives of love and affection."[101]

Escape was a short-term solution. A young and destitute girl could not make it long on the streets. She could not join one of the then-famous boy gangs, and it was not a rare occurrence that an escaped maid would be found a couple of days after her disappearance, having being raped and "deflowered." These girls had to create opportunities for themselves among strangers. When they could not do so, they were forced to return to the same household and stay until their next trial. In 1910, Emine's father came from Ereğli to Istanbul to visit his daughter. In the household where she had been entrusted, he was astonished to learn that Emine had escaped for the *third* time. The masters denied accusations of exploitation and abuse. However, the fact that they never reported the escape of the girl (until the arrival of her father) is a point to consider.[102]

Another strategy of *besleme*s was suicide. Most find it difficult to consider suicide as an effective form of expression and of agency. Yet, these girls might have seen death as their sole solution to avoid maltreatment and molestation. Attempted suicide in that respect was different, as it might serve to draw attention to the troubles of the girls and also scare their masters into creating some space for them. In September 1891, the foster daughter of an attorney was found dead in his house. There were no outside marks on her body and the police were told that she had taken pills. Since the cause of death was uncertain, the Istanbul municipality was asked to send forensic doctors from the medical school to make an autopsy.[103] In January 1909 the foster daughter of Ali Galip Bey, lieutenant colonel in the Navy, cut her throat, her stomach, and her wrists with scissors in an attempt to commit suicide. Her master argued that she was in a "state of lunacy," without explaining the reasons why.[104] A similar case took place in the household of Namık Bey, a member of the Board of Health (*Meclis-i Sıhhiye*). In 1910, his servant-daughter was found cut up from her stomach. Namık Bey claimed that she attempted to commit suicide. Yet, the police started an investigation in order to account for the genuine reason for the wounds and scars.[105] Actually many such cases carry the suspicion that murders may have been disguised as suicides.

As a third strategy, foster daughters applied to the justice of the court. Compensation cases, through which the girls wanted to receive some payment for the time they served, were already discussed in the section on unpaid labor. In addition, *besleme*s filed cases with charges of sex crimes, mainly rape. Illicit sexual relations (*zina*) in Islamic law is a crime against religion, sanctioned by punishments in the Koran. The punishments laid down for them are called *hadd*, offenses against God. The prescribed punishment for *zina* according to Sunni jurists was 100 lashes if they were free and fifty if they were slaves, followed by one year of banishment of both men and women. Capital punishment by stoning was also used under certain circumstances.[106] Ottoman codes of law (*kanunnames*), on the other hand, changed corporal penalties to fines.[107] If the woman was not married, the man was liable for the proper bride-price. If she was a slave, he had to pay damages to the owner. In addition it could be an offense punishable at the discretion of the kadi.

The rules of Islamic jurisprudence on bringing an accusation of adultery were so strict that some legal scholars have claimed that the court would never see instances of adultery, fornication, or rape. First of all, four male witnesses were required instead of the normal two, and they had to testify as eyewitnesses to the act of "unlawful intercourse" (*zina*). Moreover, the *hadd* punishment could only be brought about if the confession was made in four separate hearings.[108] Peirce calls it a paradox of Islamic jurisprudence that it set up obstacles to the enforcement of the sexual probity it mandated.[109]

For *hadd* crimes, the court was not supposed to recognize amicable settlement (*sulh*) as a legitimate form of resolution. Yet, when there was inadequate evidence for a *hadd* conviction, as in many cases of *zina* and rape, courts regularly recognized settlements.[110] In cases of rape by a master, foster daughters tried to negotiate recompense from their employers.

The crime of rape was simply disregarded and the cases were handled as compensation issues; stricter penalties could not be applied due to legal doubt. Such doubt exists if the man mistakenly, but still reasonably, assumed that sexual intercourse with his victim was legally acceptable, for example if she was bound to him in marriage or owned by him as a slave.[111] Apparently, sexual intercourse with *beslemes* raised a similar legal doubt. Masters could plausibly consider the intercourse as inherent in the job.

On August 9, 1858, a new penal code, based on the French Code of 1810, was adopted in order to reiterate the equality of all Ottoman subjects, Muslim and non-Muslim alike, in line with the promises of *Tanzimat* legal reform.[112] Laws concerning sex and sexuality were mostly subsumed under the heading "about crimes concerning violation of honor."[113] A number of articles involved sexual relations with a minor (defined under the law as a person aged twenty-one or under) by force or consent. Anyone who committed a sexual act with a minor would be imprisoned for at least six months (Art. 197). If a parent or legal guardian forced a minor to commit such an act, they were liable to be sentenced to at least five years of hard labor (Art. 199). In cases of defloration, women or their guardians sued men to pay damages equal to their bride-wealth, often negotiating the sum in court, in addition to a sentence of hard labor (Art. 200).[114]

The new penal code was incomparably modern in form and substance, marking the Empire's first clear rupture from traditional law. Still, it was not entirely free from certain Islamic legal provisions in its original form. The first article stated that the code did not abrogate the provisions of Islamic law and that it merely codified the limits of the rights of the ruler.[115] The new code was applicable only in secular (*nizamiye*) courts, using laws of procedure adopted from French models and established under the jurisdiction of the Ministry of Justice.[116] Court records point to the fact that older regulations remained remarkably intact. Multiple legal systems existed side by side in nineteenth-century Ottoman society, each offering its own vantage point on morality and sexual conduct.[117]

*Besleme*s were usually referred to the local kadi courts, where severer punishments of the new code were rarely applicable. Moreover, in these courts the testimony of the status-holder was always preferred against that of a poor, orphaned minor girl. In 1880s Egypt, a minor servant claimed that one night her master attacked and raped her. She remained with the family for some time without divulging her secret. When she realized her pregnancy, she complained to the authorities. The man denied the allegations and defended himself, saying he was an honorable man, "living next to a mosque" where he prayed regularly and that he would never commit such a crime. Since the girl could not present evidence, the court decided that she had no case against the man and asked her to keep away from him.[118]

Working girls, on the other hand, were in a highly vulnerable position. In the eyes of the judge, they were by definition "unchaste." Women whose labor was public not only faced sexual assault but were less able than wealthier women to guard their reputation and honor. Their visibility made them easier targets of social suspicion and censure. Accordingly, they were denied the honor that automatically accrued to women of greater wealth and status merely by virtue of their seclusion.[119] Maids, who were forced to work in a male environment and who were deprived of the seclusion of higher-class women, were automatically denied chastity, which was defined as the complete segregation of male and female domains.

The moral ill-repute of domestic service undoubtedly encouraged sexual abuse, but recourse to the court also reflected the absence of voluntary organizations among the servants that could provide a refuge for maltreated maids or impose informal sanctions on abusive employers.[120] Still, it is remarkable given this situation that young girls came up with accusations against masters, even when they knew that they were going to fail in their suit and pay a fine for slander due to a lack of supporting testimony.[121] Apparently, this was a strategy by the young girls to at least make the affair known to the society, even if the latter would not protect them. From this moment onward, their masters were men to whom a crime was imputed, and so they were no longer "stainless." A second accusation of the same kind could result in different action by the court.[122] Moreover, these young women also went to court as a way of solving their serious social and legal problems.[123] They most probably hoped to achieve an agreeable judicial solution, which could possibly remedy their honor and reputation, and in cases of out-of-wedlock pregnancy even offer a solution for the future of their unborn child.

Deprived of the comparatively protective environment of their own families, orphaned, destitute, and poor girls existed under three layers of subordination. First, they were materially exploited and sexually abused by their masters, who were considered to be performing a charitable act by taking them into their households. They were abused as workers and as foster daughters by their masters and fictive kin, revealing the power relations between master and servant and adult and child. Second, they were put into a disadvantaged position by the Ottoman patriarchal legal discourse, which systematically discriminated against working women and denied them fair treatment. Third, they were left powerless in the courts as judges routinely favored their masters, relying on the well-established status of the latter in society as opposed to poor and destitute girls who were unprotected orphans in a world of family, kin, and lineage relations. Nevertheless, these young women were not completely subjected, silenced, and helpless. They were able to find ways of taking the initiative in resistive strategies. The abundant mention in the records of escape stories, suicides, and accusations of abuse is a clear sign of the assumed agency on the part of *besleme*s.

Nineteenth-century Ottoman public discourse and legislation problematized the fostering of girls only to a certain extent. Intellectuals and reformers never seriously focused on children's sexuality or their unpaid labor; instead, the girls were treated as if they were adults. The imputed or real sexuality of the fostered girls was not defined as deviant. Rather, the concern centered upon the issues of morality, marriage, prostitution, and illicit relationships. The state was interested in power and in the system of controlling sexuality. The active intervention and paternalistic and disciplinary concerns of the modernizing Ottoman state in the domain of sexuality and public morality also found an echo in the discourse of the upper classes, who readily embraced matrimonial family values and accused the *besleme*s of deteriorating the public morals.

Youthful female sexuality, personified and solidified in the figure of *besleme*s, was framed in a complex and contradictory way. These girls were both sexually exploited and objects of discipline under the critical gaze of the upper classes and the state, since as sexually active, unwed, adolescent girls they disturbed the accepted rules and limits of sexual agency. Stereotypical cultural codes for young girls were dichotomized as the pure, chaste, virgin girl or the seductive, promiscuous, dangerous debauchee. The observed sexual agency of foster daughters marginalized them as indecent and fallen girls due to the well-established contention that chastity and sexual agency could not coexist.

This chapter provides a historical account of the inner world of households and the experiences of fostered girls raised by non-kin families. The source material only exists thanks to young girls' agency as legitimate historical actors. Doubtless, many tragedies concerning the abuse of young servants did not reach the archives. On the other hand, not all foster daughters were mistreated or sexually abused. There must also have been happy stories somewhere. Those, unfortunately, have rarely made it into written forms.

3

State Orphanages (*Islahhanes*)

GOING OUTSIDE of the private setting of late Ottoman households, it is now time to delineate how children became targets and actors of the politics of urbanity in the second half of the nineteenth century. The focus here is on a new educational institution, the *ıslahhane*s, first established particularly for orphans and poor children as an experimental venture in the early 1860s in the *vilayet* (province) of Danube (Tuna). In 1867, a common statute was written for *ıslahhane*s based on the one prepared by Midhat Paşa for *ıslahhane*s in the Danube.[1] This regulation, which was sent to the provinces on 21 June 1867, ordered each province to establish an *ıslahhane* for "vagrant orphans and destitute children" between the ages of five and thirteen.[2] Following this imperial order, fifteen such institutions were immediately opened all around the Empire. Again in 1873–1874, a new wave of these institutions was initiated by the Regulation on Public Administration of *Vilayets* of 1871, in compliance with an article enforcing the opening of *ıslahhane*s. A more detailed *ıslahhane* regulation was also prepared in 1871, again with reference to the Danubian model.[3] In total, more than thirty orphanages were opened within a period of thirty years (1862–1899). Taking into account the rather difficult and tardy spread of other educational establishments throughout the provinces, the penetration of the *ıslahhane*s into many different localities in the Empire deserves to be treated as a real and exceptional achievement of the late Ottoman reformers.

Their regulations, curriculum, and functions, as well as their targeted student body, made *ıslahhane*s the first modern orphanages of the Ottoman administrative authority spanning the central and provincial

TABLE 12. State Orphanages (*Islahhanes*) in the Ottoman Empire

	City	Vilayet	Year (Hijri)	Year (Gregorian)
1	Trabzon	Trabzon	1280	1864
2	Niš	Danube	1280	1864
3	Ruse	Danube	1281	1865
4	Sofia	Danube	1281	1865
5	Salonika	Salonika	1281	1865
6	Istanbul, Sultanahmet	Istanbul	1284	1868
7	Kastamonu (mixed)	Kastamonu	1285	1868
8	Bursa	Hüdavendigar	1285	1868
9	Sarajevo	Bosnia	1285	1869
10	Scutari	Scutari (Albania)	1285	1869
11	Sivas	Sivas	1285	1869
12	Aleppo	Aleppo	1285	1869
13	Baghdad	Baghdad	1285	1869
14	Izmir	Aydın	1286	1869
15	Diyarbekir	Diyarbekir	1286	1869
16	Erzurum	Erzurum	1286	1869
17	Damascus	Syria	1286	1869
18	Istanbul, Yedikule (girls)	Istanbul	1286	1870
19	Kandiye	Crete	1288	1872
20	Ruse (girls)	Danube	1289	1872
21	Harput	Mamuretülaziz	1289	1873
22	Edirne	Edirne	1290	1873
23	Adana	Adana	1290	1873
24	Konya	Konya	1290	1873
25	Jerusalem	Jerusalem	1291	1874
26	Janina	Janina	1294	1878
27	Istanbul, Üsküdar (girls)	Istanbul	1295	1878
28	Istanbul, Aksaray (girls)	Istanbul	1296	1879
29	Gümülcine (Komotini)	Edirne	1295	1879
30	Istanbul, Cağaloğlu (girls)	Istanbul	1296	1879
31	Istanbul, Sultanahmet (girls)	Istanbul	1301	1884
32	Antalya	Konya (Teke)	1306	1888
33	Skopje	Kosovo	1313	1895
34	Monastir	Monastir	1317	1899

The data has been prepared based on documentation of the Ottoman archives; dates range from 1864 to 1908.

levels. *Islahhane*s have previously been treated as institutions for juvenile delinquents.[4] This was not entirely wrong according to their Regulation. But this was still a misinterpretation resulting from institution's name, *ıslahhane*, which literally means "reform house." Midhat Pasha recounts in his memoirs that "since this was a brand new institution, with no precedent in the country," he found the name only after long consideration and finally through inspiration from a Koranic verse, which specified that the best approach to orphans was "to improve and reform them" (*salah ve ıslah*).[5] In an article that appeared in 1915 in *Tedrisat Mecmuası* (Journal of Teaching), an important educational magazine of the time, İhsan Şerif wrote that *ıslahhane* as a term simply meant "orphanage."[6] Under Abdülhamid II, *ıslahhane*s began to be called *Hamidiye Sanayi Mekteb-i Alisi*, since the organic link of the institution with Midhat Pasha was problematic. The term was still in use in official correspondence from the era.

Research in the Prime Ministry's Ottoman Archives, Ottoman laws and regulations, contemporary newspapers and journals, and Ottoman educational and provincial yearbooks shows that the idea of "reform" (*ıslah*) inherent in the term *ıslahhane* was enmeshed in the *Tanzimat* worldview and targeted more than incarceration of children under disciplinary conditions. The main objective of the institution was repeatedly and clearly formulated as "the betterment of the conditions and education of Ottoman orphans."[7] Yet the nineteenth-century institutional world of children was not defined by rigid boundaries, and many non-orphans were sheltered in these establishments. *Islahhane*s were also a form of free boarding schools, providing temporary or permanent care for children whose parents were in distress. Ottoman terminology in relation to *ıslahhane*s does not hint specifically at gender—the terms "child" (*çocuk*), "orphan" (*yetim*), and "destitute" (*bikes*) are all gender-neutral. But the reformers mostly, but not exclusively, targeted boys.

The idea of the reformatory was also present in the 1871 Regulation. Those under thirteen who were convicted of committing a crime legally necessitating a prison sentence of "one year or longer" would be put into *ıslahhane*s instead of adult prisons, together with destitute children, orphans, and children of the poor, as there were no juvenile prisons in the Empire.[8] The Regulation refers to convicted minors only a few times—three articles out of fifty-two.[9] "Criminal children," though a sheer minority, would be placed in the institution with the goals of "disciplining and punishment" (*tedib ve ceza*).

The other daring objective was to reform and discipline the outer space of the *ıslahhane*—both its specific urban surroundings and the larger Ottoman public space. The opening of *ıslahhane*s was linked to immediate considerations, such as the beautification and sterilization of urban centers by removing unattended children and youth from the streets, and the longer-term aim of urban economic progress by turning idle and wandering children into skilled and productive laborers. The institution materialized some abstract notions of Ottoman reform, such as centralization and the dissemination of Ottomanist ideals. On the local level, *ıslahhane*s were at the intersection of the process of disciplining urban spaces and the goal of economic progress in urban manufacturing and industrial activity. On the imperial and more abstract level, they were instrumental in linking the central with the provincial, and local communities with Ottoman identity.

The orphanages became significant urban landmarks with the novelties they brought into the lives of cities, namely the printing press, brass band, and edifices. Orphans became artisans, laborers, pressmen, and musicians, and orphanages operated as workshops, factories, printing houses, and conservatories. In the late Ottoman urban context, orphans and orphanages were at the very heart of the city, despite contrary tendencies that pushed them to the margins.

Wanderers, Vagrancy, and Urban Security

A series of legal and administrative reforms called the *Tanzimat* were implemented between 1839 and 1876 in the Ottoman Empire.[10] These reforms, conceived by a small and influential portion of the imperial bureaucratic elite, was closely related to foreign diplomatic pressure on the issues of right to life, liberty, and property of mainly non-Muslim subjects. Yet, they meant more over-encompassing transformation in the long-term. Different notions of "order" were at the heart of the *Tanzimat* state ideology and political idiom.[11] The term *asayiş* (public order, public tranquility) or, more narrowly defined, the technical production of security, namely *emniyet* (safety, security; the police, the law), were central to it. Especially from the 1860s onward, the new notion of order specifically meant civilization (*medeniyet*) and discipline (*inzibat*). Within this picture, any form of disobedience or breakup of the order would be corrected with *terbiye* and *tedib*, which no longer simply meant "chastisement" but super-seded the straightforward notion of punishment and assumed the larger sense of "disciplining and education." The objective was more ambitious: all that was improper or disobedient (both people and places) should suc-cumb completely to the new reforms and thus be reformed (*ıslah*) and dis-ciplined (*inzibat*).

*Islahhane*s were closely related to this new conceptualization of order and discipline in the urban space, redefining the borders of obedience and disobedience, security and danger, progress and decline, and visibil-ity and invisibility.[12] These institutions were conceived through a novel discourse of modern urban governance, which aspired to guarantee law and order, together with beautification of the city streets and progress in urban manufacturing and industrial activity.

An overview of Ottoman reform in the pilot *vilayet* of Danube may better situate the reform houses within this larger picture. The *vilayet* of Danube was created in 1864 as a proving ground for Empire-wide admin-istrative, legal, and fiscal reorganization. Under its first governor, Midhat Paşa, the province experienced a period (1864–1868) of modernization in the fields of legal and institutional reform, infrastructure, communica-tions, economic development, medical care, hygiene, and urban devel-opment.[13] The province fulfilled its role as a model reasonably well. The Danube provincial charter was used as a template by new *vilayet*s all over the Empire. It also became the basis for the comprehensive new provincial law (also known as the Law of the *Vilayet*s) in 1867. The long-term goal was to use the experience of the Danube province as the basis of future Empire-wide policies. It is not a coincidence that it was during Midhat's governorship that the first *ıslahhane* was opened in Niš (1861) for orphans and "problem children."[14]

The reorganization of the police force was part of the new urban policies that went hand-in-hand with the critical discourse targeting unattended children in public spaces. The most intriguing aspect of the

5. *Islahhane* of Salonika. Unknown photographer, İstanbul Üniversitesi Kütüphane ve Dokümantasyon Daire Başkanlığı, *Fotoğraf Albümleri Dizini*, 90423-0023.

6. Hamidiye Bursa Industrial School (1906). Unknown photographer, in *Hüda-vendigar Vilayeti Salname-yi Resmiyyesi* (Bursa: Vilayet Matbaası, 1324 [1906–1907]), 593–94.

police reform project was the restructured duties of the police officers (*zabtiye*).[15] Some *zabtiye*s in the province were retrained to enforce the new reform policies and regulations, particularly in the larger cities. Renamed "inspection officials" (*umur-i teftişiye memurları*), these policemen were given broad powers to monitor citizens' compliance with their numerous new duties in the fields of city sanitation and embellishment (such as unlawful emptying of sewage, disposing of trash, failure to sweep outside one's house or shop, or blocking traffic). More importantly, suspected minors could now be fined on the spot by the police, whereas more serious deviations were referred to the city council or to the local criminal court if necessary. The inspectors were given the authority to arrest and "remove" undesirable children, namely vagrants and beggars, from the city streets and put them into the new *ıslahhane*s.

In the nineteenth century, the "dangerous child" began to occupy a significant place in international public opinion.[16] There was public anxiety about poor children, street urchins, and underage beggars occupying newly expanding urban public spaces. According to middle-class opinion, these children should have been in school, the family home, the farm, the factory, or the workshop. The moral abandonment or neglect of children is usually attributed to material scarcity and strain on families due to rapid and forced urbanization. In the Ottoman case, while levels of industrialization, economic development, literacy, urbanization, and other measures of modernization varied considerably from place to place, accompanying social values spread more rapidly and with greater chronological coincidence. Concern and criticism regarding vagrant children in urban areas was mostly introduced and disseminated by new reform-minded cadres of administrators, most of whom worked as diplomatic representatives of the Empire in European capitals during the first half of the nineteenth century.[17] The discourses on child disciplining were partially imported and inspired from "the West," as they were part of a package of ideas regarding the modern, progressive city.[18]

The change of discourse was also partially related to the increasing circulation of commercial goods in and around cities and linked with a new conception of modern governance in urban areas.[19] The municipality and police assumed, with the interference and influence of local notables, the protection of the local community of commerce. Professional groups in the major urban centers (specifically port cities) started to promote an urban agenda in the press, local clubs, and municipalities. They supported public charity, donations, and modern education as major ways of helping the underprivileged, the poor, and the community as a whole.[20] They demanded stricter control over the city space as well as social transformation and urban reorganization. In this discourse, seasonal migrants, newcomers, and vagabonds were interpreted as threats to urban security and economy.[21] As a consequence, part of the middle-class solution was to remove and/or relocate single migrant men and vagrant children in the name of modernity and progress.[22]

In the Ottoman period, "urban reform" stressed the exclusion of unattended children from public spaces. This determination meant that the street, the square, and the city came to be conceived as "anti-child." Next to this discursive fixation, the Russo-Ottoman wars the periods 1768–1774 and 1878–1888 resulted in refugee crises that had a definite impact on the opening of *ıslahhane*s, which served as part of a major systematic and institutional initiative to take care of unattended children. As a result of the first such refugee flow in the aftermath of the Crimean War (1853–1856), destitute and vagrant children became a presence in the streets of the Danubian cities.[23] Accordingly, the refugee children of Tatars and Circassians were a majority in the first three (boys') vocational orphanages of the *vilayet* of Danube.[24] Refugee girls of mostly Abkhasian origin also constituted the majority in the girls' orphanage of Ruse.[25] A similar course was also effective in the opening of the orphanage of Trabzon. In 1864, the governorship collected the orphans and destitute children of the refugees (*muhacir*), and they were in a miserable condition. They had neither parents nor relatives and lacked the means to gain their own livelihood. Authorities established the *ıslahhane* in a rented building, where these refugee children were sheltered and educated.[26] The reason behind the opening of the *ıslahhane* of Edirne in 1873 was related to the war and occupation in the province.[27] The *ıslahhane* of Izmir admitted several refugee orphans as well.[28]

There was evidently concern and pity for the misery of refugees. Still, they were observed with a rather critical gaze as they were viewed as the chief source of crime and pauperism in the cities. Refugee children's education was problematized, and the conditions that would keep them away from delinquency became a heated topic. In the absence of genuine experts of psychology, pedagogy, or social work in the Ottoman context, the state relied on the expertise of police departments, administrative bodies, and provincial governors—especially in the person of Midhat Pasha as the "genius" behind the establishment of reform houses. These apparatuses defined juvenile delinquency and devised the methods to cure it.

According to the interpretation of the Supreme Council (*Meclis-i Vala*) in 1868, the vocational orphanages in the Danube (Niš, Ruse, Sofia) were opened primarily to collect the destitute refugee children and orphans who used to wander in the streets and perform the "ugly act of begging" (*zell-i sual*) along with other "disgraceful behavior" (*su-i efali irtikab*).[29] As apparent from the choice of words in the formulation, *zell* and *irtikab*, the council implied that the acts of these children were interpreted as almost criminal, although none of these vagrants had been charged with a specific offense. Concern and criticism about beggars and vagrants in urban areas was actually part of a novel discourse, given that begging had once been a recognized "occupation" that even had its own association in Istanbul, consisting of 7,000 men in 1638.[30] Vagrancy and begging now drew the attention of the authorities as a behavior that required policing in order to maintain public order. Neither of these activities were crimes in themselves until the passage of the Regulation on Vagabonds and Suspected Persons (1890).[31] Though the presence of child beggars can be traced back in time, perception of the issue as a "problem" and the anxiety it inspired was related to a new conception of urban areas and modern governance. In Aleppo, the governor general was worried that orphan children, unschooled, were strolling in the streets as vagrants and begging. The ones who reached puberty were also joining the ranks of the infamous boy gangs of the city.[32]

The problem of vagrant and begging refugee children came to the agenda of the government when they became numerous in Istanbul in the aftermath of the 1877—1878 Russian war. In 1881, in his report to the sultan, Saffet Pasha described how hundreds of orphaned and destitute boys and girls of the Rumelian refugees based their livelihood on begging.[33] He claimed that before the Russian attack, one could not encounter a single beggar from Rumelia in Istanbul. If these children, he continued, "who have lost their motherland and their relatives" got used to this sort of livelihood, it would be impossible in the future "to lead them into any craft or skill."[34] They should immediately be guided into a proper livelihood before their age became an impediment.

After the emergence of reform houses, children who engaged in any activity on the streets were readily seen as potential delinquents and risked being treated as such. The young were prohibited even from playing rowdy games, shouting, whistling, throwing snowballs, or sliding on wet grass or ice. The governorship of Danube, for instance, prohibited children from playing games in the streets, sledding (*kızak kaymak*), and disturbing passersby on weekdays and during school hours. In the first instance of these acts, the child and his parents would be punished by an official reprimand (*tekdir*) by the city council; the second offense was punishable by "incarcerating" the child's father (presumably for a short term); and for the third offense the child would be put into the *ıslahhane*.[35] Most commonly the children were apprehended by newly appointed police inspectors. In other cases, they were taken to the *ıslahhane* by residents of the cities.[36]

The suggested punishment stresses the need for state intervention for protecting these children, even from their own families, who were held responsible for the children's misbehavior. This new disciplinary organization of adolescents' lives therefore implied the replacement of parental authority by state authority. We know from other European examples that the disciplining and socialization of vagrant children and youth had consequences for their poor and/or immigrant families. When the streets were cleared of begging children in England and Scandinavia and they were sent to work in orphanages or workhouses, nobody asked whether their parents agreed or how they felt about it.[37] The institutions were interested in reforming not only the urban space but also the urban poor.[38]

Vagrant girls were considered less of a threat. Most descriptions of quasi-criminal bands of children on city streets refer specifically to boys. The institutions were primarily opened to educate boys; only one-tenth of them were for girls or, in rare cases, they took in both genders. Yet, the public presence of destitute girls (outside of the home, school, or factory) also informed other forms of "moral threat." The major concern was undoubtedly sexuality. Orphanages for girls were intended to protect unattended girls from sexual abuse and the presumed attractions of a life of prostitution. In 1883, an unsigned report to the sultan underlined that despite the gradual collection and institutionalization of refugee orphan boys, girls in a similar situation had been left without any provisions.[39] If these girls were deprived of decent instruction and discipline, then Istanbul would suffer from the emergence of "certain unacceptable activities."[40] The orphanage, as a result, had the duty "to protect these girls from bad behavior and to keep them under discipline."[41] The report points to the girls' possible engagement in prostitution. Yet, the need for opening a girls' orphanage was tied to the morality, order, and safety of the urban space rather than evoking pity for the girls. Girls were in danger because of their sexuality, while that same sexuality posed a corrupting threat to society in general.[42] The belief that a modern state should both protect children from danger and protect society from dangerous children was becoming established in Ottoman administrative discourse.

As a categorical representation of "policing," it became a frequent activity to chase and collect children from the streets using compulsive methods, which included brutality and force. In some cases, municipal police and gendarmes were charged with collecting children from the streets or taking them away from their poor parents. In 1862, before the opening of the Niš orphanage, the governorship first tried to convince the population with its rather directive advice (nesâyih), without any positive result. Then, the municipal police were assigned the duty of collecting children from the streets through the use of compulsion (bilicbar) or threat.[43] A similar course was followed for the Ruse Girls' Orphanage in 1872. The governorship ordered district rulers to collect orphan and destitute girls, together with daughters of very poor parents, and bring them to the center for registration in the orphanage.[44]

In 1881 consecutive orders were given for the collection of refugee orphans begging in the streets of Istanbul.[45] After a week of intense "child gathering" by the superintendents and sergeants of the municipality, 222 child beggars were collected and 34 of them were enrolled in the vocational orphanage of Istanbul, while the rest (188) were handed over to the Imperial Arsenal.[46] Throughout the 1890s and well into the early 1900s, the Istanbul municipality and security forces continued to collect beggars, vagrants, and destitute children from the streets.[47] This ongoing collection and placement effort, supported by collaboration of the government with the city's municipal units, point to the crystallization of the discourse of anti-child urban spaces and of the "governance" of poor children and families.

What is more, although the ideal solution should have been to enroll them in *ıslahhane*s, boarding schools, or vocational institutes, most of the children were transferred to the cannon foundry (*Tophane Sanayii Alayları*) or the Imperial Arsenal (*Tersane-i Amire*) due to a lack of sufficient places and the state's incapacity to open new ones.[48] This proves that education, self-development, and reform (*ıslah*) functions of the *ıslahhane*s were only of secondary importance. Their main duty was to contribute to the security, well-being, and most of all reform of the urban space by facilitating the isolation of destitute children.

The rules and regulations regarding *ıslahhane* inmates' behavior and dress code in public—at those times when they were allowed to go outside of the orphanage—are also useful indicators for the institution's contribution to urban reform and public life. Each child was provided with a jacket, a pair of trousers, and a fez for outdoor usage, in addition to indoor working clothes (Regulation, Art. 5). It was strictly forbidden to leave the premises wearing working clothes. Superintendents were responsible for scrutinizing the dressing of children, making sure that they wore their jackets and trousers (Art. 28) and that there were no stains or holes on their clothes (Art. 30). Children were also compelled "to act with good manners" (*adab üzere hareket etmek*) outside of the institution and they were not allowed "to mingle with local children" (*mahalle çocuklarıyla karışmak*) or play games with them (Art. 39).

Ottoman urban reformers imposed adult codes of dress and behavior on urban areas, and childhood practices such as playing games were denied to children. Children's public presence, in the form of wandering, begging, or simply playing, was condemned in the name of public order and new urban governance. The vocational orphanages were therefore opened to respond to a specific "orphan problem" within the cities. Children on the streets were suspected of unrest and crime and were unwanted, not because they were charged with an offense but simply because they were vagrants. The transition from "vagrant" to "criminal" was definitely linked to the changing structure of the economy. Vagrancy was criminalized in response to economic developments aiming to strengthen the "national economy."[49]

Tension of Industry and Education

New regulations and institutions of the nineteenth century assigned significant roles to orphans and destitute children in the economy. Vagrant and idle children and orphans were to acquire necessary skills in *islahhane*s and then they would be employed in new factories and industrial complexes opened by the entrepreneurs. Orphans and orphanages were part of a new project of developing the urban economy and reforming local industries to combat the Empire's foreign debt and its dependence on imported goods.

The change in the urban economic regime coincided with the decline of the guilds in the cities.[50] The guilds' role as an organizing unit of Ottoman manufacturing declined during the nineteenth century. In the aftermath of the Industrial Revolution, the Free Trade Treaties of 1838–1841 with Britain and other European countries became tools of Western intervention in the internal affairs of the Empire as well as of Western economic domination of Ottoman markets.[51] The abolition of trade monopolies, Ottoman restrictions, and lower tariffs for European merchants on imports (5%) and exports (12%) intensified the integration of the Ottoman Empire in the world economy with clear benefits to European manufacturers and merchants. Ottoman foreign trade with Western Europe expanded as the Empire became a primary exporter of foodstuffs and raw materials and an importer of manufactured goods by the early twentieth century.[52] This trend and internal setbacks further marginalized the role of Ottoman crafts in manufacturing.

In the second half of the nineteenth century, when Mediterranean trade was in decline in the face of rising Western trade, an exclusionary and protectionist discourse was evolving in the writings of Ottoman elites and intellectuals.[53] The main focus was the decline of artisan production. Namık Kemal lamented the closing down of workshops all over the Empire: "Previously, we were self-sufficient, not only in agriculture, but also in industry. We used to possess many workshops to respond our all sorts of needs. Within twenty–thirty years, all of them are ruined."[54]

The establishment of *ıslahhane*s coincides with a series of measures designed to prevent the weakening of local industries. First of all, import duties were increased from 5 to 8 percent in 1862. In the next year, in February 1863, a fair for domestic products (*Sergi-i Umumi-i Osmani*) was opened to exhibit their quality, kind, and price and to reward successful producers.[55] In 1864 the Commission for the Reformation of Industry (*Islah-ı Sanayi Komisyonu*) was formed to bolster producers in Istanbul, to "improve crafts" (*ıslah-ı sanat*), and to raise the value of their commerce.[56] The commission's first achievement was to unite artisans under a single umbrella as corporations.[57] The idea was to develop a class of Ottoman entrepreneurs who would shape a "national economy." The Empire's vocational orphanages were one of the state's new ventures to sustain and rejuvenate urban manufacturing. They would raise new generations of talented and skilled workers and ensure that certain traditional industries met quality standards. These institutions had, in consequence, a corrective role for the rehabilitation of the domestic economy, in addition to introducing new skills and industries as part of experimental teaching methods.

The opening in 1868 of Istanbul's *Islah-ı Sanayi Mektebi* (School for the Reformation of Industry), also referred to as the *ıslahhane*, was one of the commission's ventures.[58] The appearance of the same objective, the "reformation of industry" (*ıslah-ı sanayi*) in the names of the commission and the school, affirms the organic link between orphanages and urban manufacturing. When Midhat Pasha returned from Danube to Istanbul as the head of the Council of State (*Şûra-yı Devlet*), Ali and Fuat Pashas granted him the necessary funds to open an *ıslahhane* in Istanbul. According to his account, the government decided to open this school after realizing the benefits of the *ıslahhane*s in the province of Danube. These institutions played a crucial role in "protecting and educating needy and destitute children,"[59] together with providing the "rejuvenation of domestic economy and augmentation of skilled artisans."[60] The main objective of the school was declared as training a new, well-educated artisan class. They would be educated in the "arts and crafts, which definitely lag behind the quality of European artisans in terms of both production technique and commodities in the marketplace."[61]

Mourning the decline of local economies was also a leitmotiv behind the opening of orphanages in the provinces. Aleppo, the Council of State underlined, used to be "one of the superior industrial centers of the Empire with the most appreciated and valued [textile] products."[62] But many of these workshops had recently closed. The opening of the orphanage (1869) would revitalize the economy and increase the wealth of the country. The orphanage of Diyarbekir was also tied to the "revitalization of various industries."[63] Hopefully, the "benefits of this enterprise" would "not be confined to the borders of the *vilayet* of Diyarbekir but extend to the neighboring provinces."[64]

In addition to the reorganization of local industries, the complementary argument was aimed at the formation of a new skilled class of laborers. Vocational orphanages would train the inmates to become responsible and dependable workers. Fighting the idleness of the children and "turning them into productive workers" was repeatedly underlined in official correspondence as one of the main objectives behind the initiation of orphanages.[65] Together with the more often manifested objective of "saving the children," the reformers insisted that these children needed to work. One of the founding documents of the Niš orphanage criticized the ignorance of the local community for leaving children unemployed.[66] These orphanages, on the other hand, could give a measure of equal opportunity to poor orphans who had otherwise lost their chances of "acquiring education and skills" and becoming "possessors of prosperity and wealth."[67] *Islahhane*s would turn needy children into a class of skillful and talented artisans as "an act of benevolence toward the needy."[68]

Based on these aims, the curriculum of the orphanages emphasized trades rather than formal schooling. The education in vocational orphanages was limited to an introduction to reading, writing, and arithmetic.[69] Only two hours were allocated to these courses on a daily basis.[70] The school day would start in the morning with primary school education, followed by training in arts and crafts.[71] The reformers aspired to inculcate an ethic of hard work and industriousness to these previously idle and wandering children.

As a proof of the *ıslahhane*'s desired disciplinary effect on its inmates, the official local newspapers of governorships published stories of achievement. In July 1865, the official paper of the Danube, *Tuna/Dunav*, published a letter supposedly written by a fourteen-year-old student in Niš. The narrative emphasized not only the student's accomplishments but also the industrious, competitive, and "patriotic" spirit that had been sparked among the inmates.

> Some time ago, my friends and I began to learn how to cut and stitch shoes. When Süleyman Paşa, *kaymakam* of Niš, heard of this he did not believe it. His Excellency came one day to the *ıslahhane*, placed a police-man to watch over me as I worked, and ordered the policeman to give me one *lira* [gold coin] if I managed to make three pairs of shoes. I made the shoes and took the coin. Even though your newspaper reported on this matter in its thirteenth issue, your report also stated that I used a machine to make some of the stitches on those shoes. That is not true— no machines at all are used in making that kind of shoe. Thus, your report made me sorry, because my prestige among my friends was being trampled upon. . . . I beg you to publish my letter in your newspaper, so I could look again at the faces of my friends.[72]

The curricular program of the *ıslahhane*s stressed the primacy of teaching trades and skills. Children spent at least six hours a day in the ateliers.[73] In each institution there were several workshops for certain trades, and also an apprenticeship structure of teaching, namely the Lan-castrian Monitorial system, whereby more advanced students taught less advanced ones. Those who completed a certain level of instruction were used as journeymen (*kalfa*), even though they were still officially students. The masters taught them at first, then each *kalfa* instructed eight to ten children.[74] Good students of the orphanages were rotated among the provinces as *kalfa*s. For example, two students of *Mekteb-i Sanayi* of Istan-bul were sent to Salonika to be employed as *kalfa*s in shoemaking and carpentry workshops.[75] Other skilled students from the same institution were assigned to Izmir to teach tailoring and shoemaking.[76]

7. Sivas Vocational Orphanage, shoemaking workshop. Unknown photographer, in *Sivas Vilayeti Salnamesi* (Sivas: Sivas Vilayeti Matbaası, 1325 [1907]), 244–45.

The *ıslahhane*s offered vocational training in a similar set of trades, despite minor adjustments based on the specificities of the *vilayet*s for raw materials and production methods. The Adana orphanage was specialized in weaving; the children in Kastamonu were trained in carpentry and other forms of woodworking; and the Diyarbekir orphanage produced aba (a coarse woolen cloth), Persian shawls, and other traditional textile products.[77] The boys in Izmir were divided into workshops on tailoring, shoemaking, rug weaving, cabinetmaking, and printing.[78] In Aleppo, children were trained only in tailoring and shoemaking in order to manufacture the uniforms and shoes of the municipal police.[79] The *Islah-ı Sanayi Mektebi* of Istanbul was an exception. This orphanage had nineteen different trade departments, including ironworking, cabinetmaking, foundry work, architecture, tailoring, shoemaking, match manufacturing, lead pipe production, typography, lithography, and bookbinding.[80] With its well-equipped workshops, experienced masters, and large labor force, it was a veritable factory. Some children were sent to various ateliers or factories in the cities to learn other trades. The boys of the printing department of the

Niš orphanage learned it at the *vilayet* press. Leatherworking students of Istanbul were sent to the mills of Kazlıçeşme and Beykoz.[81]

*Islahhane*s quickly became important local producers, meeting vital needs of local governments and municipalities. Only three months after its opening in 1869, the *ıslahhane* of Diyarbekir was able to produce shoes for the gendarmerie together with parts of their uniforms.[82] In its later years, during the 1870s and 1880s, the orphanage provided for the needs of several governmental institutions and the local community. The vocational orphanage of Kosovo produced shoes and uniforms for officers and civil servants of the province.[83] The *ıslahhane* of Bursa specialized in weaving, producing fabric for the uniforms of the gendarmerie.[84]

The *ıslahhane* of Aleppo specifically took part in the struggle of local producers against imports. The governor of the province had previously subcontracted the manufacturing of the uniforms and shoes of the municipal police officers through a mechanism of underbidding (*münakasa*).[85] Yet, the children in the *ıslahhane* proved proficient enough both in tailoring and shoemaking. They were able to manufacture these in good quality and at a cheaper cost. Production, as a result, was transferred to the orphanage and the student labor force was increased to 400 to meet the demand. The governorship resolved that in this way the province would be relieved from the "numerous corruptions" of the subcontractors (*kontratocular*) and the treasury would spend much less. The orphanage, in that sense, actually played a role in developing local production and achieving self-sufficiency.

Large-scale producers and factories also profited from the training provided by the vocational orphanages. The opening of the first factories in the 1830s and 1840s and the resulting need for cheap labor tied orphans and orphanages to industrial production in a very curious way. The first few factories of the Empire had a remarkable orphan population to draw from as their labor force. During the mid-1830s, orphaned children worked at the imperial yarn factory (*rişte-i hane-i amire*) to maintain uninterrupted production for the Ottoman fleet.[86] Child and female workers predominated in all of the mechanized cotton-spinning and silk-reeling mills. They were an important part of the workforce in the Uşak wool yarn factories. Young women and girls also worked in the wool cloth

8. Sivas Vocational Orphanage, tailoring workshop. Unknown photographer, in *Sivas Vilayeti Salnamesi* (Sivas: Sivas Vilayeti Matbaası, 1325 [1907]), 244–45.

factories in Niausta in the Balkans and in Eyüp as well as in the umbrella workshops of Istanbul.[87]

Some of the *ıslahhane*s were particularly opened to supply laborers for large industrial complexes and factories. Midhat Pasha's industrial policies and their links with the *ıslahhane*s in Niš, Ruse, Sofia, Baghdad, and Damascus—each sheltering 150 to 250 children—were remarkable. The boys in the Ruse orphanage were employed in the coach factory of the *vilayet*'s company as producers of carts. The girls in the Ruse orphanage worked for the cloth factory, producing fabric for the army. Midhat also initiated a broadcloth factory adjacent to the Sofia Orphanage. In only two years, trained orphans replaced the masters. The enterprise was quite profitable, manufacturing 30,000 meters of broadcloth in a year.[88] The girls' orphanage of Istanbul was also opened adjacent to the Yedikule weaving factory, where the girls were employed as weavers.[89]

In addition, a "study abroad" program was planned for talented students in the institutions. The idea was to train skilled masters, who would

9. Sivas Vocational Orphanage, carpentry workshop. Unknown photographer, in *Sivas Vilayeti Salnamesi* (Sivas: Sivas Vilayeti Matbaası, 1325 [1907]), 244–45.

later come back and serve in one of the orphanages.[90] The first group of children, a total of ten boys (5 Muslims, 4 Greeks, 1 Bulgarian), were sent from the Ruse orphanage in August 1867.[91] They were all first sent to Paris, but then most of them were transferred to Liège and Le Havre. Soon after their arrival, the Ottoman ambassador in Paris, Mehmed Cemil Pasha, prepared a report where he touched upon the importance of vocational education as a part of the initiatives for rehabilitating industry.[92] The Ministries of Education and Foreign Affairs decided in December 1869 to send 20 more students from *Islah-ı Sanayi Mektebi* of Istanbul. Sixteen Muslim and 4 non-Muslim students, specialized in fourteen different trades, from engraving to tile decoration, arrived at Paris on 13 January 1870.[93] Throughout 1872 and 1873, a new mixed group of 20 apprentices were sent from the Ruse, Sofia, Niš, and Istanbul orphanages.[94] A few were enrolled in vocational schools in Paris, but most of them were placed in factories in Liège. The director of the Istanbul orphanage visited Paris in 1873 and prepared a critical report on the achievements of the children.[95] Finally, the Minister of Foreign Affairs, Safvet Pasha, declared that sending industrial students to

TABLE 13. Students Sent to Paris from the Ruse Orphanage (1867–1872)

	Name	Identity	Education	Arrival	Departure
1	Abbas	Apprentice	Paris (1867–70), Liège (1870–71), Paris (1871–72), Hâvre (1872–74)	August 1867	26 May 1874
2	Ahmed Nazif	Apprentice (mechanic)	Paris (1867–70), Liège (1870–71), Paris (1871–73), Hâvre (1873–75)	August 1867	13 February 1875
3	Ahmed Şakir	Apprentice (machine repairer)	Paris (1867–70), Liège (1870–71), Hâvre (1871–75)	August 1867	January 1875
4	Dora	Bulgarian. Apprentice (tile decoration)	Paris (1867–70), Liège (1870–71), Paris (1871–72)	August 1867	13 September 1872
5	İbrahim	Apprentice (marquetry)	Paris (1867–70), Liège (1870–71), Paris (1871–74)	August 1867	26 May 1874
6	İbrahim	Apprentice (gardener)	Paris (1867–1870), Liège (1870–71), Paris (1871–?)	August 1867	13 September 1872
7	Panayot	Greek. Apprentice (stove–maker)	Paris (1867–1870), Liège (1870–71), Paris (1871–4)	August 1867	26 May 1874
8	Stephan	Greek. Apprentice (machine repairer)	Paris (1867–1870), Liège (1870–71), Paris (1871–2)	August 1867	13 September 1872
9	Vasil	Greek. Apprentice (litograph)	Paris (1867–1870), Liège (1870–71), Paris (1871–72)	August 1867	13 September 1872
10	Yuvan	Greek. Apprentice (carpenter)	Paris (1867–1870), Liège (1870–71), Paris (1871–74)	August 1867	26 May 1874
11	Ahmed Mustafa	Apprentice (lathe operator)	Paris (1867–70), Liège (1870–74), Paris (1874)	May 1869	August 1874 (sent to Ruse with tuberculosis)
12	Yunus	Birth: Niş Apprentice (tailor)	Paris (1872–)	8 December 1872	15 July 1875
13	Todora	Bulgarian. Birth: 1860, Ruse Apprentice (printer and typesetter)	Paris (1872–)	8 December 1872	8 July 1875

Name	Identity	Education	Arrival	Departure
14 Mustafa	Birth: 1858, Crete. Apprentice (carpenter)	Paris (1872–)	8 December 1872	He paid his own expenses after 15 July 1875 and, thus, stayed.
15 Mahir	Birth: 1858 (3rd grade student) Apprentice (printer and typesetter)	Paris (1872–)	8 December 1872	15 July 1875
16 İslam	Birth: 1858, Ruse (3rd grade student). Apprentice (maker of vehicle bodies)	Paris (1872–73), Hâvre (1873–75)	8 December 1872	8 July 1875
17 Istaf	Bulgarian. Birth: 1857, Niş. Apprentice (tailor)	Paris (1872–73), Hâvre (1873)	8 December 1872	15 July 1875
18 Conné	Birth: 1858, Ruse Bulgarian, orphan. (4th grade student) Apprentice (tailor)	Paris (1872–?)	8 December 1872	8 July 1875
19 Kristo	Birth: 1858, Bulgarian (5th grade student). Apprentice (broadcloth weaver)	Paris (1872–?)	8 December 1872	8 July 1874
20 Şaban	Birth: 1862, Sofia. Apprentice (cotton fluffer)	Paris (1872–?)	8 December 1872	
21 Mitto	Birth: 1859, Sofia. Bulgarian. Apprentice (weaver)	Paris (1872–73), Hâvre (1873–75)	8 December 1872	8 July 1875

Table is prepared based on the data provided by Şişman, *Tanzimat Döneminde Fransa'ya Gönderilen Osmanlı Öğrencileri (1839–1876)*, 93–158.

TABLE 14. Students Sent to Paris from Istanbul Orphanage (1870–1872)

	Name	Identity	Education	Arrival	Departure
1	Mehmed, Fehmi Hüsnü	Birth: Istanbul. Apprentice (grater)	Paris (1870), Liège (1870–74)	13 January 1870	December 1874
2	Krikor	Armenian. Apprentice (lathe operator)	Paris (1870), Hâvre (1870–5)	13 January 1870	13 February 1875
3	Kalust, Arsen	Armenian. Birth: 1857, Tekirdağ Apprentice (foundryman)	Paris (1870), Liège (1870–75)	13 January 1870	13 February 1875
4	İbrahim, Mustafa	Birth: 1855, Gebze Apprentice (iron-maker)	Paris (1870), Liège (1870–75)	13 January 1870	13 February 1875
5	İbrahim, Hasan	Apprentice (rug-maker)	Paris (1870), Liège (1870–72)	13 January 1870	17 August 1872 (died in Liège)
6	Hüsnü, Bekir	Birth: 1857, Istanbul Apprentice (foundryman)	Paris (1870), Liège (1870–75)	13 January 1870	13 February 1875
7	Halim Hüseyin	Birth: 1854, Trabzon Apprentice (iron-maker)	Paris (1870), Liège (1870–75)	13 January 1870	13 February 1875
8	Garabet	Armenian. Apprentice (tile decoration)	Paris (1870), Liège (1870–71), Paris (1871–5)	13 January 1870	13 February 1875
9	Galib	Apprentice (engraver, sculptor)	Paris (1870), Liège (1870–71), Paris (1871–4)	13 January 1870	26 May 1874
10	Emin	Apprentice (shoemaker)	Paris (1870), Liège (1870–74)	13 January 1870	26 May 1874
11	Cavit	Apprentice (tailor)	Paris (1870), Liège (1870–71), Paris (1871–2)	13 January 1870	22 May 1872
12	Bekir	Apprentice (carpenter)	Paris (1870), Liège (1870–71), Paris (1871–5)	13 January 1870	15 July 1875
13	Aziz	Apprentice (bookbinder)	Paris (1870), Liège (1870–74)	13 January 1870	26 May 1874
14	Ali Seyid Hüseyin	Apprentice (lathe operator)	Paris (1870), Liège (1870–75)	13 January 1870	15 July 1875
15	Ali	Apprentice (shoemaker)	Paris (1870), Liège (1870–71), Paris (1871–4)	13 January 1870	26 May 1874

	Name	Identity	Education	Arrival	Departure
16	Ahmed Emin	Apprentice (jeweler) Birth: April 1854	Paris (1870), Liège (1870–71), Paris (?)	13 January 1870	?
17	Ahmed Abdi	Apprentice (harness maker)	Paris (1870), Liège (1870–71), Paris (1871–5)	13 January 1870	8 July 1875
18	Ohannes	Armenian. Apprentice (machine repairer)	Paris (1870), Hâvre (1870–5)	13 January 1870	13 February 1875
19	Salih	Apprentice (tailor)	Paris (1870), Liège (1870–71), Paris (1871–2)	13 January 1870	22 May 1872
20	Süleyman Karanfi	Birth: 1854, Tepedelen. Apprentice (machine modeler)	Paris (1870), Liège (1870–75)	13 January 1870	13 February 1875
21	Mıgırdiç	Armenian. Birth: 1859, Istanbul. Orphan.		8 December 1872	15 July 1875
22	Kristopolos	Birth: 1856, Istanbul. Greek, orphan. Apprentice (carpenter)	Paris (1872–3), Hâvre (1873–4)	8 December 1872	July 1874
23	Kadri	Apprentice (xlograph)		8 December 1872	8 July 1875
24	Halim	Birth: 1857, Istanbul Apprentice (tailor)	Paris (1872–?)	8 December 1872	15 July 1875
25	Cafer	Apprentice (harness maker)	Paris (1872–3), Hâvre (1873–5)	8 December 1872	8 July 1875
26	Bilal	Apprentice (maker of vehicle bodies)	Paris (1872–3), Hâvre (1873–5)	8 December 1872	8 July 1875
27	Mihal	Birth: 1855, Istanbul. Orphan. Apprentice (carpenter)	Paris (1872–3), Hâvre (1873–5)	8 December 1872	8 July 1875
28	Nazif	Birth: 1858, Istanbul. Apprentice (glazier)	Paris (1872 –)	8 December 1872	8 July 1875
29	Süleyman	Birth: 1860, Istanbul. Apprentice (carpenter)	Paris	8 December 1872	8 July 1875
30	Şakir	Birth: 1856, Istanbul. Apprentice (foundryman)	Paris	8 December 1872	15 July 1875

Table is prepared based on the data provided by Şişman, *Tanzimat Döneminde Fransa'ya Gönderilen Osmanlı Öğrencileri (1839–1876)*, 93–158.

Europe did not bring about the intended results, despite generating significant costs. As a result, most of the students were brought back in July 1875.[96]

The regulation of the *ıslahhane*s stipulated that students were entitled to a daily wage (*yevmiye*), which was supposedly saved for them by the government lending agency (*emniyet sandığı*) till the day they left the institution. This sum would theoretically serve as capital for those who wanted to start their own businesses.[97] However, school administrations and local governments could be reluctant to release these virtual sums. In 1900, there were a series of complaints from former graduates of the Ruse girls' orphanage.[98] Eugenie Yorgiyef claimed her accumulated wages, which had been entrusted to the Ruse treasury (*Rusçuk Sandığı*), along with accumulated interest.[99] Fatma Hatun, mother of Mustafa, a now-deceased orphan, demanded his accumulated "salaries" (*maaş*) from the Bursa orphanage where he had been "employed" (*istihdam*) for nine years.[100] The choice of words like *istihdam* and *maaş* indicate the ambivalence of children's status in the *ıslahhane*. They were not only students but also the labor force. The fact that Mustafa remained in the orphanage much longer than the formal five years of training also implies that these institutions were not simply centers of education but also operated as workshops offering employment.

Those who successfully finished their five years of study were given the chance to be employed in the orphanage on either a daily basis (*yevmiye*) or a long-term contract (*müddet*).[101] It is possible to track the reverberations of the policy in the local applications. In the *ıslahhane* of Izmir, former students were employed as masters for the instruction of smaller children. From among the former students of the school, Eşref Efendi later became the master of a sock-making workshop, and Bedros Efendi became the journeyman in a carpentry workshop.[102] The Regulation of the Diyarbekir orphanage mentioned that those who completed their courses successfully could be employed as assistant teachers (Art. 9).[103]

Children in the orphanages were also used as helpers for the institution. They were the ones who took care of their wards/dormitories by sweeping the floors, carrying water, rolling up their beds, and doing all the other necessary chores. Those who were punished for misbehavior in the institution were also responsible for cleaning the toilets. Yet, it was forbidden for janitors (*mubassır*) to use children to fulfill their own duties.[104]

The 1869 Ordinance of General Education (*Maarif-i Umumiye Nizam-namesi*) attempted to establish a modern educational infrastructure. In parallel with the recent developments in educating and employing orphans and destitute children in arts and crafts, the ordinance stressed the necessity of vocational training for the development and modernization of the country.[105] It was not a coincidence that pioneering educational reforms of the *Tanzimat* era were in areas of technical-vocational, professional, and informal public education.[106] In this context, *ıslahhane*s and their inmates were expected to "reaffirm the eminence of the industry and to reinforce the wealth of the nation and the country," as the governor of the province of Aleppo, Naşid Rüşdü Bey, put it in his report to the grand vizier.[107]

Negotiation of Ethnoreligious Heterogeneity

Ottomanism germinated from the recognition of the notion of citizenship as part of the *Tanzimat* reforms. Its proponents believed that it could solve the political and social issues that the Empire was facing. Influenced by the French Revolution and such thinkers as Montesquieu and Rousseau, the ideology promoted equality among the *millet*s. Political elites used Ottomanism to achieve consensus among different ethnic and religious communities and to foster political and social unity. In terms of policy development and governmentality, Ottomanist thought supported the equality of Muslims and non-Muslims, and a series of laws followed to put that into effect. Non-Muslims were admitted to secular schools and allowed to serve in the bureaucracy after graduation. New institutions and bodies were created in which all the elements of the Empire served alike.[108] The Regulation of General Education of 1869 had certain articles supporting the mixed education of Muslims and non-Muslims in *idadi* (high) schools, female teacher-training colleges (*darülmuallimat*), and *rüşdiyye* (middle) schools.[109] With their religiously mixed character, the *ıslahhane*s were a part of this Ottomanist trend of the educational policies of the *Tanzimat* era. From another perspective, it has also been suggested that the opening of the first *ıslahhane*s in the *vilayet* of Danube was related to the efforts of the Sublime Porte to counter the influence of Russia in educating Bulgarian children and the emergence of separatist ideas among the Bulgarians.[110] Children without families or with families of precarious means were among the first to be included within the new citizenship paradigm. These fragile subjects of the Empire were thought to be strong candidates as the new "Ottoman citizens."

The first article of the 1871 Regulation of the *ıslahhane*s underlined that these institutions were opened "for Muslims and Christians alike under rules of equality."[111] The directors of the orphanages were supposed to "treat each Muslim and non-Muslim child without exception as their own children" (Art. 24).[112] The articles outlining the daily routine specify that after waking up and making their beds, Muslim children should perform ablution and go to the morning prayer. Non-Muslims were exempt from Muslim prayer, but they were also allowed to worship according to their beliefs (Art. 32).[113] The curriculum underlined that the two hours of formal education would be done separately in different classrooms (Art. 9) and with different teachers. Muslims would be taught by a Muslim teacher, and non-Muslims by their own coreligionists (Art. 8). Since this formal part of education mainly comprised reading and writing, teachers were called "language teachers" (*lisan hocası*) in the Regulation (Art. 12). Non-Muslim children who could speak Turkish would be instructed together with Muslims (Art. 35).

In line with the general Regulation, non-Muslim teachers were hired for formal language courses. A Bulgarian instructor was hired to teach non-Muslim children in the Niš orphanage.[114] There was also a "teacher for Bulgarian children" (*Bulgar etfal muallimi*), Raskal Nikola Efendi, in the boys' orphanage of Ruse.[115] The yearbook for the province of Aydın for 1901–1902 notes a certain İvan Keşişoğlu as the teacher of Greek students.[116] In some cases, teachers were recruited based on the demand and financial support of the communities. For instance, in Edirne, the Jewish community agreed to pay for the salary of a Jewish instructor so that Jewish refugee orphans (*mülteci*) would be admitted to the orphanage and educated.[117] The materials printed on the orphanages' presses bear witness to multiple-language education. The printing presses of the Izmir orphanage, for example, undertook publications in both Ottoman Turkish and Greek.[118] The official newspaper of the *vilayet* of Danube, *Tuna*, was published within the *ıslahhane* and was half in Turkish and half in Bulgarian.[119]

*Islahhane*s were among the first examples of mixed education in the Empire. The orphanage in Niš had an orphan population of 150 Muslim and Christian boys.[120] The *ıslahhane* of Diyarbekir sheltered 60 Muslim and Christian boys right after its opening in 1869.[121] The Girls' Orphanage of Ruse also had a mixed group with 30 Muslims and 21 Christians in 1872.[122] The student body of the Izmir boys' orphanage was also religiously heterogeneous (Greeks and one or two Armenians and Jews), although the majority was Muslim.[123] The orphanage of Damascus, which was first opened in 1869 but discontinued for lack of funds, was reinitiated after the appointment of Midhat Pasha in 1878 with a collection of 200 Muslim and non-Muslim orphans.[124] The student population of the boys' *ıslahhane* of Istanbul was also always mixed.

Centrally dictated rules and regulations declared these institutions as multilingual and multireligious schools. Still, negotiation and bargaining on the local level was possible. The governor of Aleppo claimed that, despite the official regulations stipulating mixed education on a boarding basis, the admittance of children affiliated with different religious communities (Muslims, Christians, and Jews) as boarding students would create very serious problems in the province. In his report to the grand vizier, he wrote that the boarding (*beytutet*) of the children of different communities seemed impossible, since it would be "in contradiction with the prevalence of fanaticism among the *millet*s."[125] Children from all these three religions were admitted. But the governor was reluctant to board them together, arguing that "religious leaders of the communities would create several crises" and even alienate children from the orphanage.[126] It was decided that there would be "no reference to religions"[127] and the common language of the orphanage would be Turkish. The governor was hopeful that in the future "their jaundice and antagonism would wither away"[128] and that "a real friendship would develop among them,"[129] at which time the school administration might reinstitute the article on the boarding of children. This was the single *ıslahhane* that was established on a nonboarding basis.

Ottoman Urban Reform in the Center and Provinces

The rich and complex institutional history of *ıslahhane*s embodies such concepts as modernity, the modern state, and "Ottoman reform." Vocational orphanages were significant educational and economic apparatuses of the nascent modern state in the provinces. They were conceived as part of a series of reforms to change the urban space and local economic relations throughout the Empire and to solidify central governmental authority. In the case of the *ıslahhane*s, the relation between the center and the provinces was usually smooth and coordinated. But there was still continuous negotiation based on the specific needs of the localities. Both provincial governments and the central authority had certain powers of jurisdiction and spheres of influence regarding the administration of the institution. Vocational orphanages were both a product of central planning and a provincial enterprise.

The *ıslahhane*s in the provinces owed their existence and legal justification to centrally enforced orders and central planning. Their operations, as well, implied ongoing dialogue with the center. Here it is necessary to underline that the concept of "the center" is somewhat misleading. It is apparent that, at the beginning, the *vilayet* of Danube was the center of the idea and supplied the knowhow for its actual application. However, the center of the institutional structure was reappropriated at the core of the Empire, shortly after the opening of the *Islah-ı Sanayi Mektebi* of Istanbul in 1868. This top-down relationship materialized in a number of ways. The uniforms designed for Istanbul boys were taken as a model for other institutions.[130] Curricular books and other educational material (Korans, tracts, maps, etc.) were published in Istanbul and then sent to the provinces free of charge.[131] The competent students of the Istanbul orphanage were assigned as journeymen or masters in the provincial orphanages.[132] *Islahhane*s in the provinces had to send to Istanbul their student registers, which collected information on the student's name, physical description, entry date, and skill specialization.[133]

Moreover, as a part of the efforts to evaluate "the dissemination of recent progress in eminent arts and crafts in the provinces," a "sample inventory" (*numunehane*) was organized in the Istanbul orphanage in the early 1870s.[134] The idea was to compare the yearly progress or decline of the quality of products of these institutions in different corners of the Empire. The inventory was meticulously organized, with separate sections for different sorts of products, and divided into years and provinces.[135] The first such samples were sent from the Danubian orphanages in 1873.[136] This initiative was important in reinforcing the central planning of the rejuvenation of the economy. The central authorities scrutinized the overall situation and progress of these institutions, despite their obviously local character.

Notwithstanding their strong links to the Ministry of Education and the *Mekteb-i Sanayi* of Istanbul, the *ıslahhane*s were also deeply rooted in their provincial settings. Orphanages were repeatedly asserted to be "under the authority of the provincial governments."[137] When the central government was approached with applications for the enrollment of children, the petitions were forwarded to the provincial authorities "since they were in charge of the orphanages."[138] As an expected outcome of this, the personnel of the orphanages were dependent on local governments for their recruitment and compensation. When these employees applied for different matters to the Ministries of the Interior and/or Education, they were referred back to the governorship, since the matter had to be solved by the local authorities (*mahallince*).[139] The relative autonomy of the provinces is also apparent from their exceptional regulations, such as the case of Kastamonu, where boys and girls were coeducated.[140]

Aside from administrative independence, the most obvious proof of the orphanages' local character was the organization and sources of their finances. The *ıslahhane*s, in most cases, were opened with the "benevolent contributions" (*iane*) of local notables. These were defined as "men of means" (*erbab-ı şürut*), "possessors of wealth and riches" (*eshab-ı servet ve yesar*), "charitable persons" (*zevat-ı kiram*), or generally "philanthropists" (*eshab-ı hayr ve hamiyyet, eshab-ı hayrat ve hasenat*).[141] The local population, together with the governors, contributed with donations of buildings, grounds, or rent revenues. The 1869 register, which includes the names of contributors to the orphanage of Diyarbekir, reaffirms the importance of the officials. The largest sum was donated by the governor of the province. Yet, the contribution of local notables cannot be disregarded. Other philanthropists (*eshab-ı hamiyyet*) undertook the construction of a complex with six shops, built next to the Governor's Residence (*Hükümet Konağı*). Another complex was erected adjacent to the newly built public offices outside the walled city. The rents of all would be used as revenues for the orphanage.[142]

One might question whether these were genuinely voluntary donations or quasi-tax contributions, as in the case of nine tribal sheiks from the district of Amara, who donated a total of 6,000 kuruş, or of Nasreddin Shah, who donated 2,000 lira to the *ıslahhane* of Baghdad (1869).[143] Actually it is very likely that the officials compelled the population to contribute to the budget of the orphanage. At least part of the revenues of the *avarız*[144] was spent on these institutions.[145]

In other cases, wakf land or property (*müsakkafat-ı mevkufe*) was transferred to the orphanages. For the construction of the orphanage of Edirne, a large and expensive plot of land close to the imperial mosque of Selimiye was donated by a certain Ayşe Sıdıka Hanım, who was the trustee of the wakf owning that territory.[146] When the orphanage was opened in 1873, the state expropriated many houses and plots around the land to enlarge the area. The act was always presented as one of benevolence. Nevertheless, trustees of wakfs also donated property in order to be relieved from their accumulated tax debts. In Damascus, for instance, rent-yielding property was transferred to the orphanage in exchange for a pledge that the former debts of the original owner would be cleared so that "the sustenance of the destitute would not be interrupted."[147] The benevolence of the notables was understandably related to their immediate economic interests.

Next to the contributions of the notables, the largest part of the orphanages' income came from the central budget of the *vilayet*. Some rent and tax revenues (*mahsulat, varidat, öşriyye, aşar, akar*) were transferred to the orphanage as the institution's permanent income.[148] In order to cover the operational expenses of the *ıslahhane* of Kastamonu, the rent revenues from twenty-five shops, khans, and coffeehouses were dedicated to the orphanage, as were the revenues of the boat that carried rough rice (*çeltik*) on the Kızılırmak.[149] The governorship of Aydın allocated the revenues of the thermal spring of Balçova and the bath of the Karantina district to the orphanage. Two percent of the tithe of the surrounding districts was also transferred to the institution with a decree in 1893.[150] In Bursa, several shops were built on state-owned (*emlak-ı emiriyeden*) land of the road house (*menzilhane*) and the rents were granted to the orphanage.[151] In Salonika, the grounds on which the orphanage was built were on a main street (*Hamidiye Caddesi*) and were donated by the municipality to bring rent revenue to the institution.[152]

The sale of student handiwork provided the bulk of the daily operating expenses of the *ıslahhane*s, and through the labor of their inmates orphanages largely could pay for their own costs. The 1867 Regulation for Provinces mentioned that the annual revenues of the first two *ıslahhane*s in Ruse and Niš were around 250,000 kuruş, 70,000–80,000 of which were covered by the volume of production in the orphanage.[153] In some instances, as in the case of Baghdad, a shop selling the goods produced in the orphanage was connected to the school. Most of the *ıslahhane*s manufactured a range of products for local or central governments. This was done to make sure that these institutions had a permanent income from their contracts with state institutions. The same type of relationship was true for provincial printing presses and newspapers. Not only were these presses organically linked to orphanages in terms of their physical location and labor force but also the revenues of local newspapers were frequently part of the budget of *ıslahhane*s.[154]

The orphanages and orphans had a new meaning within the changing and developing urban context. Local populations embraced the *ıslahhane*s as a valuable part of urban life. The awareness of the benefits of a reformed urban infrastructure was growing quickly among the population, and this contributed to the increased interest in *ıslahhane*s. They definitely meant something novel for the reformed city administrations, for new projects of city planning, for new actors such as businessmen and merchants, and for inhabitants of the cities who passed by these new institutions. These institutions also brought significant urban landmarks into the lives of the cities: the printing press, brass bands, and the edifice of the orphanage itself.

In addition to traditional arts and crafts, the orphanages also offered modern industrial skills. The practice of printing was an important departure from the classics. Printing presses were often part of the orphanage curricula and had an organic link with the establishment of provincial printing houses. The precedent was set with the governorship of Midhat Pasha, first in the Danube and then in Damascus and Baghdad. The orphans in the Ruse Orphanage were employed in the printing house of the governorship as bookbinders and lithographers. They published the bureaucratic documents for the *vilayet* in addition to the official newspaper, *Tuna*.[155] The orphanage of Baghdad was also tied to the printing house of the *vilayet*, which primarily published the official newspaper, *Zevra*.[156]

The first printing press of the governorship of Kastamonu was also installed within the *ıslahhane* in 1867.[157] The press of the *vilayet* of Salonika was part of the orphanage, and all documentation of the province, including the yearbooks, were published by the children.[158] There was a printing press in the orphanage of Izmir as well. On the first anniversary of the institution, the boys were proficient enough to print a letter of gratitude to the sultan, typed in both Ottoman and Greek.[159] The formation of the press in the provinces also had significant meaning in light of such concerns as modern ways of communication, literacy, and construction of an imagined community. As a surprising coincidence, one of the key figures of modernity, the press, was entrusted to the hands of the orphans.

The instruction of musical knowledge and the formation of brass bands were also indispensable parts of the curriculum in the *ıslahhane*s. Established under the authority of the provincial governments, most of the orphanages had quite large and successful brass bands that performed particular duties as representatives of the local administration. The musical bands and the children forming them acted as functionaries of the governorship with an assigned role to celebrate and accompany certain days and events with their music and marching in the streets. The band was a symbol of the merger of the orphanage with the city's identity.

The orphanage of Skopje even had its own anthem, written by Mustafa Şekip Tunç and composed by the music teacher of the school, Ali Fevzi.[160] Music courses were initiated and a brass band was formed in the *ıslahhane* of Bursa in the 1900s. The music class of the Salonika orphanage was attended by only "eager and talented children."[161] They received two hours of theoretical and practical music courses on a daily basis. In the 1890s their teacher was Alfons Biçoto Efendi, and 35 of 114 students were part of the band.[162] The *ıslahhane* of Salonika also was the precursor of the conservatory of the city. Many of the "graduates" were competent musicians, playing at least one instrument. In an oral history interview, Yaşar Ürük

10. Brass band and pupils of the *Islahhane* of Salonika. Unknown photographer, İstanbul Üniversitesi Kütüphane ve Dokümantasyon Daire Başkanlığı, *Fotoğraf Albümleri Dizini*, 90852-0009.

tells that his grandfather was one of the inmates of the orphanage of Salonika, where he became both a shoemaker and a clarinet player.[163] With the population exchange of 1923, he migrated to Izmir and started playing for the city's brass band. He immediately noticed that almost all the musicians in the band were practicing shoemaking for a living! Actually they were all graduates of the orphanage of Izmir, and just like himself they received vocational and musical training at the same time. It is also true that the *ıslahhane* of Izmir had a large band with 35 musicians in the 1890s and also a populous shoemaking workshop.[164] The band grew bigger through the decade, and in 1901 it comprised 42 boys under the direction of the music teacher, Hidayet Bey, and his assistant, Viktor Kaleya Vecnarino.[165]

The physical appearance of the orphanage buildings in the urban matrix had significant impacts for the urban population and the urban milieu at large. These orphanages quickly became landmarks in the historical memories of cities. This is actually understandable, since most of them had grand, remarkable, and memorable edifices, especially compared to other educational institutions such as primary or secondary schools. These structures themselves point to the vested interests of Ottoman reformers in these institutions. The *ıslahhane*s were not opened in small, rented, temporary buildings. They had multistoried stone buildings with complex architectural features. Some of those former orphanage buildings are still in use today, usually reserved for educational purposes but also for other uses. The one in Konya now serves as the Special Provincial Administration (*İl Özel İdaresi*). The building of the orphanage of Izmir is now the vocational school of the city, Mithatpaşa Endüstri Meslek Lisesi.

Even after all the firsthand witnesses of the actual building have passed away, the institutions are remembered by the new generations in the neighborhood, since places have a form of memory that is passed on to newcomers.[166] The centrality of the orphanages in the public urban space is clear from the appearance of their names in street or district names. For example, one street and an entire neighborhood are named after the orphanage in Salonika (*Islahhane Caddesi, Islahhane Mahallesi*).[167] In a similar respect, *Islahhane Sokak* of Trabzon, in the district of Ortahisar, was named after the orphanage there. Also in Skopje, the orphanage still seems to be kept in urban memory. As early as 1906 there was already an *Islahhane Caddesi* in the Gazimenteş district of the city. Furthermore, as late as the 1980s there was a park carrying the same name, *İslahane Parkı.*[168]

11. Skopje Vocational Orphanage. Unknown photographer, İstanbul Üniversitesi Kütüphane ve Dokümantasyon Daire Başkanlığı, *Fotoğraf Albümleri Dizini*, 93216-0004.

As an outcome of a well-implemented central order, a large network of *ıslahhane*s emerged in the last quarter of the nineteenth century.

The establishment of the institution was linked to tangible aspirations, such as disciplining urban spaces and promoting progress in urban manufacturing and industrial activity. The attitude of nineteenth-century Ottoman reformers toward disciplining and rehabilitating orphans and vagrant children was twofold. Although the publicly prevalent discourse highlighted the desire to save destitute children from the dangers to which they were prey, a stronger and deeper discourse stressed that the public, political, and economic order of the society was threatened by "dangerous children." As a first priority, the vagrant and idle children were to be removed from the streets—so *ıslahhane*s were opened as a means of political control and exclusion from the society. But the reformers also aspired to make these children productive and useful in artisanal positions, as a means of (re)inclusion in the society. The *ıslahhane*s, therefore, not only solved a public-order problem but also suggested a possibility of reintegration—of reshaping civic responsibility among children who had either lost or never embraced it.

On a more abstract and Empire-wide level, the opening of *ıslahhane*s was part of the larger context of "Ottoman reform." These institutions were instrumental in strengthening the ties between the center and the provinces and in disseminating Ottomanist ideals among local communities. These children offered opportunities to those who aspired to turn them into laborious workers and loyal Ottomans. They could spread a new form of allegiance to the state, closer to the notion of citizenship. It was this prospect that made children the actors of several social and political developments of the nineteenth century. Analyzing the establishment and operations of the *ıslahhane*s from a perspective of the history of children and youth reveals obscure corners and unnoticed aspects of Ottoman modernization, urbanization, economic development, and welfare policies.

It is easier to discuss the motivations of the state, the schools, the city planners, the industrial reformers, or even the families. Hearing the real and direct voices of the children who were educated in these vocational orphanages is trickier. Source materials rarely hint on their overall satisfaction, their living standards in the orphanages (compared to their former experiences of poverty on the streets), or their emotional needs and shortcomings. All these require the testimony of the children who spent a part of their lives in the orphanages. Although writing autobiographies and memoirs has become fashionable in the twentieth century, the accounts of former students of these institutions are not represented by such efforts. The paucity of sources that give direct agency to the orphaned children is not only because children rarely have a voice but also because the orphans belonged to lower classes and did not have the cultural capital through which to express themselves in memoirs. Silenced people of the past, such as peasants, artisans, slaves, women, and children, very rarely left letters or memoirs.[169]

The silence of the sources hints that *ıslahhane* children had slim chances of upward mobility. The education they received was predominantly vocational, which did not truly equip them for written expression. Reformers frequently stressed that orphans, street children, and vagrants were the target population for the *ıslahhane*s. Still, these institutions were also frequently used by families in need who tried actively to benefit from state assistance options by voluntarily sending their children. There is a voluminous body of petitions written by parents for the enrollment of their children in *ıslahhane*s. Many poor families tried to provide the necessary documentation of their poverty and destitution so that they could be relieved of the extra burden of their children through state welfare.[170] The training they had in the orphanages made these poor children skilled workers and self-sufficient household heads, but it rarely opened doors to the more affluent sections of society.

The only firsthand "voice" of these children comes in the form of petitions and notes of gratitude to the sultan, where his philanthropy and benevolence is praised. The boys at the Izmir orphanage wrote a letter in 1869 in order to express their thankfulness to the sultan, together with the *vali* and the notables of the province. They said, "Deprived of our mothers and fathers, we were previously creeping naked in the streets, crawling in the mud. We had no one to help, no one to give a hand. We had no one to educate us in order to reach salvation. Many thanks to God that now we are saved from that misery and we attained this bliss."[171]

It is unlikely that *islahhane* children wrote these letters themselves. The sophisticated language suggests that the words were dictated by their masters. This is not surprising, since subalterns tend to speak in the voice of their superior.[172] This form of evidence only projects the self-image of state and school administrators as if it was the supposed viewpoint of the children. In this picture, the state wanted to depict them as rescued from danger, happy, fulfilled, and grateful.

Petitions present a more accurate picture of the viewpoint of the sub-ordinates. Letters of remission, or letters of grievance and petitions, are one of the best sources "of relatively uninterrupted narrative from the lips of the lower orders."[173] In March 1914 Ali bin Ahmed, a second-year student of the Salonika orphanage, wrote a petition. He was forced to migrate to the capital as a result of the Balkan wars and had to interrupt his education. He pledged to be transferred to the orphanage of Damascus, where some of his former co-scholars had already been enrolled.[174] This petition points to Ali's willingness to be in an *islahhane*. His motivation to go as far as Damascus might be a sign of his destitution and desperation in Istanbul as an orphan with no one to rely on.

The presence of orphans and unattended children in the urban space became an issue for urban administrators, local notables, and the central state. Their collection and education was related to urban and economic aspects of internal politics and the Ottoman reform era. In the next part, the focus will reach beyond the borders of the Empire to concentrate on the international controversy that humanitarian relief for orphans had the potential to create. This way, the book will complete its journey from the most inner/intimate sphere to the most global/international, from the realm of unwanted pregnancy and childbirth to interstate diplomacy.

4

The Internationalization of Orphans

PHILANTHROPY, charity, and charitable institutions have traditionally been interpreted as manifestations of religious values. Lately, historians of the Middle East have begun to assert the importance of self-interest, or collective self-interest, in motivating elites to offer charitable assistance.[1] Charity reflects a donor's wishes, inspired by spiritual, social, economic, and political motives, together with self-interest and ambition. Attaining paradise in the afterlife, securing social standing, seeking economic advantage through tax reductions or protection of property, and consolidating political support could all be possible motives for charitable or beneficent acts.[2] For elites, poor relief had a number of social and economic benefits, including maintenance of a reserve of workers, confirmation of the proper place of the poor, keeping public order, control of epidemic infections, and moral improvement, or "civilizing," of the poor.[3]

Orphan care in the Ottoman Empire included these traditional forms, such as raising orphans within a larger family, foster care, or apprenticeship. Thus the opening of orphanages in the Ottoman Empire can be explained through a complex web of interrelated forces, including economic, social, political, and ideological factors, which lay behind the establishment and maintenance of both architectural and human monuments. An institutional solution for orphaned children was related to the emergence of an increasingly modern capitalist economy in urban areas, as in the example of *ıslahhane*s. Here we come across the inevitable relationship between orphanages and workshops, with the identities of orphans conflated with those of apprentices. An alternative theoretical approach is that of the "the great confinement."[4]

The analysis of charity needs to take into consideration agents on both sides, namely, those who provide charity and those who receive it. The economically favored, on the supply side, give to the disadvantaged out of self-interest. Charity indirectly and elaborately helps the privileged to maintain a fundamental inequality in all spheres of life. Still, the demand side can achieve power over the favored and force them to engage in redistribution of resources. Therefore, charity has the added benefit of eliciting from the poor respect for the very social system that keeps them in poverty.[5] From the supply/demand perspective, charity often requires the presence of needy people or specific recipients. Yet, it is not necessarily dependent on the number or condition of those who are the potential "customers" of charity. Sometimes, the relation between the two is of an inverse nature: the demand is created after the emergence of the supply. More importantly, charity is offered only in response to a giver's perception of both the need and the deservedness of the recipient.

The number of orphans in general oscillated from decade to decade, and from place to place, due to political, military, and social problems. In the case of orphans, the pressing need for some sort of orphan relief, either in the form of orphanages or foster care, emerged in emergency situations. Warfare, especially an endemic state of guerrilla conflict, could create a larger number of homeless children and necessitate the opening of many new orphanages.[6] In these circumstances, the number of destitute children became so great that their institutional or private care was regarded as inevitable by interested parties. Still, in these crisis periods, only *certain* parties took actual measures to tackle only *certain* orphan problems. The volume of destitute children is a meaningful variable, but the engagement in orphan relief also had more intricate motivations.

Based on the sheer number of orphans, the nineteenth-century Ottoman Empire should have witnessed the mushrooming of orphanages all over the place. The entire country was shaking with independence movements, regional conflicts, intervention of the Great Powers, shrinking territories, and floods of refugees. But this was not the case. First, not every "orphan problem" led to the opening of orphanages. Second, different actors were active in various orphan crises. Third, some orphans were more important than others depending on the perception of the parties who assumed their "relief and rescue."

A comparison of different crisis periods may help clarify this line of interpretation. The Armenian massacres in the Eastern *vilayet*s of the Ottoman Empire during 1894–1896 evolved into a major arena through which the missionaries and the Sublime Porte fought for legitimacy, power, prestige, and hegemony over a seemingly philanthropic field of establishing orphanages.[7] However, the victims of the Crimean War of 1853–1856 and the Russo-Ottoman War of 1877–1878 were not treated as such. Actually, both wars had caused the entry of enormous numbers of refugees into the Empire, especially from the Black Sea region. Hundreds of thousands of people were forced to leave their homes, and most of them were widows and orphans. The arrival of refugees into the cities caused a real crisis in providing for these hungry, naked, sick, and destitute people who apparently needed to be sheltered, fed, and educated. However, the relief measures for these refugees had never become a serious matter of rivalry among the Sublime Porte, the missionaries, and other relevant parties.

In actuality, the missionary activities for Muslim refugees were rather limited. The missionaries of the American Board of Commissioners for Foreign Missions (ABCFM)[8] were not really involved in providing for these miserable people.[9] This was definitely related to the fact that the missionary societies operating in the Ottoman Empire subconsciously knew that they had no chances of converting, or even educating, the Muslims due to administrative and political obstacles put forward by the authorities and their previous experience of failure with the Muslims.

In contrast to this previous disengaged attitude toward "humanitarian relief," the Armenian massacres of 1894–1896 pushed the ABCFM to open approximately sixty orphanages in about thirty mission stations. Why did they put themselves under such a huge burden? And why did "the charitable works" of the missionaries disturb the Sublime Porte, such that they struggled to obstruct these initiatives? This chapter, situated at the crossroads of charity, missionary activity, the modern state, nationalism, and the history of education, dwells upon the intricacies of orphan relief in the Ottoman Empire in the last decade of the 1890s.

The initial focus will be on practical issues relating to the orphanages of the Catholic and Protestant missionaries, such as their geographical dispersion, number of orphans educated, basic components of the education, and motives of the missionaries in orphan relief. The chapter also elaborates on the competitive environment created by the opening of missionary orphanages, since foreign relief activities, especially in the realm of orphans, created hostility on the side of the Sublime Porte due to religious and nationalistic reasons. Ottoman authorities were disturbed by the effectiveness of missionaries in the fields of education and orphan relief because they were convinced that orphans, torn apart from their families and their social environment, were perfect targets for religious and nationalistic aims. With regard to orphans, all sides were amazed at—or in dread of, depending on their position—the ease of "converting" these children and "gaining" them. The Porte was not alone in its disgust of the missionary competition. The Gregorian Armenians were also in a very difficult position. Being in theory the legitimate guardian of the Armenian orphans, the Patriarchate was weak in many ways. Although criticism toward the activities of the state and the missionaries was strong, the Patriarchate was still dependent on the charities of these adversaries for the survival of the remnants of the massacres.

Interestingly, all actors playing a part in the orphan crisis during the aftermath of the massacres—missionaries, the Gregorian Armenian Patriarchate, foreign consular officers, and the Sublime Porte—had regarded the others as accomplices in this matter, despite their deeply felt conflicts in general. Perceiving the issue from the standpoint of each, it was felt that the other two or three were in some form of alliance. Each side felt a strong threat from the others or believed that the others were in alliance to hinder them. This relatively paranoid perception had some truth in it. Unlikely parties were actually getting closer to each other to eliminate rivals.

Missionary Rivalry in Post-1896 Orphan Relief

Humanitarian involvement of the European Powers in the Ottoman Empire actually started as the West's earliest and most universal engagement to address a distant suffering, with the Armenian massacres, beginning in

1894 and continuing for more than two years.[10] Observers were talking about 50,000 Armenian orphans scattered all over the Empire, below the age of twelve.[11] In a number of countries, "human rights of the Armenians" attracted significant political support. The place and importance of religious groups in this panorama was also quite large. The constituency that the Armenian massacres found in Germany was millenarian Christians, part of a broader international Protestant impulse. These brought the events in Anatolia to the attention of the mainstream Protestant religious press, which eventually joined the cause. As defendants of the movement for Armenian relief in Germany, they organized rallies, took up collections for clinics and orphanages (amassing well over 600,000 marks by January 1897), and "adopted" children and paid the salaries of doctors and nurses.[12]

The entrance of the ABCFM into the picture is understandable, as philanthropy was always a part of the American missionary mandate. Specifically four departments of missionary work were emphasized. The evangelistic work, which developed into churches, the department of publication, educational work, and philanthropy, included free medical service, hospitals, famine relief, and the like.[13] Yet, the opening of orphanages en masse started only after the Armenian massacres of 1894–1896. Before the massacres the American missions only had three small-scale Homes. After these events the missionaries opened close to sixty orphanages (see Tables 17 and 18). In 1898, the American missionaries reported that they were able to take care of 4,000 orphans in twenty different mission centers.[14] The orphanages, though already grown into a serious mission field, were still defined as "emergency work."[15] The feeling of emergency and crisis was forced by the volume of needy. Mr. Sanders of Urfa reported that between 40 to 60 percent of the population of the city was made up of orphans and widows.[16]

In the pages of the *Missionary Herald* or in the reports of missionaries from 1894 to 1898, the main subject was the orphanages and general relief work. The extent of the work is also clear from the ratio of it in expenditures and from the interruption of general educational work in some stations for almost two years. Even if this was an unexpected situation, the missionaries in the field were content with their operations, despite many inconveniences they had to face. In the end, they had a great opportunity to make a massive impact on the local population.

> Very few have failed to meet the expectations of friends who succored them, and some of them are doing admirable work as *Disciples of Christ*. There is a quiet, yet deep, religious awakening throughout the orphanage, giving promise of blessed results. When we remember that *these young people are in a special sense being "saved to serve,"*, the value of these orphanages in our mission field is most apparent.[17]

Although American missionaries took hesitant steps toward orphan care, their establishment was remarkable by the end of the century. The ABCFM had about sixty orphanages in thirty districts. The number of orphans in these establishments ranged from 50 to 1,000, but on average most of the orphanages had some 100 children. The orphan asylums of the ABCFM are thought to have provided for around 10,000 orphans in the following decade after the massacres. In his trip throughout Turkey, Dr. Cornelius H. Patton was surprised by the orphanage work, since this was "not an integral part of the work of American missionaries."[18]

The ABCFM was involved in orphan relief only when faced with a crisis, and declaredly on a temporary basis, while the Catholic missionaries had equivalent operations starting from their early years in the Empire. There were several groups of Catholic missionaries in the Ottoman Empire: Jesuits, Lazaristes, Assumptionists, Franciscans, Brothers of the Christian Schools (*Frères des écoles Chrétiennes*), Capucins, Carmelites, Sisters of St. Vincent de Paul (*Filles de la Charité*), Sisters of Notre Dame of Sion, and Dominicans, among others. Most of these missions were politically and financially under French protection, although there were some Italian missions connected to *Propaganda Fide*. The orphan care was mostly left to female missionaries. Together with Sisters of the Assumptionists and Franciscans, the most important female missionary group in the Ottoman Empire was *Filles de la Charité*.[19]

In contrast with the ABCFM, the missionary work of the Catholics was strongly linked to orphan care from the start. *Filles de la Charité* established their mission station in Istanbul in 1840, and in a year they were able to run a small orphanage of twenty-four girls.[20] Long before the

Armenian massacres of the 1890s, there was a large network of Catholic orphanages (around forty) in relatively urban areas and port cities (see Table 15). Orphan relief was part of the regular operations of Catholic missionary groups. Interestingly, they could not *benefit* from the post-massacre situation and opened only eight very small orphanages (see Table 16). This was because well-established Catholic missions were in geographically distant areas. The missions in the vicinity had only a few orphanages, and the capacity was too small to shelter large numbers of orphans. As a result the main strategy of Catholic missionaries was to transfer as many orphans as they could to their large, established orphanages in Beirut, Jerusalem, and Istanbul. They also called Catholic families to foster Armenian orphans in order to bypass their weakness.[21]

Protestant and Catholic missionaries differed in their involvement in orphan care and their approach and strategies, based on their past experiences and present-day capabilities. In geographical terms, while the Catholics had control of the western coast and port cities in the Balkans and Arab provinces, the American missionaries had their stronghold in the inner and remote areas of Eastern Anatolia. The Americans, when they first developed their missions, were in a much weaker position compared to the Catholics, who had been a presence in those lands for around two hundred years.[22] The most important advantage possessed by Roman Catholic schools was that they taught French, the official language of foreign diplomacy in the Empire. So they were able to draw more children to their schools and orphanages.[23] The rights of consular representation and political intervention in the matters of protection of the Christians, given to the European powers after the Congress of Berlin, were also other important factors envied by the Americans. The Americans argued that the Catholic influence and success in Mardin, Siirt, and Diyarbekir resulted from their consular representatives.[24] Protestants also believed that many native peoples were converted to Catholicism by "promises of temporal advantage," namely the rights and privileges of French or Italian citizenship. French protection, or protégé status, meant to be freed from taxation and liability of imprisonment.[25]

Despite their "inexperience" and "delay" in entering the field, the Americans were successful enough to surpass their adversaries. In the end, the volume of American engagement in post-massacre orphan care was significantly higher. Catholics were quite discontented with the Protestants' achievement. The Dominican missionary of Van, Galland, wrote to his superior in Paris that he did not know how to fight with an orphanage of 12 children against equivalent institutions of the Protestants sheltering more than 300.[26] This unprecedented success was related to the ABCFM's well-developed missions—with its schools, churches, congregations, and staff—in the afflicted areas. They were able to channel their entire activity into a neighboring realm very quickly. In terms of finances, Protestants utilized a range of methods for private fundraising, from personal subscriptions to large donations, which quickly responded to immediate needs. The Catholic missionary enterprise had an alliance with French diplomacy and was dependent on the state treasury (and also the papacy) for their income.[27]

The involvement of several philanthropic societies for the care of the Armenian orphans—and not Bulgarian, Circassian, or Crimean ones—is significant. The "popularity" of Armenian orphans was related to the issues of religion, nationality, identity, and conversion. They were hungry, miserable, and poor creatures of the present but they were also seen as a projection of future. The struggle focused on the definition of prospects that lay ahead of orphans. Armenian orphans both promised hope and generated fear in the minds of those interested, based on what they could do and what they failed to do. All sides of the controversy, including the state, missionaries, foreign consular agents, and the Armenian Patriarchate, sensed the potential and treated the realm of orphan relief as an arena of competition. All were aspiring to save the Armenian orphans and they all devised the same strategies, accusing one another on the same basis.

Conversion and Mobility of Orphans within the Empire

For the missionaries of the eastern provinces of the Empire, the Armenians were regarded as the most appropriate targets of missionary activity due to their previous record of conversion. Yet, even among the Armenians, the missionaries were coming across problems in entering into communities and in breaking the negative attitude of the local community. Crisis periods, such as epidemics, earthquakes, wars, or massacres, when the community was in utter need, were crucial moments for the missionaries during which they turned the misery of the population into an opportunity to gain recognition. In the aftermath of many such events, the missionary correspondence reflects hopefulness. The Armenian massacres of 1894–1896 also created an atmosphere of heightened visions for conversion.

The missionaries in Bitlis were targets of jealousy after the first massacres in Sasun in 1894. The missionary of Van, Dr. Raynolds, seeing this "glorious field" for "gospel work," wrote, "I almost envy our Bitlis associates the work that awaits them."[28] In some instances, the discourse was disturbingly joyful, disregarding the suffering and loss of the people. Dr. Barnum of Harput even claimed that orphans were "glad" to lose their families during the massacres, since they found salvation.

> 13 months ago not one of these boys and girls who are so much interested in spiritual things knew how to pray, or had any knowledge of Christ and his salvation. One of the little girls, in writing the other day to a man who had adopted her, said that she was *glad she lost everything, for in that day she had found Christ*, whom she could not lose.[29]

After the spread of the massacres to the entire eastern provinces, the missionaries were on equal terms with their Bitlis associates and they were all offered the same *opportunity*. Feeding the hungry, caring for the sick, sheltering the orphans and widows, the missionaries had a much larger constituency at their disposal, not only to help but also to "mold under their religious influence."[30] The orphans were the most precious opportunity among them, since they supposedly held the future in their hands.

> The future of this blighted country must be very largely *in the hands of the Armenian children* who have survived, for as always hitherto, this Mohammedan country must owe its economic and intellectual development to the Christians. These children, *these orphans, can be trained* now for that stupendous task. *Behold America's opportunity!*[31]

Post-massacre relief measures were hardly selflessly benevolent. All interested parties had political calculations and objectives.[32] They

12. Shoemaking workshop for orphan boys, American Orphanage at Harput (1897). Unknown photographer, "The Orphans of Turkey," *Missionary Herald* 93 (December 1897): 501–3.

deliberately employed a policy that was shaped within the lines of the "deserving and undeserving needy." Denial of access to relief worked on a number of levels. First, both Protestant and Catholic missionaries selected Armenian massacre victims as their target group for philanthropic action, instead of another group also in need of such provisions. Second, among Armenians, they prioritized the orphans over other groups of adults or children, since the orphans supposedly had the potential to be easily converted and saved from the "filth and ignorance" of their society.

> VAN: While it is worth much to be able to keep the multitudes from starving, *little can be done to lift them out of their filth and ignorance*. But *the orphans can be put under such influences* as may change their whole destiny for time and eternity.[33]

As a third level, Armenian orphans were also subjected to a serious selection process that the missionaries called "sifting." Not all orphans

13. Carpentry workshop, Sivas American Orphanage (1908). Unknown photographer, *Missionary Herald* 104 (May 1908): 210.

deserved their philanthropy. The missionaries made planned trips to many districts, and after careful examination they selected only a few of these children to be accepted in their orphanages. Although the particulars of the "sifting process" are not elaborated, clearly it was not based on need or destitution. What mattered was the assumed ease of conversion.

> VAN: These [boys] are selected from the most *promising* and advanced
> . . .[34]

> SIVAS: We selected the *cream* of them, now no longer with parents and relatives to keep them back.[35]

> MARDIN: These orphans *have been gathered from 34 places* after careful *sifting*, and that only after various trips for the purpose.[36]

> VAN: As we must *select a few from the many*, this was the class that presented the *strongest claim on our sympathy* both from their utter helplessness and *because of the hopeful future they promise* if now cared for and educated.[37]

The declared objective of "saving the orphans" was only meaningful in the context of religious indoctrination and conversion. Benevolence and humanistic help was in no way blindly distributed and was directly related to the desire for proselytizing. All those involved were aware that Armenian orphans would become targets of proselytizing efforts. The missionaries criticized Ottoman rescue efforts from a racist perspective, arguing that "they were interested in adding intelligent minds to their degenerate race."[38] In missionary discourse, the work meant not only evangelization but also rescuing Armenian orphans from conversion to Islam. They depicted the crisis and the need for intervention with Crusade jargon. In reality, Armenian orphans were under threat of "losing their faith" in either hands, be it Muslim or Protestant.

> The thought that thousands of poor children are today without father or mother and that they try to escape an inevitable death that awaits them or Islamism that watches for them, makes a very profound and painful impact. . . . [39]
>
> We understand that the situation of these unsupported orphans was disturbing, deplorable: they ran the risk to lose their life and their faith.[40]

The Ottoman state was pressured on the issue of conversions to Islam due to interference rights of the Western powers resulting from the Treaty of Berlin (1878). A Government Inquiry Commission was established in order to investigate forcible conversions during the massacres.[41] The British vice-consul at Urfa, Mr. Fitzmaurice, was appointed to the commission together with two state officials. In his report to the British Parliament, Fitzmaurice declared that although the government claimed that these converts "had found salvation of their own free will,"[42] there was overwhelming evidence that it was made quite clear to Christians that to espouse Islam was the sole escape from instant and horrible death. He put the number of forced converts at considerably over 6,000.[43] Another issue that the missionaries touched upon was the adoption of orphan girls into Muslim households. Catholic missionaries underlined that they opened the girls' orphanage in Siirt due to the dangers of conversion to Islam and sexual abuse.

> It was necessary to provide for these poor little girls, whose parents had disappeared in one way or another during the massacres, and who, completely abandoned or received into Muslim houses, were in danger of losing their faith and their innocence.[44]

14. Orphan girls doing housework with the house mother, American Orphanage at Harput (1897). Unknown photographer, "The Orphans of Turkey," *Missionary Herald* 93 (December 1897): 501–3.

When a few German and American Protestant orphanages were disbanded in Diyarbekir, the Protestant missionaries worked hard to make the consular officials solve the issue since they were worried that some of these orphans could "take refuge in Muslim houses, and [be] lost to moral and Christian influences."[45]

There were different mechanisms of care for the Armenian orphans of 1894–1896. The largest number of orphans was sheltered in the newly opened orphanages of the ABCFM. A relatively small number was taken into private households. A third option was to send orphans to already established and permanent orphanages in Istanbul, Izmir, Bursa, Jerusalem, and Beirut. Many were even sent to Germany, Switzerland, and elsewhere to the care of those individuals who had been working for succoring these orphans.[46] All sides of the "orphan problem," the Armenian Patriarchate, the Sublime Porte, and different missionary groups, attempted to transfer at least some of the orphans from the area. Thanks to their orphanage network, American missionaries were the least interested in the practice. Gregorian Armenians, Catholics, and German Deaconesses, on the other hand, lacking the necessary local sources and manpower, devised this strategy to be able to compete. The Sublime Porte, in its turn, invented obstructive measures to stop the flow of Armenian orphans from one place to another.

The initiating parties seem to disregard it, but these journeys would have been painful for children. Some of them were as little as four-years-old. They were taken from mountainous eastern regions under hard winter conditions to be sent away as far as Izmir. Their trip to Trabzon, the closest port to northeastern Anatolia, whether on horseback or by foot, usually took more than a week. There was always tension at the port before embarkation to the ships. While missionaries, the English consul, and local security officials at the port were discussing and deliberating on their fates, these uprooted orphans were shuttled back and forth between these different authorities. Frequently the missionaries were the winners. So Armenian orphans were loaded onto a ship to Istanbul and had to suffer a long sea voyage on a crowded deck with limited food and water. These aspects never became a concern for the missionaries, who were supposedly acting as saviors of the children. When the Sublime Porte intervened, they rarely referred to painful road trips or to the sadness of taking children so far away from their families and homelands. Usually orphans were permanently separated from their families. The distance from home was remarkable, and visits were unlikely. For instance, Diruhi Jernazian had been sent in 1898 to the German missionary orphanage in Izmir, as a six-year-old, leaving her brothers and sisters in Maraş. When she died of tuberculosis in 1906, the director of the orphanage sent back only a small photograph of her.[47] The state's discourse emphasized the harms of missionary operations. The fight was not centered on the actual needs of the orphans but over their futures.

At the height of the Armenian massacres of 1896, the head organization in the German Reich took a pro-Armenian position and decided to exclusively dedicate the Izmir orphanage of the German Deaconesses, a Protestant women's organization, to massacre survivors and *"to serve the Armenian people."*[48] Donations from Germany allowed the expansion of the orphanage to accommodate 120 Armenian orphans. There were also orphans from massacre-unaffected western Anatolia. The Deaconesses were ordered to maintain a high number of Armenian children in the institution, no matter where they came from. There was also a considerable traffic toward Jerusalem, where the Deaconesses also had an orphanage. In May 1898 the government authorized the sending of a score of children from Harput and Diyarbekir to the orphanage of the Deaconesses in Jerusalem, following the request of the German consul there.[49]

Traveling from one place to another within the Empire could only be done with a valid travel permit (*tezkere*), and the transfer of orphans always generated diplomatic controversies. In the case of the Armenian orphans, the Ottoman state was alarmed by the increasing activities of foreign missionaries and determined to impede their activities. The American missionary in Bitlis, Mr. Cole, had to apply a number of times during the second half of 1896 for the transfer of 23 Armenian orphans (12 boys, 11 girls) to the orphanage of the German Deaconesses in Izmir.[50] The children finally arrived at Trabzon in November and were to embark on a Greek ship to Istanbul. On the very last moment, they were stopped by the inspector at the port, who thought "the reasons behind their transfer were incomprehensible" (*mahall-i mezkureye sevklerindeki maksad anlaşılamadığı*). New problems were encountered with every new group of orphans. In December 1896, the American missionaries asked for the interference of the British consul of Erzurum to send more than forty orphans to Izmir and Bursa by way of Trabzon. The Ministry of Police (Zabtiye Nezareti) thought that it would be impossible to stop them once they reached the port and wrote to the governorship of Erzurum to hinder their departure from the province.[51] Despite all these obstructions, quite a few orphans were actually transported to the permanent orphanages in Bursa, Izmir, Bardezag (Izmit), and Jerusalem.[52]

Leaving aside the transfer of orphans to the big cities of the Empire, there was also a circulation of orphans going on within eastern Anatolia. The missionary in Maraş, a certain Mrs. Lee, was opening a new orphanage and demanded the transfer of some orphans from the Zeytun region. The local authorities initially objected, yet the issue was favorably decided in the end.[53] Actually there were more than enough massacre orphans everywhere in eastern Anatolia. If this was the case, then why was Mrs. Lee particularly interested in bringing orphans from Zeytun? At least two dynamics were at work. First, the Protestant missionaries found it useful to separate children from their families and relatives who were thought to continuously exert "unchristian influences." The native homes were thought to cancel out the Protestant influence of mission schools and orphanages.

> However faithfully we labor for the girls in our boarding schools, there is always this drawback, that the home influence is against us and much of our work is there undone. This is not the case with the orphans [in West Broussa Orphanage for Girls]; for them *there is no vacation and there is no force drawing them down* while we are trying to lift them up.[54]

Second, the Protestant missionaries wanted to make sure that they raised orphans from different geographical regions. This way they could go back to their native villages as teachers or preachers and act as "a well-trained native agency" enlightening the village community in the future. By 1904, the Eastern Turkey mission reported that their orphans had started to fill up the ranks of each station. Orphans, for that reason, were significant investments for the missions, solving the problem of recruitment.

> Since the well remembered events of 1895, the [Eastern Turkey] mission has been engaged in the care and instruction of some 2,550 orphans of both sexes. . . . On the whole each station has had its *corps of teachers and general helpers enriched from the ranks of these orphans*, and many are still in the higher schools in course of preparation for labor in these station fields on evangelistic and educational lines. The orphans have proved *a grand investment for the regular work of the mission*—one way in which the lord has made the wrath of men to praise him.[55]

Catholic missionaries used the same method of transferring massacre orphans to their well-established orphanages. They had only eight orphanages in the region, and the total number under their care did not exceed a few hundred. Their biggest project was the Sainte Anne orphanage of the Armenian Catholic Patriarchate, opened in 1898 in Istanbul. Sixty-two massacre orphans were brought from various parts of the Empire to this orphanage.[56] The adoption of the Armenian orphans by volunteering parties in France was also discussed in the second half of 1896.[57] The Capucin Fathers in Mezre, who had 28 boys and 18 girls in their orphanage, hoped to see some of these children educated in France so that they would return to their villages as "catechists and schoolmasters," as "apostles" to "do good for their unhappy compatriots."[58]

Response of the Armenian Patriarchate

After the massacres of 1894–1896, which put the Armenian population in the area into a catastrophic socioeconomic situation, Ottoman Armenians devised modern forms of charity and benevolence, such as private charity associations, fundraising campaigns, and orphanages. Before that, orphan care was provided under the roofs of churches, in monasteries, and more recently in hospitals. The patriarch Maghakia Ormanian, elected right after the massacres, was under serious pressure from the community since the orphans' future was perceived to be at stake. He was expected to reorganize the administration of the orphan problem by erecting a network of orphanages. This bold project required significant financial resources. Local charity organizations of the Patriarchate and communities could not meet the pressing needs in afflicted areas. Despite communal resistance against foreign involvement, the Patriarchate was only partially successful in "saving" the orphans from Protestant hands and was forced to consent to the opening of missionary establishments.

The Patriarchate opened a dozen orphanages, thanks to the benevolent contributions of the Armenians of Istanbul and from areas spared from violence. A special subcommittee was formed in order to execute these relief measures. They were charged with taking an inventory of orphans, controlling the management of the establishments, and distributing subsidies. Large monasteries also opened orphanages on their own premises. Based on the investigation of the Ministry of Interior, the Armenian Gregorian clerical authorities had orphanages in Urfa (with 50–60 orphans), Zeytun (6), Aintab (40), Mamuretülaziz (33), Malatya (30), Arabkir (32), Van (130), Erzurum (160), Sivas (63), and Diyarbekir (520).[59]

The Patriarchate also worked on the transfer of orphans from the provinces to Istanbul and their consequent admittance to the Armenian Orphanage in Yedikule, affiliated with the Surp Prgiç Armenian Hospital.[60]

There were around a hundred of them in the capital city. Twenty were enrolled in the Kalealtı (Levon Vartuhian) Armenian School, while eighty were under the supervision of the vice-prelate (*Reis-i Ruhani Vekili*).[61] Ormanian also launched an adoption campaign and invited financially well-off Armenian families to take care of at least one child until the day that s/he would be able to earn his/her own living.[62] The Patriarchate also worked around many obstacles created by local or central authorities to bring orphans to the capital. In mid-1897, continuous requests were made for the transfer of 345 children from several provinces[63] to be sheltered in the Armenian Orphanage in Istanbul and in the houses of charitable persons.[64] At first, the Ministry of Justice and Sects, under an order from the Ministry of Interior, refused to give these children travel permits on the pretext that the trip was too long and that the Patriarchate should work to take care of them in their home towns.[65] The Patriarchate replied that they also wished for the provisioning of orphans in their native localities but, given the emergency of the circumstances and their weakness in terms of budget, such an option would force them to ask for the generosity of the benevolent sultan.[66] Arguing that the total number (345) was quite small compared to the general orphan population, the Patriarchate insisted on the release of permission. The final authorization was delayed until March 1900 and was given with the precondition that the orphans were divided into groups of five or six. This curiously meant the transfer of orphans in 69 separate convoys.[67]

This orphan relief project altered relations between the missionaries and Gregorian Armenians. In some instances, the American missionaries argued that, due to gratitude and sympathy, relief work created brotherly relations with the Gregorians. They saw the realm of philanthropy as an opportunity to break the prejudices of communities, to gain legitimacy, and to enlarge spheres of influence.[68] The same hope existed also among the Catholic missionaries. They believed that their involvement in orphan care increased the sympathies of the local population and served as a mechanism to break their prejudices.[69] Orphan care was considered to be crucial for furthering operations in conversion. As religious education had always been an integral part of missionary education, raising orphans as Protestants or Catholics was their primary goal. Missionaries assumed that it was possible to mold the character of these children and make a decided mark on their future lives such that they would give "a higher and nobler life to the Armenian people."[70]

> BURSA: God's providence has placed the choicest of the youth of the land
> of both sexes in our hands, and the work of *molding their characters* is,
> so to speak, entirely committed to us, and the prospect is . . . to *make*
> *a decided mark* on their future lives and characters.[71]

> MERZIFON: The orphanage work has furnished an unusual opportunity
> for impressing truths upon the men and women of the next genera-
> tion in Turkey.[72]

> VAN: [They] were never so easily collected than today after the massa-
> cres. Wouldn't these children become one day our best auxiliaries
> within the Armenian society, for the conversion of their compatri-
> ots? Indeed, a movement of conversion or rather rapprochement
> towards Catholicism takes place in Van since the events of June of
> last year. . . . There is not a more effective means than the complete
> Catholic education of Armenian youth, who were raised by us from
> early on, cleared away from prejudices of the milieu, will remain
> firmly attached to us without being prone to the concerns of the
> politics nor to the fluctuations of opinion.[73]

The Armenian Patriarchate became very critical of the missionary proselytizing efforts. It was feared that the gathering of thousands of orphan children into missionary institutions might result in the with-drawal of great numbers of children from the "national church." They tried to follow closely what form of instruction these children received so as to prevent their alienation from their own community. This was a matter of life and death, as the community's youngest generation was at stake. The Armenian ecclesiastical authorities were concerned about the evangelization of children when they were informed that apostolic priests were not allowed in these institutions. In the end, the patriarch filed a long complaint.

> Mr. Chambers [an Erzurum missionary] allows the orphans to go to
> the Armenian church, but will not permit a priest to be received in the

establishment in order to teach the Armenian children the belief and ceremonies of their church. He says that he already teaches the Bible in the institution, and that the priest may visit the institution, but without being charged with the religious and moral instruction of the children.

The committee [of Gürün] in charge of the orphanage raises many difficulties about the attendance of the orphans at the Armenian church, and this notwithstanding the promises made when the orphanage was opened. At Easter they sent only the smaller children and that on the second day of Easter, declaring that the larger boys were free to go or not. As to the orphan girls, the committee insists that they must receive the communion at the holy altar of the Protestant church, which the girls refuse to do. The professors and servants in the orphanage sneer at the children for praying, kneeling, and for making the sign of cross, and require them to pray with the eyes shut. They do these things in order to bring up the children as Protestants.

MARAŞ: The missionaries have commenced not to send the orphans to the Armenian church and deprive them of the privilege of attending church and of communing. They sneer at the manner in which the children pray and forbid them to make the sign of cross or to kneel at prayer.[74]

Orphans were generally permitted to attend the service at the Armenian church. But, they were also compelled to attend Sabbath and midweek services in the Protestant chapel and Bible instruction was a part of the regular curriculum in the school. Faced with patriarchal criticisms, they pursued a conciliatory policy.[75] They could in no way consent to the omission of biblical instruction from daily studies. Yet, the missionaries declared that they recognized the right of the mother church to continue her ecclesiastical care of the Gregorian orphans.[76]

It is strongly desired that Gregorian Armenian orphans be kept to their connection with the national church. And we recognize the reasonableness of this desire to provide against any influences of the nature of proselytizing efforts, *under cover of charitable care for the helpless.* Yet on our part, and on the part of all supporters of this work, it will be regarded as a "sin qua non" that the *whole care of the mental, moral and religious train-ing of these children be in the hands of the superintendents of the orphanages,* left quite untrammeled of course, Armenian visitors, clergy or lay, will always find a welcome at the orphanages. . . . *We do not aim to make Prot-estants of them,* that considering their condition *as minors,* most of them very young, we will not recommend their becoming Protestants while in the orphanages, and that we will give the children facilities for attend-ing their church on Sunday morning and on special occasions during the week.[77]

[M]uch talk has been made by the Gregorians as to these children becoming Protestants if left entirely under our charge. This will not be our effort in any respect, but it is simply *impossible not to surround them by an atmosphere redolent of the Bible, prayer and Christian principles,* while they attend our school. We cannot but hope that many of these children will come out of the orphanages consecrated, educated Christians to bless this land.[78]

On the one hand the missionaries were making open declarations against proselytizing or denationalizing; on the other, their education was solely based on evangelical truths and they were aiming to train these orphans as bearers of the Protestant faith. Dr. Raynolds even spoke of a form of hidden conversion, not in name but in essence. As outright con-version proved politically difficult, they devised a strategy of "indirect conversion" through schooling.

Certainly no effort is made to estrange the children from the mother church, but very *constant effort is made to establish them in true Christian-ity,* and it seems to me that the effort is quite as successful as could be expected. Several of the boys are now about ready to go forth as gradu-ates of the school and teachers of their people and *if they can go as mem-bers of the mother church and find entrance to the hearts of the people whom they go,* and be freed from restrictions on their consciences, and all this *without having the handicap of Protestant name,* we might hope far greater results in the way of really extending the master's kingdom than could come for sending preachers and teachers as Protestants.[79]

Tension between the Sublime Porte and the Missionaries

In his memo regarding the rejection of the reinstitution of a German orphanage in Diyarbekir, the governor of the province described the missionaries as "a herd of locusts" dispersed in the area.[80] This description is priceless in understanding the perception of the Ottoman administration. Missionaries were numerous, they were hard workers, they were essentially harmful to the country, and they were bypassing the jurisdiction of the state. The missionaries were actually limiting the reach of Ottoman rule in some areas thanks to their success in fields of education and health. The uneasiness of the Ottoman state had an older history, yet the 1894–1896 Armenian massacres escalated the tension.[81]

The graveness of the orphan crisis, coupled with the rivalry and efficiency of the American missionaries in remote provinces, forced the Sublime Porte to devise a number of defensive and offensive strategies. As the simplest excuse to hinder missionary activity, the government disavowed the need for relief in the provinces, claiming that accounts of massacres and suffering were either exaggerated or false. In order to refuse the missionaries the authorization to open orphanages, officials claimed that there were no killings in these places and therefore no poverty, no hunger, no misery, and no orphans. The Ministry of Foreign Affairs argued in December 1897 that there was never a massacre in Hadjin and there were no orphans in the area. The American missionaries were making "intentional, delusive publications" on the issue and "deluding the European and American public.".[82] The denial strategy was only rarely used and relatively short-lived. Ottoman authorities usually acknowledged that some events (*olaylar, hadise*) or turmoil (*iğtişâş*) took place, though they refrained from using the word "massacres" and assuming responsibility for them. Still, they claimed that missionary relief was unnecessary and that the Ottoman state had the means to provide for its subjects.

A second frantic defensive strategy of the state was to hinder the distribution of foreign aid. Throughout the summer of 1895, right after the massacres in Sasun, a commission of relief was sent by the English to assist missionaries in the distribution and help with the general work. However, they were constantly hampered by the opposition of the Official

Aid Commission (*İane Komisyonu*).[83] The commission denied the American intermediacy in relief work and declared itself as the legitimate accredites of aid distribution.[84] The same scenario was repeated when Clara Barton[85] was about to arrive at Istanbul in March 1896 with a mission to distribute, via the Red Cross, a serious sum collected by the National Armenian Relief Committee. The Ottoman state refused to allow the Red Cross to do the work, insisting that the necessary relief was already provided by the state and the corresponding organization in the Empire, namely the Red Crescent. After unofficial pressure from the U.S. Congress and president, objections were overridden and Clara Barton started the work.[86] Controversies of the same sort often reoccurred. In September 1897, the Porte was informed that Armenian orphans and widows were given money, grain, and other necessities by a mixed commission through the agency of American missionaries.[87] Arguing that "the seditious acts of the foreigners were blatant," the governor was ordered to prevent such breaches of state authority.[88]

The Armenian Patriarchate also had grave problems in receiving relief funds. A significant amount of money was collected *exclusively* for the Armenian needy with the sale of donation tickets to "charitable persons" by an Aid Commission that the Sublime Porte declared as the responsible organ. The Armenian Patriarchate was entitled, by imperial decree, to receive the donations directly from the Aid Commission and to use them for reparation expenses of churches and schools that were set on fire and/or demolished, for support of the needy, and for feeding and sheltering orphans and widows.[89] However, seeing the huge sum, the Porte decided that "the damage was not restricted to Armenians only and that Muslim schools and mosques also got their share of the violence."[90] The commission was separated into two branches (Muslim, Armenian) to distribute the money accordingly. This bifurcation complicated the Patriarchate's receipt of donations. The clerks neglected to note the benefactor of each donation and for that reason they did not know the real share of the Armenians in the total amount. In an arbitrary way, the Porte consented to send 65,000 kuruş to the Patriarchate.[91]

Ottoman authorities were the most concerned that the missionaries would enlarge their constituencies by converting Armenian orphans.

Then these Ottoman subjects would be completely lost to foreign causes. A mixed commission (made up of three Muslims from Sheikh ul-Islam, the Ministry of Education, and the Ministry of Interior, two Armenians, and one Greek Orthodox) was established in September 1897 in order to hinder the conversion of Ottoman subjects to Protestantism and to control the growing influence of foreign missions.[92] It had the duty of assuring that everyone remain in their own religion.

> In order to use the poor, the helpless of the non-Muslim subjects by supporting and curing them and in order to steal the orphan and the destitute to Russia, to England and to France with a *vesika*, the societies, Palestine of Russia, Protestants of England, and Jésuits of France, are opening numerous establishments in all parts of the Empire with so-called humanitarian causes. It is necessary to impede the harmful impacts of these establishments, since those extremely destitute and desperate orphans, who are not yet capable of *comprehending the honor and essence of religion or sect*, understandably *seek refuge anywhere to feed themselves.*[93]

Orphanages were seen as centers of missionary mischief. Officials were disturbed that American orphanages were increasing their inmates each day and the missionaries were "physically and spiritually working to spread the Protestant faith."[94] The Sublime Porte was aware that the main targets of the conversion attempts were non-Muslim subjects, particularly the Armenians. There was only minor concern for the conversion of Muslim subjects.[95] Still, as the missionaries were undermining and surpassing state jurisdiction as part of their routine work, the government was on the defensive. In April 1899 it was ordered to stop the "evil doings" of the missionaries, since if inculcation and instruction continued in the orphanages, "the morality and thinking of the local population would be so corrupted that they would eventually lose their nationality."[96]

Despite the abundance of decrees and orders for the prevention of missionary activities, it was rare that they were successfully implemented. Financial deadlock and the weakness of the state bureaucracy and educational network in the provinces might explain the inertia. In addition, foreign diplomacy almost always hindered the Ottoman authorities in taking effective action. Severe sanctions were reversed after the pressuring of the

Western powers. One exception was the closure of four American orphanages (in Diyarbakır, Palu, and Çüngüş) and two German orphanages (in Palu and Diyarbekir) in early 1899. The decision was taken in mid-1897 after the regional inspection trip of the new governor, Halid Bey, which took him to Mardin, Çan, Maden, Çermik, and Palu.[97] The actual closure was delayed until January 1899.[98]

The governorship investigated the complaints of the Armenian Prelate of Diyarbekir that only 44 of 95 orphans in Diyarbekir orphanages had permission from Gregorian religious authorities. The authorizations were given with the promise that "their mother tongue would be preserved" and they would not be removed from their church.[99] The Armenian Patriarchate only agreed to the "daily maintenance" of children and did not approve further educational aspirations.[100] The Directorate of Education informed the governorship that these orphans attended the Protestant school wearing a special school uniform.[101] The ambassador of the United States denied the charges, arguing that the orphanages in Diyarbekir did not provide any sort of instruction. Yet, the police department confirmed the assertion with its "secret investigation" (tahkikat-ı hafiye) and reported that there was a man in the orphanage, whom the children called varjabet, meaning "teacher" in Armenian.[102]

The governorship asked for official communications from the Ministries of Foreign Affairs and the Interior on the prohibition of foreigners to open educational establishments, such as orphanages, without obtaining authorization from relevant authorities.[103] In the disbandment order, institutions were declared illegal based on Article 129 of the Regulation of General Education, failing to obtain the imperial firman.[104] Two orphanages in Diyarbakır (50 boys and 45 girls),[105] two in Çüngüş (34 boys and 35 girls), and two in Palu (one with 30 boys, the other with 150 boys and girls) were closed.[106]

The event led to the immediate visit of the ambassador of the United States to the Minister of the Foreign Affairs. In defense of the conduct of missionaries, the ambassador argued once more that "these charitable institutions could not be considered as educational establishments."[107] They only had the "philanthropic objective of saving orphan and destitute children from misery."[108] The ambassador also underlined the temporary (*muvakkat*) nature of the institutions. They all would soon be closed as the orphans gained their own livelihoods. More critically, the ambassador warned the minister that the issue might turn into an international crisis, putting the Ottoman state into the position of a cruel despot working against the prosperity of its subjects.

In order to avoid negative international opinion, the ambassador suggested the ministry obtain an official complaint from the Armenian Patriarchate, wherein "detriment and mischief of the Americans," such as the instruction and inculcation of the Protestant faith, were discussed.[109] In this way, the governorship would put the liability of the closure of orphanages onto the shoulders of the Armenian authorities as a scapegoat in the matter. The threats of the ambassador were taken seriously and a complaint letter was demanded from the Patriarchate. In a remarkably subtle way, the embassy found a way to paralyze both the state and the Patriarchate, tacitly legitimizing the presence of the missionaries in the field.

The Patriarchate informed the authorities that they had already filed a complaint eleven days before (2 July 1899) on the issue of proselytizing efforts of the missionaries. In it, the patriarch asked the government not to overlook the "population hunting" (*sayd-ı nüfus*) activities of Protestant and Catholic missionaries; he said they were abusing the poverty and misery of the Armenian people in the provinces, who were still unrecovered from the calamity.[110] When he read the real complaint, the American ambassador was very angry at the Armenian clergymen. How could they unashamedly dare to lodge a complaint against the "Protestants, the only ones to rescue their orphans from starvation"?[111] As the true whipping boy of the matter, in the end the patriarch was compelled to write a letter of excuse to the American authorities, declaring his and his people's gratitude and appreciation of the missionaries in the eastern provinces.[112]

> The Armenian Patriarchate hurries on to bring forth to the knowledge of the Legation of the United States of America, regarding the rumors that circulate on the foreign orphanages in the provinces of Turkey:
>
> that no step is made on behalf of the Patriarchate, neither against the existence nor against an unspecified act regarding the mentioned orphanages;

that the Patriarchate from time immemorial followed with a feeling of full gratitude the care and the sacrifices that the pious hearts of Europe and America showed towards the Armenian widows and orphans, the poor stricken people;

. . . that the Patriarchate, relying on the philanthropic intentions of these benefactors, remained and remains convinced that the benevolent aids should serve neither for proselytism, nor against the Armenian national church.

There is evidence that other Ottoman governors attempted to close missionary orphanages in the province of Mamüretülaziz (Harput, Eğin, Arabkir, and Malatya). But after an application of the German Embassy to the Ministry of Interior, the execution of the decision was at first postponed and finally dropped.[113]

Even after the closure of orphanages and the dispersion of around ninety orphans to private homes, the German missionaries in Diyarbekir never lost touch with the orphans. One German missionary, Herr Baenisch, "continued to provide for them."[114] Later, Ottoman authorities discovered that he "secretly kidnapped" the children and illegally reopened his orphanage in a rented house in the center of the province.[115] There were numerous complaints in the police records, arguing that he did not let mothers see their children and that he converted these orphans to Protestantism. When a police officer was sent to the house, Baenisch refused to let him in for inspection and "acted disobediently by insulting and expelling the officer."[116]

In parallel to de facto openings, missionaries also applied for authorizations. German missionaries, disappointed by the effectiveness of their own government, counted on British diplomacy to convince the Ottoman authorities, since the orphanages were funded by British benefactors as well.[117] The British ambassador applied to the Sublime Porte on 17 August 1899 with an official communication (muhtıra), which underlined that these orphanages were established only with humanitarian purposes to use and distribute funds sent from America, Britain, and Switzerland.[118] The ambassador also pointed to the unhampered functioning of many American orphanages in the province of Mamüretülaziz (in Harput,

Hüseynik, Hülaküğ, Malatya, Arabkir, and Eğin) criticizing the nonstandard and arbitrary nature of governance in the Empire—a very common complaint of the missionaries.[119] In order to circumvent the jurisdiction of the Regulation of Education, the ambassador also claimed that though they were called as such, these institutions were not orphanages (*eytamhane*) but rather abodes (*mesken*), where the orphans were only boarded, fed, and sheltered but in no way instructed.[120] By the end of August 1899, the Porte ordered the governorship to give permission for the reestablishment of the orphanages in Palu and Çüngüş.[121]

The German orphanage of Dr. Johannes Lepsius in Diyarbekir, upon its attempted reopening, was also subject to strict investigation. The Commissariat of Police first asked for a detailed inventory of the orphans (94 boys and girls) containing information on each orphan's name, sex, neighborhood, nationality/religion (*millet*), age, and their guardians. The police interrogated all the guardians regarding their consent. It was found that only 26 guardians gave their assent with promises of material gain, while 61 orphans were taken without such consent (the remaining 7 were indeterminate).[122] In December 1899 the governor reported to the grand vizier that the authorization of this orphanage would lead to the multiplication of these "schools of sedition."[123] He suggested the appointment of the "director-in-charge from among Ottoman subjects" so as to keep the administration of the orphanage under "continuous surveillance."[124]

This exceptional crisis over the closure of some missionary orphanages reveals the power distribution among different actors. There was a major struggle between the state and the missionaries, the latter playing the active part and the former striving to curb its power. The Armenian Patriarchate, on the other hand, was usually pushed and pulled by the wills of others.

The policy of closing foreign orphanages was limited in scope and short-lived. The government acknowledged that it would be "really hard, if not, impossible" to disband foreign schools, for they were very numerous, they had functioned all around the Empire for quite a long time, and "some even had a government license," though others did not.[125] Realizing the limits of its sovereignty, given the actual influence of the Great Powers in internal politics, the Porte settled for arbitrary obstructions, hindrances, and obstacles. Yet, as a more courageous attempt, opening equivalent institutions in the eastern provinces to compete with the missionaries on the same grounds was also discussed. These institutions would improve the state's presence in the eastern provinces and strengthen the ties of patriotism as charity works of a modern state.[126]

The decision to open compensatory educational institutions in the eastern provinces, especially primary schools and orphanages, was directly related to the closure of the orphanages in Diyarbekir and Palu. In the face of ongoing complaints of the foreign embassies about closed orphanages and international public opinion on the misery of orphans and widows, the Porte assumed that if compensatory welfare was offered, then the criticisms would be rendered superfluous. A series of orders called for the enumeration of government schools and establishment of state orphanages in order to resist the (re)opening of orphanages by the missionaries. The state's entry into the field would render the foreign involvement redundant, inhibit missionary influence, and decrease the tension in diplomatic relations.[127] The Minister of the Interior openly discussed in his report in April 1899 that the only way to silence the British, German, and American embassies was to open asylums for orphaned Armenian children and to shelter, feed, and educate them with state resources.[128] In May 1899, the ministers of Foreign Affairs and Education claimed that "foreigners would have no legitimate right to interfere" if the orphans in the provinces were educated in prospective state orphanages.[129] The Porte, so to say, acknowledged its incapability in preventing missionary activities with prohibitive measures. It was in this climate that a competitive strategy was formulated.

In May 1899 a small commission, made up of the ministers of Foreign Affairs and Education, Tevfik Pasha and Zühdü Pasha, legal adviser of the Sublime Porte, Hakkı Beyefendi, and the head of secondary schools, Celal Bey, convened to work on the establishment of primary schools and "houses of cultivation for orphans" (*eytama mahsus darütterbiyeler*) in all necessary localities in the eastern provinces for Ottoman children of all creeds, so that the pernicious work of the missionaries could be stopped.[130] In addition to mixed and gratis orphanages,[131] the report also proposed the opening of primary schools, industrial schools, teachers' institutes, and secondary schools for boys and girls.[132] It was once more underlined that these schools and orphanages were crucial for "fighting back the mischiefs of foreign institutions"[133] and for the "conservation of morals [religion] and language of the people of the Empire."[134] Introduction of a curriculum that would respond to the needs of all religious faiths would guarantee a "mixed and united" (*muhteliten ve müttehiden*) educational program and students' minds would be protected from "foreign indoctrination" (*telkinat-ı hariciyye*).[135]

Consequently, orders were sent to the provinces.[136] The governor of Diyarbekir, Halid, who already shown that he took the fight against the missionaries most seriously, was the first to act. Without even asking for financial support from the central treasury or the Ministry of Education, he opened an industrial school for the orphans of the region. The school was designed to house a religiously mixed body of 400 orphaned and poor boys who would learn one or more of seven trades offered in the curriculum.[137] The costly construction of the school (a spacious building with an area of 1,280 square meters) was finished in May 1900, and it opened with 30 Muslim and non-Muslim boys.[138] The necessary amount (300,000 kuruş) was collected in the form of benevolent contributions from civil servants and the population of the province. As a gesture to please the sultan, and in line with other industrial schools, the governor asked for permission to use the "exalted name of *Hamidiye.*"[139] According to the Regulation prepared by the governorship, the school would be on a boarding basis with two sections (primary school and trades) and would prioritize orphans from five to fifteen years of age.[140]

Despite a long series of orders and plans from the Porte to enter into the field of orphan relief, this was the only rival institution opened to combat the missionaries. It is also interesting that by 1902, as the issue of Armenian orphans slowly faded out, the institution was redefined as a center for "the revival of domestic industries."[141] Actually, already in 1899 the scheme of instituting orphanages in the provinces was reduced to opening "just one orphanage" at a central place. The orphanage would welcome "the Ottoman orphans of all creeds" not only for "the conservation of their nationalities" but also for "the correction of their morality."[142] The Porte wanted to make sure that religious and national allegiances of Ottoman subjects were not altered in missionary and other foreign orphanages. In

August 1899 the Ministries of Education and Foreign Affairs proposed the establishment of a boys' orphanage in the capital. Given the impossibility of bringing the entire provincial orphan population to Istanbul, an urban center already having problems of destitute children, two categories of orphan boys were privileged: those who were "in the hands of the missionaries" and those who had no family or relatives to care for them.[143]

The authorities assumed that the orphanage would have a religiously mixed group of 2,500 boys between the ages of 6 and 10 who came from Istanbul and the provinces. There were plans to construct five separate buildings, housing 400–500 orphans each, on a very large piece of land in Acıbadem (Haydarpaşa).[144] By November 1899, the planned Acıbadem orphanage was redefined as "reserved for the destitute children of the Muslim community."[145] However, this project remained unaccomplished.

Abdülhamid II's Imperial Orphanage (*Dar'ülhayr-ı Ali*), which was opened in 1903 in Sultanahmet, appears to be the continuation of the initial idea to open an orphan asylum for the Armenian children of the eastern provinces.[146] However, in the records of the orphanage, there is no mention of Armenian orphans transported from massacre areas. Furthermore, the idea to have a religiously mixed student body was abandoned and the institution only admitted Muslim orphans, some of whom were converted before entering the orphanage.[147]

Unusual Accomplices

Philanthropy takes its color and shape from the vessels into which it is poured. "I need to provide help!" is a decision about oneself and about "the other," a question of identification and rejection, of affection and distance. As a result, humanitarian relief campaigns are always campaigns for particular humans, even when advocates speak the language of universality. They entail only a particular commitment to a particular group of people.[148] Although the relief bodies claim to be antipolitical, in practice activism means taking sides and mobilizing powerful constituencies. So they are bound to be partial and political.[149]

The involvement of the foreign missionaries in the relief of the victims of the Armenian massacres of 1894–1896 manifests these intricacies of relief. The missionaries, by privileging Armenians against other Muslim or non-Muslim groups, by preferring orphans as their primary target of relief, and finally by sifting only certain Armenian orphans with reference to their inclination toward conversion, clearly exhibit their partial engagement in the realm of humanitarian aid. Their philanthropic works were motivated and determined by their loyalty to the cause of proselytizing.

The interest of many states, societies, social and religious groups, and political figures for the care of Armenian orphans generated a competitive and insecure environment for the immediate actors of the controversy. From all three angles of the triangle, namely the missionaries, the Sublime Porte, and the Gregorian Armenians, the other two were seen as accomplices. The missionaries tended to assume that the Armenians were allies with the Ottoman state, united to hinder the operations of the missionaries.[150] The Sublime Porte was also inclined to view the interests of Armenians and American missionaries as being in tune with one another. Armenians, stirred up by nationalist aspirations, were longing for independence, while the missionaries, by providing such facilities as education, health, and orphan relief, were reinforcing their alienation from the state. Charges were made by Ottoman officials that American missionaries in the Empire incited the Armenians to sedition.[151]

> The charge has frequently been made by officials in Turkey that missionaries are responsible for the uprisings which have resulted in massacres. The charge has been repeated so frequently that it has apparently been believed by a few representatives of some European governments.[152]

The Armenian community also felt threatened from both sides. According to the Armenian authorities, both the missionaries and the Sublime Porte had a stake in the control of Armenian orphans. Both had visions for converting the Armenian Apostolic community. The missionaries threatened their religious identity by obstructing the children in practicing their faith; the Porte targeted their national survival. The integration of orphan children in the establishments of the missionaries (American, German, Swiss, and French) created a feeling that the nation's survival was under threat, since two generations had been lost at the same time. The fathers were killed by the state, while their children were under the influence of foreigners.[153]

TABLE 15. Pre-Massacre Orphanages of Catholic Missionaries

	Place/Name	Date of Opening	Institutional Features	Number of Orphans (by year)
1	Constantinople–Galata Saint-Benoît	1783	Center of the Lazaristes, next to La Providence of Soeurs.	(1851) 25 abandoned children (1915) 120 orphan girls
2	Constantinople–Galata *Couvent de La Providence* (Maison Centrale des filles de la Charité) (Maison de Notre Dame de Providence)	1839	A crèche and an orphanage, opened in the neighborhood of the College, under the patronage of Saint Joseph	(1839) 9 girls (1840) 40 girls (1880) 60 (1883) 70 boys (1894) 70 (1900) 150 in the crèche
3	Izmir Maison de Marie	1840		(1880) 65–70 orphan boys (1894) 45 orphan girls
4	Constantinople–Bebek Maison de St. Joseph	1841	The terrain was bought in 1836. Crèche de Bebek, Orphelinat (with foundlings)	(1883) 40 girls (1894) 270 orphans (1920) 55 abandoned children
5	Colonie Agricole de St. Vincent d'Asie (Bithynie)	1854	Belonged to the Lazaristes	(1854) 20 orphan girls
6	Constantinople Hopital de la Paix Orphelinat de Notre Dame de la Paix	1856	Orphanage. At a certain age, orphans were taught a trade, such as iron-work, carpentry, tailoring, shoe-making, weaving. They helped the girls around 15 for marriage.	(1870) Opening of girls' section with 40–50 girls. (1873) 85–90 (1878) 80–90 (1883) 90 (1886) 130 (1900) 200 (1915) 50
7	Kula (Izmir) Établissements des Orphelins, Orphelines et Enfants Trouvés, de Saint-Joseph au Kula	1859	A vocational education for boys, in the trades of the carpenter, blacksmith, tailor, shoemaker, gardener, and baker.	(1876) 18 (1916) 72 orphan girls, 42 boys
8	Izmir Orphelinat des Soeurs de St. Joseph de l'Apparition à Cordelie [AlayBey]	1860		

	Place/Name	Date of Opening	Institutional Features	Number of Orphans (by year)
9	Izmir Orphelinat de la providence des Soeurs de Charité	1860		(1867) 200 orphans (1916) 43 orphan girls, 26 abandoned children
10	Calamari (Salonika)	1860s		(1900) 40 girls
11	Zeytinlik (Salonika) Orphelinat de Saint-Vincent de Macédonie (two kilometers to Salonika, in the countryside)	1861	They received both orphans and abandoned children.	(1873) 28–30 boys (1894) 25 (1900) 40 orphans (1916) 20 orphans, 15 abandoned children
12	Beyrouth Orphelinat Saint Charles	1861		(1861) 20 abandoned children (1891) 300 girls (1900) 120
13	Salonika	1864	(1873) orphanage of foundlings	(1873) 30 (1894) 22 girls (1916) 30 girls
14	Izmir Orphelinat de Dames de Sion	1864		
15	Orphelinat de St. Joseph (Çukurbostan, Péra)	1865	Section for abandoned children until 1886 (then they were transferred to la Paix).	(1883) 200 girls
16	Buca Orphelinat des Soeurs de Charité	1867		
17	Aydın Maison de Charité des Soeurs de Charité	1868 (rebuilt in 1875)	Maison de Saint-Vincent (orphanage for boys and girls)	
18	Izmir Nazareth de St. Roch (Mortzkia)	1870–71	Asylum for the abandoned children of Fille de la Charité	

(continued)

TABLE 15. Pre-Massacre Orphanages of Catholic Missionaries (*cont.*)

	Place/Name	Date of Opening	Institutional Features	Number of Orphans (by year)
19	Constantinople *La Maison de l'Artigiana* (Hospice des Artisans)	1871	It was founded by an Austrian in 1838, and then transferred to the Lazarists in 1871.	Asylum for 150 small children
20	Association des Demoiselles Patronesses de la Créche	1872		(1874) 560 orphans
21	Bornova (Bournabat) Orphelinat de Soeurs de Charité	1873		(1873) 33 (1916) 64 girls
22	Jerusalem (by Mlle Colomb)	1875	Asile Français de Jérusalem	(1881) 50–60 orphans
23	Bursa	1875	Orphelinat (Fille de la Charité) Opened in 1857, closed after a few years. Reinstallated in 1875.	(1883) 6 orphan girls
24	Alexandrie	1878		
25	Karaağaç	1879	Orphanage for boys and girls	(1879) 26 girls, 30 boys
26	Andrinople	1879	(1881) Industrial work: textile work, embroidery, rug-making, crochet, etc. A small workshop was slowly developing.	(1886) 30–40 boys
27	Bethléem	1879		(1881) 70 orphan boys
28	Mardin	1879	Orphanage of Capucins; school and nursery of SS. Franciscaines	Orphan girls
29	Khosrova	1880		(1880) 25 orphans, 130–150 young boys

	Place/Name	Date of Opening	Institutional Features	Number of Orphans (by year)
30	Trabzon	1882	Capucins of Trébizonde 3 December 1882, they had a nursery for the foundlings.	
31	Diyarbekir (Les Religieuses franciscaines de Lons-le-Saunier)	1882	For orphan girls.	
32	Urfa	1885		
33	Terre Sainte (Jerusalem)	1886	A crèche for the abandoned children. In 15 years, 486 children were received.	(1886) 36 (1890) 23 (1900) 116
34	Jerusalem L'orphelinat Saint-Joseph	1887	Soeurs de Saint-Joseph de l'Apparition	(1889) 50 girls
35	Mosul	1889		275
36	Constantinople– Kadıkoy l'orphelinat de Saint-Jacques	1889	Mékitaristes de Venise	
37	Koukouch/Kılkış (Salonika)	1890		(1916) 20 girls
38	Cilicia, Adana	1895		(1895) 4 girls (1900) 30 (1901) 60

This table is deduced from Catholic missionary journals (*Les Missions catholiques: bulletin hebdomadaire de l'Oeuvre de la propagation de la foi, Annales de la Congrégation de la Mission, Oeuvres des écoles d'orient*); some official annuals and summaries (Père J. B. Piolet, *La France au Dehors Les Missions Catholiques Françaises au XIXe Siècle, Tome Premier, Missions d'Orient* [Paris: Librairie Armand Colin, 1900]); and French diplomatic documents (MAE Quai d'Orsay, Correspondance Politique et Commerciale, Nouvelle Série, 1897–1918, Turquie).

TABLE 16. Post-Massacre Orphanages of Catholic Missionaries

	Place/Name	Date of Opening	Institutional Features	Number of Orphans by Years
1	Siirt (Orphelinat de filles à Siirt)	1896	(la Mission Dominicaine) Older orphan girls rendered services such as assistance for day pupils.	(1897) 10 girls (1898) 17 (1899) 18 (1900) 20
2	Malatya (Orphelinat Arménien de Malatya)	1896–97	Orphanage of SS. Franciscaines	Around 25 boys and girls
3	Erzurum	1897		(1897) 150 girls
4	Kayseri	1897	Foster care Rug-making workshop	(1897) 20 girls (1900) 20–25 girls
5	Van (Orphelinat de filles à Van)	1898		(1898) 16 Girls (1899) 30 (1900) 25
6	Van (Orphelinat de garçons à Van)	1898	(la Mission Dominicaine) Boys received Catholic religious instruction and attended the chapel of the mission. Older orphan boys were employed in the city as apprentices.	(1898) 35 boys (all Armenians) (1899) 30 (1900) 35 (1904) 26
7	Constantinople (Orphelinat Sainte Anne)	1898	(de Patriarcat Arménien Catholique)	62
8	Mezre	1898	(Mission des Capucins, orphelinat des SS. Franciscaines)	28 boys, 18 girls

This table is deduced from Catholic missionary journals (*Les Missions catholiques: bulletin hebdomadaire de l'Oeuvre de la propagation de la foi, Annales de la Congrégation de la Mission, Oeuvres des écoles d'orient*); some official annuals and summaries (Père J. B. Piolet, *La France au Dehors Les Missions Catholiques Françaises au XIXe Siècle, Tome Premier, Missions d'Orient* [Paris: Librairie Armand Colin, 1900]); and French diplomatic documents (MAE Quai d'Orsay, Correspondance Politique et Commerciale, Nouvelle Série, 1897–1918, Turquie).

TABLE 17. Pre-Massacre Orphanages of ABCFM Missionaries

	Place/Name	Date of Opening	Institutional Features	Number of Orphans by Years
1	Izmir German Protestant Orphanage	1851		(1887) 25 orphans
2	Bursa	1875	Bursa Orphanage (mixed), founded by Rev. Mr. Gregory Baghdasarian and his wife after the famine of 1874. Curriculum: Scripture, German, geography, drawings, needlework.	(1883)70 (1887) around 100 children (1890) more than 600 children had been admitted in 15 years. (1890) 50 children
3	Tarsus (Christie, Jenanyan) St. Paul	1888	Opened with 17 students. After 1895, Jenanyan assisted 11 communities, aiding 5,000 widows and children. Boys worked as carpenters, bookbinders, laundrymen, stable boys, sweepers of the rooms, waiters at table, cleaners, and nursing the sick.	(1901) over 30 orphans (1905–1906) 50 orphans in the school (1910) 41 orphans
4	Üsküdar, Istanbul Orphans' Home Scutari	1888	Orphan girls, from various parts of Constantinople and its vicinity, were accepted (1889).	In its first year, over 100 orphan girls had applied, but only 25 could be taken

The data for this table was deduced from thorough research of the official journal of the ABCFM (*Missionary Herald*, from 1850s to 1914); of the archive of internal correspondence (Papers of the American Board of Commissioners for Foreign Missions [microform]. Unit 5, The Near East, 1817–1919); and from various memoirs and books of the missionaries in the field.

TABLE 18. Post-Massacre Orphanages of ABCFM Missionaries

	Place/Name	Date of Opening	Institutional Features	Number of Orphans
1	Antep Girls' Seminary and orphanage Boys' Home	1897	Boys: carpet and rug work Girls: Aintab drawn work, lace; help in housework; do all the washing.	(1911) 129 boys in boys' home (1911) 133 girls
2	Arabkir	1897	Two homes Swiss support, ABCFM administration	(1897) 100 children
3	Bardezag (Adapazarı) The Bardezag Orphanage for Boys	February 12, 1897	Boys, mostly from Constantinople massacre. Financial support from England, Switzerland, and the USA. Regular school courses and industrial training (tailoring, shoemaking, carpentry, bookbinding, tin-smithing, iron working, rug making, sock-knitting, sericulture)	Opened with 9 orphans (1898) 101 orphans (1902) The total number received so far was 164 (1906) 101 boys
4	Bitlis (Mr. Cole)	1897	Industrial training	(1897) 250 boys and girls
5	Bursa West Bursa Orphanage (for girls)	1897	Financed by Comités Suisses de Secours aux Arméniens, directed by Rev. G. L. Garabedian and wife. French lessons and training in cutting, fitting, and sewing of garments; knitting, mending, use of sewing machine; housework, cooking.	(1897) 48 girls (1898) 55 girls (1902) 52 girls
6	Çüngüş	1897	Both a girls' and a boys' orphanage. Closed by the government in February 1899, reopened in August 1899.	(1897) over a 100 girls (1899) 69 boys and girls
7	Diyarbekir	1897	Two homes (girls, boys), supported by the Germans and English, closed by the government in February 1899	(1897) less than 100 children
8	Eğin	1897	Two homes (English funds)	(July 1897) 100 orphans
9	Erzurum	1897	Erzurum Orphanage There were 2,000–3,000 orphans in the province.	(1897) 60

	Place/Name	Date of Opening	Institutional Features	Number of Orphans
10	Geghi (Kiği)	1897		50 orphans
11	Gürün (Hubbards)	After 1895	2 orphanages at Gürün, supported by Swiss funds (1901) The Swiss took over the orphanages "Gürün Relief Industry" (1897), 130 looms in operation	(1895) 50 boys (1901) 25 boys
12	Hadjin (Mrs. Coffing)	After 1895	2 orphanages (1899) Pastor Lohmann (of Germany) agreed to support 100 orphans at Hadjin.	(1898) 75 orphans in each
13	Harput (Caroline E. Bush)	After 1895	(1897) 1,711 orphan boys and girls in Harput (1909) Some 1,400 orphans cared for in Harput station field. Boys' trades: shoemaking, tailoring, carpenter. The girls trained in sewing, knitting, spinning, crochet. They helped in cooking and housework. (1907) The orphanage produced silk and lace to be sold in the market.	(1897) 7 homes in the city of Harput, 150 boys and girsl (1899) over 1000 Armenian orphans in the orphan homes, 350 are in the kindergarten and primary departments of the college school. (1902) number under care reduced to about 900
14	Kayseri	1896	Relatively small orphanages.	30–40 (in the school)
15	Konya (Jenanian Apostolic Institute)			(1903) over 500 boys and girls
16	Malatya	1897	(English funds)	(1897) 10 more orphans
17	Maraş (Miss Agnes C. Salmonds) (Mrs. Clara Hamlin Lee)	1898–9	6 orphanages (3 for girls, 3 for boys) (1899) Marash Orphanage Farm, producing grapes, tomatoes, beans, eggplants, onions, etc. (1906) 200 mulberry trees and silk worms. Cotton was used for beds and mattresses of 100 boys.	(1898) 228 children (1903) 360 boys and girls (1911) over 1000 orphans in Maraş orphanages

(continued)

TABLE 18. Post-Massacre Orphanages of ABCFM Missionaries (*cont.*)

Place/Name	Date of Opening	Institutional Features	Number of Orphans
18 Mardin (Helen Thom, Mr. Andrus)	September 1896	Girls' department: home-economics Boys' department: general formal education	(1897) 72 boys, 40 girls (1898) 53 boys, 37 girls (1899) 62 boys, 31 girls (1900) 38 boys, 30 girls
Mardin Hill Orphanage			(1898) 65 in Mardin Hill (1911) 24 boys in Mardin Hill
19 Merzifon	After 1896	Orphanage for boys (Mrs. Carrington) Orphanage for girls (Mrs. Tracy) Orphans in Anatolia College (C. C. Tracy) Girls trained in "art of making a good home" and weaving; and boys in shoemaking, tailoring, cabinet-making, weaving cotton cloth.	(1897) over 50 girls, nearly 60 boys (1898) 160 children (1900) 42 girls, 70 boys (1900) over 100 orphans in Anatolia College
20 Mezre	1897	Two homes (German involvement)	(Feb. 1897) 60 children (July 1897) 166 orphans
21 Palu	1897	Boys' orphanage of the ABCFM (English funds) Mixed orphanage of the Germans. Closed by the government in February 1899, reopened in August.	(1899) 30 in boys orphanage, the other had 150 boys and girls
22 Peri	1897		
23 Sasun	1897	Sassoun Branch Orphanage near Muş. Industrial training	
24 Sivas (Hubbards)	After 1895	5 orphanages in the city: Emma Hubbard's Boys Orphanage; Jenan-yan orphanage; Swiss Orphanage; 2 other mission orphanages. Boys were trained in tailoring, shoemaking, carpentry, bookbinding, cabinet making; girls in weaving clothes, rug making, sewing, housework, nursing for the sick.	(1897) 280 orphans in Sivas and Gürün (1898) 200 orphans (1900) 320 orphans in Sivas and Gürün (1901) 273 orphans

	Place/Name	Date of Opening	Institutional Features	Number of Orphans
25	Talas	1896	Talas orphanage	
26	Urfa (Mr. Chambers, Ms. Shattuck) Orphanage at Urfa, Shattuck	After 1895	Urfa mission furnished work for widows and orphan girls in lace making, embroidery, and rug making. Boys were trained in carpentry, cabinet-making, iron work, smithing, tailoring, boot and shoemaking. Boys' orphanage owned two large farms in Harran producing wheat.	(1897) 80 orphans in two orphanages; 3325 more on the relief list (1906) 60 orphans (1907) 75 orphans (1908) 61 orphans, only 15 girls (1910) 45 orphan boys
27	Van (G.C. Raynolds)	After 1895	The boys were instructed in shoemaking, blacksmithing, carpentering and other useful trades, while the girls were prepared to be useful in homes and schools. The girls made a large part of their own clothing and learned to sew and mend, besides taking part in housework.	(1897) 250 in orphanage, also the oversight of 300 children (1899) 400 orphans (1900) 300 boys, 200 girls (1901) 509 (1902) 425
28	Zeytun	1897		(1898) 30 orphans (1903) 30 orphans

The data for this table was deduced from thorough research of the official journal of the ABCFM (*Missionary Herald*, from 1850s to 1914); of the archive of internal correspondence (Papers of the American Board of Commissioners for Foreign Missions [microform], Unit 5, The Near East, 1817–1919); and from various memoirs and books of the missionaries in the field.

This book, following an itinerary based on the heightened politicization of different groups of destitute children, started its journey with the most inner sphere of infant and mother. Then, the focus moved to the household level by directing attention toward the adoption/employment of foster daughters. The third chapter suggested a new interpretation of Ottoman urban reform, with particular reference to security, education, and economy. The lead actors of this last chapter were Armenian massacre orphans, as they became the targets of "humanitarian" campaigns and an international dispute. This way, the voyage from the most intimate/private sphere to the most international/public one comes to an end.

Conclusion

Ottoman Children as Historical Actors

SIXTEEN TEENAGERS, ages fourteen to eighteen, were detained on December 26, 1995, in the western city of Manisa, about 30 miles east of the Aegean port of Izmir, on the grounds that they had put up leftist posters and were members of a subversive leftist organization. They were held in custody at the Anti-Terrorism Branch of the Manisa Police Department for five days. When they were released, they pressed charges against the police officers, claiming that they had been subjected to torture. Defense lawyers said their clients were stripped naked, beaten, subjected to electric shocks, hosed down with pressurized water, and sexually abused. Their so-called confessions were extracted under these circumstances. They were charged with writing slogans on walls, distributing manifestos, throwing molotov cocktails, and being members of a secret organization. Despite medical reports of torture, the teenagers' trial lasted for years.

During the trial, one scene became inscribed in social memory, as it was repeatedly aired in news reports on national TV channels. The TV footage showed a prison vehicle slowly moving away from the court building, as the mothers of the Manisa children wailed. One of them, clinging to the back door of the vehicle, tearing her hair and beating her breast, says, "Do not take away my daughter. . . . Please do not take her away, she is just a child!"

What she actually meant was that her daughter was too little to have anything to do with politics. Her assumption is typical of the social and political roles that are attached (or not attached) to children and youth.

Most people see children as innocent, ignorant, and vulnerable. This vision is anachronistically romantic and incapable of seeing children as active agents, while there is ample proof of the contrary. In the past few years, groups of children and youth in Turkey challenged conventional power relations within their families as well as other forms of subordination in the society resulting from class, ethnicity, or gender identities. Since the early 2000s, Kurdish children, often referred to as "stone-throwing children," have entered the public discourse as central political actors in the urban Kurdish movement. More recently, during the Gezi Park Resistance of June 2013, commentators repeatedly referred to the role of youth, specifically the generation of the 1990s, in the outbreak and culmination of the movement. These teenagers were usually the ones who put tents in the park, who built barricades, and who resisted the brutality of police forces, especially their widespread use of pepper gas and pressurized water.

In the last decade, there has been a debate about the increasing political subjectivity of children in the urban centers of Turkey. The stereotypical public discourse in Turkey, produced by mainstream journalists, politicians, and prosecutors, acknowledges that there are different versions and examples of the politicization of children and that these children had some form of political agency. In this interpretation, children are portrayed as simply being deceived, manipulated, and exploited by certain politicized adults, since politics is conceived as a sphere in which children have no place. And interestingly, children are considered political only if they are positioned against the state. They are either terrorists, members of secret organizations, anarchists, or *chapullers*.[1]

Their families, friends, and sympathizers argue that these children are innocent and cannot be political (i.e., cannot have agency). Those who see them as politicized disapprove of their acts as arising from manipulation and targeting the established order. The possibility for children's agency is either denied or portrayed as being motivated by others. These contemporary opinions are not very different from those of mainstream history-writing, which has failed to add children to its account. History has endlessly recorded and commented on wars, the rise and fall of empires, royal dynasties, and all the intricacies surrounding power. It did much less for those who were far away from these spheres of officialdom.

Abandoned, orphaned, and destitute children are precisely the ones furthest removed from these circles, and we only come to know of their existence as anomalies or simply as passing comments, and so they remain an indiscernible mass in the makeup of history.

My main motivation behind the writing of this book was to show that children are legitimate historical actors who triggered, if not contributed to, the emergence of a new, modern social order. They are not necessarily imitators of adult choices and actions. Both historical researches and recent ethnographic studies prove that they can subvert the agendas and norms of the political scene.[2] Accordingly, this research puts children in the center of the narrative, making them the main actors in late Ottoman history. In this book, I reevaluate a well-researched historical era through children's experiences, a result of my conviction that the enumeration and multiplication of accounts relating to the same events, eras, and processes contributes to an enriched perception and comprehension of history. Such a reading and interpretation is especially relevant since the nineteenth century was a period of decisive importance in the modern history of European-Muslim relations, the future of the Levant, and Europe. It was also the period that led to the quartering of the "sick man" by colonial powers, paving the way to the *Tanzimat* and the rise of nationalist Turkey. These historical shifts and reorganizations have been repeatedly read in political or strategic terms, but they need to be reread as lived realities bearing on the lives of humans who are rarely heard from or listened to.

This effort is similar to those of labor historians, feminist historians, or historians of colonialism in the 1960s, 1970s, and 1980s, respectively, who worked to recover the place of labor, women, and the colonized in history. The agency of these groups have been recognized and their voices, which had been lost in the depths of a forgotten past, have been recovered. In a similar manner, the reintroduction of children into the general picture as partakers, witnesses, and actors of history brings forth unnoticed and unelaborated aspects of seemingly exhausted subjects of nineteenth-century Ottoman history. Instead of focusing on childhood as an idea or a distinct phase in the human life-cycle, this research focuses on real children and treats them as active agents.

The nineteenth century was a period during which children assumed new roles as future citizens, workers, or believers. The particular stress on unprotected children results from their potential to take part in distinct facets of life, in different corners of social history—from the orphanage to factory lines, from the streets to non-kin households. In the post-*Tanzimat* era, namely in an epoch of exceptional change, reform, and transformation, orphans assumed a novel form of significance. As the climate of uncertainty and turbulence reinforced the tendency to experiment, the experiences of rootless and poor children became a proving ground in essentially novel or experimental undertakings.[3] Midhat Paşa targeted orphans and children of the very poor for his *ıslahhane* project, which is discussed in detail in chapter 3 on state orphanages. This was a brand new educational technique, combining harsh discipline with hard work as a way of both punishing children and helping them become self-sufficient. This could only been tried out on a disadvantaged group of children without a strong family network. As the experiment proved to be successful, it generated in the minds of the middle and upper classes a consciousness of the benefits of vocational training, and such courses were incorporated into the curricular programs of a number of institutions. Thus orphans served as "test subjects" to essay pilot projects during a period of reform imbued with ambitious initiatives of change.

Children lacking the protective reflexes of a family to support them were also ideal candidates for those who had transforming aims to construct a new communal or national identity through indoctrination or conversion. For instance, the Catholic Sisters found it more plausible to concentrate on the care and education of abandoned babies, since these infants, having no family or relatives to reclaim them from the Sisters, could be directly proselytized by spontaneous baptism at entry to the institution. Both Catholic and Protestant missionaries wanted to take hold of as many Armenian orphans as they could, based on their conviction that these children would become the most reliable members of their congregations in the foreseeable future.

Due to their vulnerability and defenselessness, orphans and destitute children were under threat from various dangers and misfortunes, which in the end made them more experienced in the face of nineteenth-century social questions such as begging, exploitation, or abuse. Foster daughters, for that reason, were well-informed witnesses who could speak about child circulation, enslavement, and the dynamics of middle-class households. The concerns and fears of different actors, such as poor parents and relatives, Ottoman authorities, and intellectuals, were also concentrated more on unprotected children rather than minors in general.

Destitute children offered chance and menace at the same time. Unattended minors were seen opportunistically by the state, missionaries, communal leaders, local notables, provincial governors, and household masters. They could become threats when placed in the wrong hands. Child-saving projects and campaigns, therefore, were designed not only to protect and shelter children but also to inhibit other rival groups that might attempt to supply the same provisions for them. For instance, street children and unprotected waifs in the urban centers were collected into state orphanages by provincial governments not only to prevent the growth of beggars and the wandering urban poor, who were seen as threats to the order, security, and economy of the cities, but also to establish productive workshops and skilled laborers. Though always involving the language of pity and sympathy, relief measures were never selflessly benevolent. Those who provided charity pursued certain opportunities, defined by their own political calculations and objectives. Relief policies also discriminated among various groups of needy people.

Giving orphans and destitute children a voice and making them visible adds delicate nuances to the history of Ottoman modernity. As the target of a range of political, economic, and religious actors in local, communal, national, and international realms, these children were part of various facets of nineteenth-century Ottoman history. The four cases studied in this book—the shelter, the home, the school, and international orphanages—bring into the light the children who occupied them. Institutional structures were redefined by their real, lived historical subjects.

Parallel with the new scholarship on modern governmental institutions and practices in the late Ottoman Empire, which widened the array of historical agents to include central, local, domestic, and international actors, this study conceives orphans as historical actors positioned significantly in relation to the central state, provincial governors, municipal heads, missionaries, communal leadership, and local elites.[4] Following this trajectory, my book offers an analysis of modernity, based on the complicated relations, positioning, and practices of real historical agents, and as an outcome of social and political struggles and negotiations between these numerous, dynamic agents.

There is also discussion on the emergence of practices and conceptions that are related to the modern state. Several themes discussed in separate chapters point to the emergence of a solidly structured, bureaucratized, and relatively centralized administrative apparatus. The controversy over nationality and citizenship of the foundlings, discussed in chapter 1, resulted from the obsession and preoccupation of the nascent modern state authority with properly registering newborn babies and also resistance from religious heads of the communities to accept a new administrative reform that challenged their customary authority and autonomy over their own members. The crisis was typical of the convulsions of transforming a communally divided, multinational empire into a centrally administered modern state.

The establishment of *ıslahhane*s in the provinces of the Empire also points to centrally conceived state policies, which were later disseminated in an organized manner to the remotest corners of the Empire. Other administrative decisions and solutions that were discussed in chapter 3, such as the revitalization of urban trades and industry or the maintenance of stricter order in the cities, were also examples of increased state power on municipal, provincial, and imperial levels.

The original purpose of this study was to hear and see the children—the quiet invisible ones. It is not easy, though, to write the history of those who personally leave almost no evidence behind. The same deterrent is encountered by other researchers writing "history from below" of traditionally subordinated groups and identities. In the case of children, in addition to various subservient positions created by class, gender, social status, and ethnicity, there was another level of dependence created by age and seniority that continuously left children and youth out of the historical narrative.

Most of the time, it was almost impossible to find sufficient, satisfactory sources that provided actual first-person narratives of destitute children. Sources consulted for chapter 2 were the most appropriate source materials to achieve the goal of "listening to children," since with the help of many court cases and official grievance applications the testimonies of fostered girls could be directly heard. Admittedly, chapter 1 offers the least amount of testimonies from children themselves. The protagonists in this chapter are exposed infants who were unable to reflect on their own situation. Yet, the chapter succeeds in taking heed of the completely silenced voices of these abandoned children with an expressed concern for their lives and circumstances, which made it impossible for them to speak for themselves. The period of the earliest years of their life-course is discerned in this chapter, especially with reference to a range of provisions offered to them and to certain serious disputes in which they became the main subjects.

Although chapters 1, 3, and 4 could not have relied on equivalents of the source material used for chapter 2, what the book aims to accomplish is to show the viewpoint of children regarding various phenomena that affected them. All the chapters succeed in exposing children's experiences and bringing into view their perception of general trends and decisions. In chapter 4, for instance, the transfer of children from Eastern Anatolia to the western regions of the Empire is questioned by emphasizing how such long trips would have been painful, even deadly, for them. Also in chapter 1, the suffering of foundlings caused by the endless genealogy fights between municipalities, police departments, birth registrars, and religious officials is problematized, with the aim of exhibiting the mortal impacts of modernized administrative apparatuses and discourses of the state and communities on actual subjects. In chapter 3, it is also noted that orphaned and poor children on the streets were possibly institutionalized in involuntary terms. Street children or beggars were collected from the streets with the intermediation of the police and put into orphanages through coercion. Their relatives or parents were also pressured to agree to send orphaned and poor children into these newly established, vaguely known environments.

There is also space for optimism. Orphans might have been happier in institutions than they were in the homes of their relatives or non-kin members. Ephraim K. Jernazian, one of the orphans of the 1896 massacres, tells in his memoirs that he was physically, intellectually, and morally satisfied in an orphanage of the ABCFM in Maraş (the Ebenezer Home), and that thanks to the missionaries he had the opportunity to receive a very good education.[5] The autobiography of Nissim Benezra, who became an orphan during World War I, also affirms the increased quality of life during his attendance at the orphanage of the Alliance Israélite in Ortaköy (Istanbul) compared to the starvation and poverty he was faced with at his relatives' houses.[6] These accounts are precious sources that challenge the generalized perception of orphan asylums, usually equated with coercion, discipline, and coldness. The evidence at hand suggests that the contrary could also be the case based on the viewpoint of children.

The very effort of unearthing the histories of these children deserves to be legitimately considered as "seeing the invisible." In many respects, the book accomplished to put orphans and destitute children into a prominent position within nineteenth-century Ottoman history. Various groups of destitute children—foundlings, foster daughters, inmates of orphanages, and orphans of an ethnic conflicts—were invaluable historical actors in elaborating upon different aspects of Ottoman modernization, including urbanization, citizenship, welfare policies, the growth of urban child labor, maintenance of order and security, and ethnic and national awareness. Many of these topics have already been the subject of numerous studies. The accomplishment of this book is rescuing from oblivion voices and experiences that have contributed to the making of history. It offers a new and original historical account of the nineteenth-century history of the Ottoman Empire, introducing the testimony of neglected, forgotten, unnoticed observers—the children.

Notes ❧ Bibliography ❧ Index

Notes

Introduction: Ottoman Children's "History from Below"

1. The story is told by Haşim's son, Hayrettin Günercan, born in 1912 in Istanbul. Mine Göğüş Tan, Özlem Şahin, Mustafa Sever, and Aksu Bora, *Cumhuriyet'te Çocuktular* (İstanbul: Boğaziçi Üniversitesi Yayınevi, 2007), 203–10.

2. For instance, in Başbakanlık Osmanlı Arşivi (BOA), irade, Maarif (İ. MF.), 8/1320.C.1, 5/C/1320 (8.10.1902); BOA, İrade, Hususi (İ. HUS.), 99/1320.C.32, 4/C/1320 (7.10.1902).

3. Karen Sanchez-Eppler, *Dependent States: The Child's Part in Nineteenth-Century American Culture* (Chicago: Univ. of Chicago Press, 2005).

4. Leena Alanen, *Modern Childhood?: Exploring the "Child Question" in Sociology* (Jyvaskyla: University of Jyvaskyla, 1992), 59.

5. Harry Hendrick, "The Child as a Social Actor in Historical Sources: Problems of Identification and Interpretation," in *Research With Children: Perspectives and Practices*, ed. Pia Christensen and Allison James (New York: Routledge, 2008), 40–63.

6. Philip L. Safford and Elizabeth J. Safford, *Children with Disabilities in America: A Historical Handbook and Guide* (Westport: Greenwood Press, 2006).

7. Joan Wallach Scott, *Gender and the Politics of History* (New York: Columbia University Press, 1988), 18.

8. Though not specifically dealing with the Ottoman Empire, edited volumes of Fernea are valuable. Elizabeth W. Fernea, ed., *Children in the Muslim Middle East* (Austin: Univ. of Texas Press, 1996); and Fernea, *Remembering Childhood in the Middle East: Memoirs from a Century of Change* (Austin: Univ. of Texas Press, 2003). Another important book on Southeastern Europe is Slobodan Naumović and Miroslav Jovanović, eds., *Childhood in South East Europe: Historical Perspectives on Growing Up in the 19th and 20th Century* (Belgrade: Graz, 2001).

9. We have to underline the importance of the work of Behar and Duben, despite the geographical (Istanbul) and religious (Muslims) limits of the analysis. Alan Duben and Cem Behar, *Istanbul Households: Marriage, Family and Fertility, 1880–1940* (Cambridge: Cambridge Univ. Press, 1991).

10. Abdurrahman Kurt, *Bursa Sicillerine Göre Osmanlı Ailesi, 1839–1876* (Bursa: Uludağ Üniversitesi Yayınları, 1998); Hayri Erten, *Konya Şeriyye Sicilleri Işığında Ailenin Sosyo-Ekonomik ve Kültürel Yapısı (XVIII. yy'in İlk Yarısı)* (Ankara: Kültür Bakanlığı Kültür Eserleri, 2001); Eyal Ginio, "18. Yüzyıl Selanikinde Yoksul Kadınlar," *Toplum ve Bilim* 89 (2001): 190–204; Nuri Köstüklü, *Sosyal Tarih Perspektifinden Yalvaç'ta Aile (1892–1908): Bir Osmanlı Kazası Örneğinde Türk Ailesinin Temel Bazı Özellikleri* (Konya: Günay Ofset, 1996); Leslie Peirce, *Morality Tales: Law and Gender in the Ottoman Court of Aintab* (Berkeley: Univ. of California Press, 2003); Cafer Çiftçi, *Bursa'da Vakıfların Sosyo-Ekonomik İşlevleri* (Bursa: Gaye Kitabevi, 2004); Margaret L. Meriwether, "The Rights of Children and the Responsibilities of Women: Women as Wasis in Ottoman Aleppo, 1770–1840," in *Women, the Family, and Divorce Laws in Islamic History*, ed. Amira al-Azhary Sonbol (Syracuse: Syracuse Univ. Press, 1996), 219–35.

11. Harald Motzki, "Child Marriage in Seventeenth-Century Palestine," in *Islamic Legal Interpretation: Muftis and Their Fatwas*, ed. Muhammad Khalid Masud, Brinkley Messick, and David S. Powers (Cambridge: Harvard Univ. Press, 1996), 129–40; Mahmoud Yazbak, "Minor Marriages and Khiyar al-Bulugh in Ottoman Palestine: A Note on Women's Strategies in a Patriarchal Society," *Islamic Law and Society* 9, no. 3 (2002): 386–409; Judith E. Tucker, "If She Were Ready for Men: Sexuality and Reproduction," *In the House of the Law: Gender and Islamic Law in Ottoman Syria and Palestine* (Berkeley: Univ. of California Press, 1998), 148–78; Avner Giladi, "History of Childhood in Premodern Muslim Societies," in *Individu et Société dans le Monde Méditerranéen Musulman: Questions et Sources*, ed. Robert Ilbert and Randi Deguilhem (Strasbourg: European Science Foundation, 1998), 57–68.

12. Haim Gerber, "Anthropology and Family History: the Ottoman and Turkish Families," *Journal of Family History* 14, no. 4 (1989): 409–21; Margaret L. Meriwether, *The Kin Who Count: Family and Society in Ottoman Aleppo, 1770–1840* (Austin: Univ. of Texas Press, 1999); Iris Agmon, *Family and Court: Legal Culture and Modernity in Late Ottoman Palestine* (Syracuse: Syracuse Univ. Press, 2006); Margaret L. Meriwether and Judith E. Tucker, eds., *Social History of Women and Gender in the Modern Middle East* (Boulder: Westview Press, 1999); and Beth Baron, *Egypt as a Woman: Nationalism, Gender, and Politics* (Berkeley: Univ. of California Press, 2005).

13. Bekir Onur, ed., *Toplumsal Tarihte Çocuk: Sempozyum, 23–24 Nisan 1993* (Istanbul: Tarih Vakfı Yurt Yayınları, 1994); *Türkiye'de Çocukluğun Tarihi* (Ankara: İmge, 2005); *Çocuk Tarih ve Toplum* (Ankara: İmge, 2007). See the Bibliography for a fuller account of his works.

14. Mine Göğüş Tan, Özlem Şahin, Mustafa Sever, and Aksu Bora, eds., *Cumhuriyet'te Çocuktular* (Istanbul: Boğaziçi Üniversitesi Yayınevi, 2007). See the Bibliography for a fuller account of her works.

15. Cüneyd Okay, *Osmanlı Çocuk Hayatında Yenileşmeler 1850–1900* (Istanbul: Kırkambar Yayınları, 1998); "War and Child in the Second Constitutional Period," in *Childhood and Youth in the Muslim World*, ed. François Georgeon and Klaus Kreiser (Paris: Maisonneuve & Larose, 2007), 219–32. See the Bibliography for a fuller account of his works.

16. Philippe Ariès, *Centuries of Childhood: A Social History of Family Life* (New York: Vintage, 1962); John Demos, *Family Life in a Plymouth Colony* (Oxford: Oxford Univ. Press, 1970); Lloyd de Mause, ed., *The History of Childhood* (London: Souvenir Press, 1976); Martin Hoyles, ed., *Changing Childhood* (London: Writers' and Readers' Co-operative, 1979); David Hunt, *Parents and Children in History* (New York: Harper & Row, 1972); Edward Shorter, *The Making of the Modern Family* (London: William Collins, 1976); and Lawrence Stone, *The Family, Sex, and Marriage in England 1500–1800* (London: Wiedenfield & Nicolson, 1977).

17. The study of Marianna Yerasimos analyzing Ottoman children in paintings from the sixteenth to nineteenth centuries, for example, is a replica of an Ariès study. Marianna Yerasimos, "16.–19. Yüzyılda Batı Kaynaklı Gravürlerde Osmanlı Çocuk Figürleri," in Onur, *Toplumsal Tarihte Çocuk*, 65–75.

18. Linda A. Pollock, *Forgotten Children: Parent–Child Relations from 1500 to 1900* (Cambridge: Cambridge Univ. Press, 1983); Nicholas Orme, *Medieval Children* (New Haven: Yale Univ. Press, 2001).

19. Okay, *Osmanlı Çocuk Hayatında Yenileşmeler*; Onur, *Dünyada ve Türkiye'de Değişen Çocukluk*; Onur, *Türkiye'de Çocukluğun Tarihi*; Duben and Behar, *Istanbul Households*.

20. Norbert Finzsch and Robert Jütte, *Institutions of Confinement: Hospitals, Asylums, and Prisons in Western Europe and North America, 1500–1950* (New York: Cambridge Univ. Press, 1996); Bertrand Taithe, "Algerian Orphans and Colonial Christianity in Algeria, 1866–1939," *French History* 20, no. 3 (2006): 240–59; David J. Rothman, *The Discovery of the Asylum: Social Order and Disorder in the New Republic* (New York: Aldine de Gruyter, 2002); Jacques Donzelot, *The Policing of Families*, trans. Robert Hurley (New York: Pantheon Books, 1979); Erving Goffman, *Asylums: Essays of the Social Situation of Mental Patients and Other Inmates* (Garden City: Anchor Books, 1961).

21. Zafer Toprak, "II. Meşrutiyet Döneminde Paramiliter Gençlik Örgütleri," in *Tanzimattan Cumhuriyet'e Türkiye Ansiklopedisi* (Istanbul: İletişim Yayınları, 1985), 531–36; Yiğit Akın, *Gürbüz ve Yavuz Evlatlar: Erken Cumhuriyet'te Beden Terbiyesi ve Spor* (Istanbul: İletişim, 2004); Rıfat N. Bali, *Sports and Physical Education in Turkey in the 1930s* (Istanbul: ISIS Press, 2009).

22. Kathryn R. Libal, "'The Child Question': The Politics of Child Welfare in Early Republican Turkey," in *Poverty and Charity in Middle Eastern Contexts*, ed. Mine Ener, Michael Bonner, and Amy Singer (Binghamton: State Univ. of New York Press, 2003), 255–72; "Realizing Modernity through the Robust Turkish Child, 1923–1938," in *Symbolic Childhood*, ed. Daniel Cook (New York: Peter Lang, 2002), 109–30; "The Children's Protection Society: Nationalizing Child Welfare in Early Republican Turkey," *New Perspectives on Turkey* 23 (2000): 53–78.

23. Duygu Köksal, "İsmayıl Hakkı Baltacıoğlu, İnkilap ve Terbiye: Ulusun 'Çocukluğu,'" *Toplumsal Tarih* 40 (1997): 7–12.

24. Selçuk Akşin Somel, *The Modernization of Public Education in the Ottoman Empire, 1839–1908: Islamization, Autocracy and Discipline* (Leiden: Brill, 2001); Benjamin C. Fortna,

Imperial Classroom: Islam, the State, and Education in the Late Ottoman Empire (Oxford: Oxford Univ. Press, 2002); Benjamin C. Fortna, *Learning to Read in the Late Ottoman Empire and the Early Turkish Republic* (New York: Palgrave Macmillan, 2011); Benjamin Fortna, "Kindergartens in the Ottoman Empire and the Turkish Republic," in *Kindergartens and Cultures: The Global Diffusion of an Idea*, ed. Roberta Wollons (New Haven: Yale Univ. Press, 2000), 252–73.

25. Tuba Kancı and Ayşe Gül Altınay, "Educating Little Soldiers and Little Ayşes: Militarised and Gendered Citizenship in Turkish Textbooks," and Fatma Gök, "The Girls' Institutes in the Early Period of the Turkish Republic," in *Education in "Multicultural" Societies: Turkish and Swedish Perspectives*, ed. Marie Carlson, Annika Rabo, and Fatma Gök (Stockholm: Swedish Research Institute in Istanbul, 2007), 51–71 and 95–107.

26. Nadir Özbek, "Osmanlı İmparatorluğu'nda 'Sosyal Yardım' Uygulamaları, 1839–1918," *Toplum ve Bilim* 83 (2000): 111–32; "Philanthropic Activity, Ottoman Patriotism, and The Hamidian Regime, 1876–1909," *IJMES* 37 (2005): 59–81; "The Politics of Poor Relief in the Late Ottoman Empire: 1876–1914," *New Perspectives on Turkey* 21 (1999): 1–33; *Osmanlı İmparatorluğu'nda Sosyal Devlet: Siyaset, İktidar ve Meşruiyet 1876–1914* (Istanbul: İletişim Yayınları, 2002); Mine Ener, *Managing Egypt's Poor and the Politics of Benevolence, 1800–1952* (Princeton: Princeton Univ. Press, 2003).

27. Carl Ipsen, *Italy in the Age of Pinocchio: Children and Danger in the Liberal Era* (New York: Palgrave Macmillan, 2006), 10.

28. The Foucauldian concept of governmentality is widely used by Ottoman historians as an analytical tool. Khaled Fahmy, *All the Pasha's Men: Mehmed Ali, His Army and the Making of Modern Egypt* (Cambridge: Cambridge Univ. Press, 1997); Ener, *Managing Egypt's Poor*; Nadir Özbek, "The Politics of Welfare: Philanthropy, Voluntarism and Legitimacy in the Ottoman Empire, 1876–1914," Ph.D. diss., Binghamton Univ., 2001; and Fariba Zarinebaf, *Crime and Punishment in Istanbul, 1700–1800* (Berkeley: University of California Press, 2010).

29. Kent F. Schull, *Prisons in the Late Ottoman Empire: Microcosms of Modernity* (Edinburgh: Edinburgh University Press, 2014).

30. Anna Davin, *Growing Up Poor: Home, School, and Street in London* (London: Rivers Oram Press, 1996), 7.

31. During my researches from 2005 to 2008, the American Board Archives were located in the American Board Library at the Bible House in Istanbul (50 Rızapaşa Yokuşu, Mercan, Eminönü, Istanbul). It held the original documents of the Western Turkey Mission of the ABCFM, for Istanbul was the head office of the mission. As of 2010, the library and the archives have been moved to the American Research Institute (ARIT) at Arnavutköy (Istanbul).

32. The original archives of the ABCFM are held at the Houghton Library, Harvard College Library, in Harvard University, Cambridge, Massachusetts. Yet, Research Publications Ltd. filmed a considerable part of the collection in the early 1980s, preparing in the end 858 rolls of film. The Near East section covers the reels from 502 to 720.

33. During my researches in 2007, the Archives of the French Foreign Ministry were divided into three parts: Paris, Nantes, and Colmar. My concentration was in the collections held in Paris and in Nantes.

34. Archives des Capucins, Paris. Registries of baptisms, marriages, burials, and marriage contracts of French citizens, who had resided in Anatolia in the eighteenth and nineteenth centuries, are kept in the Capucin Archives.

35. Archives Historiques de La Congrégation de la Mission (Lazaristes), Paris.

36. Nearly half of the volumes of the *Missionary Herald* are held in the library of Center for Islamic Studies (İSAM). However, the complete collection can be reached at the ARIT Library, Istanbul.

37. *The Orient* and Annual Reports from 1839 to 1932 are held at the ARIT Library, Istanbul.

38. The complete microfilm archive of the journal is held at the Bibliothèque Sainte-Geneviève, Paris.

39. The complete digitalized archive of the periodical is housed at the Bibliothèque National de France, Paris.

40. Partial collections of *Annales de la Congrégation de la Mission* exist in the Bibliothèque Sainte-Geneviève and Bibliothèque National de France. The complete collection can be found in the Archives Historiques de La Congrégation de la Mission.

1. The Politics of Child Abandonment

1. BOA, Dahiliye, Mektubi Kalemi (DH.MKT.), 549/2, 3/S/1320 (12.05.1902).

2. The Foucauldian concept of governmentality is widely used by Ottoman historians as an analytical tool. See Khaled Fahmy, *All the Pasha's Men: Mehmed Ali, His Army and the Making of Modern Egypt* (Cambridge: Cambridge Univ. Press, 1997); Ener, *Managing Egypt's Poor*; Nadir Özbek, "The Politics of Welfare: Philanthropy, Voluntarism and Legitimacy in the Ottoman Empire, 1876–1914," Ph.D. diss., Binghamton Univ., 2001.

3. John Boswell, *The Kindness of Strangers: The Abandonment of Children in Western Europe from Late Antiquity to the Renaissance* (Chicago: Univ. of Chicago Press, 1998); David Ransel, *Mothers of Misery: Child Abandonment in Russia* (Princeton: Princeton Univ. Press, 1988); Rachel Fuchs, *Abandoned Children: Foundlings and Child Welfare in Nineteenth Century France* (Albany: SUNY Press, 1984); Peter Laslett, Karla Oosterveen, and Richard M. Smith, eds., *Bastardy and Its Comparative History: Studies in the History of Illegitimacy and Marital Non-conformism in Britain, France, Germany, Sweden, North America, Jamaica, and Japan* (Cambridge: Harvard Univ. Press, 1980); Nicholas Terpstra, *Abandoned Children of the Italian Renaissance: Orphan Care in Florence and Bologna* (Baltimore: Johns Hopkins Univ. Press, 2005); David I. Kertzer, *Sacrificed for Honor: Italian Infant Abandonment and the Politics of Reproductive Control* (Boston: Beacon Press, 1993).

4. It is possible to find rich information in related areas. Avner Giladi, *Infants, Parents, and Wet Nurses: Medieval Islamic Views on Breast-Feeding and Their Social Implications* (Leiden:

Brill, 1999); Badra Moutassem-Mimouni, *Naissances et abandons en Algérie* (Paris: Éd. Karthala, 2001); Jamila Bargach, *Orphans of Islam: Family, Abandonment, and Secret Adoption in Morocco* (Lanham: Rowman & Littlefield, 2002); Amira al-Azhary Sonbol, "Adoption in Islamic Society: A Historical Survey," and Andrea B. Rugh, "Orphanages in Egypt: Contradiction or Affirmation in a Family-Oriented Society," in *Children in the Muslim Middle East*, ed. Fernea, 45–67, 24–41; Ener, *Managing Egypt's Poor*; Özbek, *Osmanlı İmparatorluğu'nda Sosyal Devlet*. Recent studies by Beth Baron are also very important: "Nile Mother: Lillian Trasher and Egypt's Orphans," in *Competing Kingdoms: Women, Mission, Nation, and American Empire, 1776–1960*, ed. Barbara Reeves Ellington et al. (Durham: Duke Univ. Press, 2010), 240–68; "Orphans and Abandoned Children in Modern Egypt," in *Interpreting Welfare and Relief in the Middle East*, ed. Nefissa Neguib and Inger Marie Okkenhaug (Leiden: Brill, 2008), 12–34.

5. Thomas W. Gallant, "Agency, Structure, and Explanation in Social History: The Case of the Foundling Home on Kephallenia, Greece, during the 1830s," *Social Science History* 15 (1991): 479–508; Méropi Anastassiadou, "La protection de l'enfance abandonnée dans l'Empire ottoman au XIXe siècle. Le cas de la communauté grecque orthodoxe de Beyoğlu (Istanbul)," *Südost-Forschungen* 59–60 (2000–2001): 272–322; Nazan Maksudyan, "Fight over 'Nobody's Children': Religion, Nationality, and Citizenship of Foundlings in Nineteenth-Century Ottoman Empire," *New Perspectives on Turkey* 41, no. 2 (2009): 151–80; "Modernization of Welfare or Further Deprivation? State Provisions for Foundlings in the Late Ottoman Empire," *Journal of History of Childhood and Youth* 2, no. 3 (2009): 361–92.

6. Lakit describes any object including a "human infant" found in a public place. In the Ottoman documents, these children were simply defined as "abandoned" (*metruk, terk edilmiş, bırakılmış, bulunmuş*).

7. Mouradgea d'Ohsson, *Tableau Général de l'Empire Othoman: Divisé en Deux Parties, dont l'une Comprend la Législation Mahométane; l'Autre, l'Histoire de l'Empire Othoman*, vol. 5 (Istanbul: Les Editions ISIS, 2001), 119–20.

8. Avner Giladi, *Children of Islam: Concepts of Childhood in Medieval Muslim Society* (New York: St. Martin's Press, 1992), 71.

9. Anastassiadou, "La protection de l'enfance abandonnée," 293.

10. *The Levant Herald and Eastern Express*, 8:6 (February 6, 1893), 65. I thank Julia Phillips Cohen for this reference.

11. Adrian Wilson, "Illegitimacy and Its Implications in Mid-Eighteenth-Century London: The Evidence of the Foundling Hospital," *Continuity and Change* 4 (1989): 103–64.

12. BOA, DH.MKT., 1573/83, 07/R /1306 (11.12.1888); BOA, Cevdet Belediye (C.BLD.), 90/4467, 29/Za/1255 (03.02.1840); BOA, *Bab-ı Ali Evrak Odası Amedi Kalemi* (A.AMD.), 48/37, 08/Za/1269 (13/08/1853); BOA, DH.MKT., 1440/10, 26/Za/1304 (16.08.1887).

13. For instance, BOA, DH.MKT., 1007/53, 19/B/1323 (19.9.1905); BOA, DH.MKT., 2235/92, 12/R/1317, (19.8.1899); BOA, DH.MKT., 1553/12, 4/S/1306 (10.10.1888).

14. Anastassiadou, "La protection de l'enfance abandonnée," 294: "Dear Sir . . . he is a bastard and we ask you to baptize him immediately, because he has pain."

15. Ahmet Midhat Efendi, *Müşahedat* (Ankara: Türk Dil Kurumu, 2000), 196.

16. Etienne van de Walle, "Illegitimacy in France during the Nineteenth Century," in Laslett, Oosterveen, and Smith, *Bastardy*, 264–77.

17. Khaled Fahmy, "Modernizing Cairo: A Revisionist Narrative," in *Making Cairo Medieval*, ed. Nasser O. Rabbat, Irene A. Bierman, and Nezar Alsayyad (Lanham: Lexington Books, 2005), 173–200.

18. In France, Rachel Fuchs found that the sex of the baby was not a significant factor; from 1830 to 1869 roughly half of all babies abandoned were male (Fuchs, *Abandoned Children*, 65). The same held true in Spain; see Joan Sherwood, *Poverty in Eighteenth-Century Spain: The Women and Children of the Inclusa* (Toronto: Univ. of Toronto Press, 1988), 138–39. Ransel also found that in Russia, as time passed, boys and girls were abandoned in equal numbers (Ransel, *Mothers of Misery*, 132–34).

19. Anastassiadou, "La protection de l'enfance abandonnée," 285.

20. Vangelis Kechriotis, "The Greek Community in Izmir, 1897–1914," Ph.D. diss., Leiden Univ., 2005.

21. Carolyn Flueh-Lobban, *Islamic Society in Practice* (Tallahassee: Univ. Press of Florida, 1994), 74.

22. D'Ohsson, *Tableau Général de l'Empire Othoman*, 119.

23. M. S. Sujimon, "The Treatment of the Foundling (al-laqit) according to the Hanafis," *Islamic Law and Society* 9 (2002): 358–85.

24. Sujimon, "The Treatment of the Foundling," 361–62.

25. "suret-i hafiyede enzar-ı ammeden gizli bir yere," BOA, Dahiliye, Umur-ı Mahalliye-i Vilayat Müdüriyeti (DH.UMVM.), 114/44, 23/Ra/1340 (24.11.1921).

26. There are a few examples where the infants were abandoned in cemeteries. In 1893 a baby girl was found in the cemetery of the İshakpaşa mosque in Salonika (BOA, DH.MKT., 146/25, 27/Ra/1311 [7.10.1893]). In another example, in 1907, a foundling was discovered in the Muslim cemetery of Salonika, and he was delivered to the municipal guard (*belediye çavuşu*) (BOA, DH.MKT., 1146/88, 30/Z /1324 [13.2.1907]). In 1911 a six-month-old baby was found in Karacaahmet Cemetery in Istanbul (BOA, Dahiliye Nezareti Kalem-i Adliye DH.EUM. KADL., 7/3, 01/S/1329 [1.2.1911]). In 1905 a baby was found in the cellar of the bastion (Toprak Tabya) in Okmeydanı (BOA, Zabtiye Nezareti (ZB.), 372/111, 5/Ts/1321 [18.11.1905]).

27. In 1906 a baby was abandoned in front of a grocer's (*bakkal*) house in Tarlabaşı (BOA, ZB., 373/34, 20/Ni/1322 [3.5.1906]). In 1903 a girl was left at a moneychanger's door (BOA, DH.MKT., 783/6, 15/Ş /1321 [5.1.1903]). In 1910 a boy was abandoned at a candymaker's door in Kumkapı (BOA, DH.MKT., 95/89, 29/Ra/1328 [10.4.1910]).

28. Anastassiadou, "La protection de l'enfance abandonnée," 307. In Istanbul they were living in Hasköy, Balat, Fener, Tatavla, and Dolapdere.

29. M. S. Sujimon, "The Treatment of the Foundling," 358–85.

30. Eyal Ginio, "Living on the Margins of Charity," in Ener, Singer, and Bonner, *Poverty and Charity*, 165–84.

31. Bayle St. John, *The Turks in Europe: A Sketch of Manners and Politics in the Ottoman Empire* (London: Chapman & Hall, 1853), 64.

32. Ehud R. Toledano, *Slavery and Abolition in the Ottoman Middle East* (Seattle: Univ. of Washington Press, 1998), 26; Halil İnalcık, *İslam Ansiklopedisi*, vol. 5 (Istanbul: Milli Eğitim Basımevin, 1950), 613; Avigdor Levy, "The Officer Corps in Sultan Mahmud's New Army 1826–1839," *IJMES* 2 (1971): 21–39.

33. Mehmet Zeki Pakalın, *Son Sadrazamlar ve Başvekiller*, vol. 2 (Istanbul: Ahmet Sait Matbaası, 1942), 403–4.

34. Ahmet Midhat Efendi, *Dürdane Hanım* (Ankara: Türk Dil Kurumu, 2000), 43, 47, 108.

35. Ahmet Midhat, *Müşahedat*, 196–97.

36. d'Ohsson, *Tableau Général de l'Empire Othoman*, 120.

37. "sokaklara bırakılan çocukların hıfz-ı sıhhatleri ile ırza ve infakı vazife-yi hükümet iktizasından olmasına," BOA, *İrade, Meclis-i Vala* (İ.MVL.), 519/23345, 22/Ca/1281 (23.10.1864).

38. Sujimon, "The Treatment of the Foundling," 362–63.

39. In 1811 an infant was found near Kovacılar (Fatih, Istanbul) and taken by a woman. The baby was granted a monthly allowance of 10 kuruş (BOA, C.BLD., 76/3746, 26/M /1226 [20.02.1811]). In 1888 wet nurse stipends were increased to 55 kuruş in Salonika (BOA, DH.MKT., 1573/83, 07/R /1306 [11.12.1888]).

40. *İstanbul Mahkemesi 121 Numaralı Şer'iyye Sicili* (Istanbul: Sabancı Üniversitesi, 2006), 35.

41. BOA, C.BLD., 76/3746, 26/M /1226 (20.02.1811).

42. I thank Suraiya Faroqhi for correcting my translation.

43. BOA, İ.MVL., 290/11567, 18/S /1270 (20.11.1853).

44. Mahmoud Yazbak, "Muslim Orphans and the Sharia in Ottoman Palestine According to *Sijill* Records," *Journal of Economic and Social History of the Orient* 44 (2001): 123–40.

45. BOA, DH.MKT., 1353/36, 04/L /1303 (06.07.1886).

46. For Trabzon: BOA, DH.MKT., 1351/45, 16/N /1303 (18.06.1886). For Mardin: BOA, DH.MKT., 1514/45, 10/L /1305 (20.06.1888). For Rize: BOA, DH.MKT., 1772/33, 02/Ra/1308 (16.10.1890); BOA, DH.MKT., 422/67, 14/Ra/1313 (04.09.1895); BOA, DH.MKT., 111/40, 01/S /1311 (13.08.1893). For Beirut: BOA, DH.MKT., 2480/113, 17/M /1319 (6.5.1901). For Salonika: BOA, DH.MKT., 1573/83, 07/R /1306 (11.12.1888); BOA, DH.MKT., 2224/40, 14/Ra/1317 (22.07.1899).

47. BOA, DH.MKT., 1986/123, 20/M/1310 (14.8.1892).

48. A baby boy, found in 1858 in the street in Üsküdar, was granted a temporary stipend and given to Emine Hanım for nursing (BOA., İ.MVL., 397/17286, 23/Za/1274 [05.07. 1858]). An infant girl, found in Sultan Bayezid Camii, was granted a temporary stipend of 50 kuruş (BOA, İ.MVL., 351/15313, 18/B/1272 [25.3.1856]). A girl was found in Ankara, Hatuniye district. She was given to a wet nurse with a temporary stipend of 30 kuruş (BOA, İ.MVL., 342/14761, 04/S/1272 [16.10.1855]).

49. "müddet-i ırzaiyesi tekmil olmuş olmasına nazaran maaş tahsisi bazı emsaline tevafuk etmez," BOA, İ.MVL., 233/8108, 02/C /1268 (24.03.1852).

50. BOA, İ.MVL., 233/8108, 02/C /1268 (24.03.1852). Also in 1865 Mehmed was found in a mosque in Serez (Serres) and granted a monthly stipend of 30 kuruş until he could take care of himself (*kendini idare edinceye kadar*) (BOA, C.BLD., 90/4485, 24/Ş /1281 [22.01.1865]). In 1865 İsmail Hakkı was found in Çürüklük (Topkapı, Istanbul) and granted a monthly stipend of 50 kuruş until his puberty (*hadd-ı buluğ*) (BOA, C.BLD., 18/854, 19/Za/1281 [15.04.1865]).

51. Some examples may be BOA, C.BLD., 8/396, 18/S/1282 (11.07.1865); BOA, DH.MKT. 1573/83, 07/R /1306 (11.12.1888); BOA, İ.MVL., 290/11567, 18/S /1270 (20.11.1853); BOA, A.AMD., 48/37, 08/Za/1269 (13/08/1853). The state retains the guardianship of the child, and it may act as the marriage guardian (*veli*) of a female foundling, represented by the person of the kadi.

52. "hükümet marifetiyle istekli olan kadınlara teslim edilerek," BOA, İ.MVL, 519/23345, 22/Ca/1281 (23.10.1864). There are earlier examples. In 1840 two-day-old Mehmed Nuri was found in Kumkapı (Istanbul) at the Atik Nişancı Mehmed Paşa mosque. He was given to a wet nurse with a monthly stipend of 30 kuruş (BOA, C.BLD., 90/4467, 29/Za/1255 [03.02.1840]).

53. BOA, Maliyeden Müdevver Defterler (MAD.d.) MAD. d. 1/13894; BOA, MAD.d. 1/13578; BOA, MAD.d. 1/14192.

54. BOA, İ.MVL., 519/23345, 22/Ca/1281 (23.10.1864).

55. "galâ-yı es'âra nazaran dûn," BOA, DH.MKT., 1573/83, 07/R /1306 (11.12.1888).

56. In 1899 a baby was given to a black wet nurse (Zenciye Fatıma bint-i Abdullah), and she was offered a stipend by the municipality as one of its employees. BOA, DH.MKT., 2235/92, 12/R/1317, (19.8.1899).

57. In the Ottoman Empire, day laborers received 60 to 150 kuruş a month. A wet nurse stipend was one-third of this, ranging between 30 and 50 kuruş a month. Charles Issawi, *The Fertile Crescent, 1800–1914: A Documentary Economic History* (New York: Oxford Univ. Press, 1988), 400.

58. BOA, DH.MKT., 1227/77, 25/Z /1325 (29.01.1908).

59. BOA, DH.MKT., 1249/74, 22/Ra/1326 (23.04.1908). BOA, DH.MKT., 816/40, 6/My/1325 (19.5.1909).

60. BOA, DH.MKT., 1986/123, 20/M/1310 (14.8.1892).

61. *Règlement de l'orphelinat grec à Smyrne, fondé en février 1870* (Smyrne: n.p., 1874), 7, in Hervé Georgelin, *La Fin de Smyrne: Du Cosmopolitisme aux Nationalismes* (Paris: CNRS, 2005), 128.

62. Hayrullah Efendi, *Avrupa Seyahatnamesi*, ed. Belkıs Altuniş-Gürsoy (Ankara: T. C. Kültür Bakanlığı, 2002), 119–21.

63. Charles John Murray (Firm), *Handbook for Travellers in Asia Minor, Transcaucasia, Persia, Etc.* (1895), 75.

64. Today, the building serves as the Izmir Ethnography Museum and the same term, *piçhane*, is still in use. Doğan Kuban, *İzmir ve Ege'den Mimari İzlenimler: Kaybolan bir Geçmişten Görüntüler (Mimari Çizimler)* (Izmir: Çimentaş Vakfı Yayınları, 1994), 125; İnci Ersoy Kuyulu, "Orientalist Buildings in Izmir: The Case of the Kemeraltı, Çorakkapı, Keçeciler and Kemer Police Stations," *Electronic Journal of Oriental Studies* 4, no. 29 (2001): 1–24, 8.

65. Ahmet Midhat Efendi, *Acayib-i Alem* (Ankara: Türk Dil Kurumu, 2000), 155–57.

66. William Deans, *History of the Ottoman Empire: From the Earliest Period to the Present Time* (Edinburgh: A. Fullarton, 1854), 322.

67. Dror Ze'evi, *Producing Desire: Changing Sexual Discourse in the Ottoman Middle East, 1500–1900* (Berkeley: Univ. of California Press, 2006), 161–63.

68. For more information on Besim Ömer, see Yeşim Işıl Ülman, "Besim Ömer Akalın (1862–1940): ange gardien des femmes et des enfants; L'acclimatation d'un savoir venu d'ailleurs," in *Médecins et ingénieurs ottomans à l'âge des nationalismes*, ed. Méropi Anastassiadou (Paris: Maisonneuve & Larose, 2003), 101–21. For more information on his birth clinic, see Nuran Yıldırım, "Viladethane," *İstanbul Ansiklopedisi* 7 (1994): 388–89; Ayten Altınbaş and Oğuz Ceylan, "Viladethane," *Tombak* 17 (1997): 26–32.

69. Rachel G. Fuchs, *Poor and Pregnant in Paris: Strategies for Survival in the Nineteenth Century* (New Brunswick: Rutgers Univ. Press, 1992), 220.

70. Maternities and foundling asylums had traditionally been located next to one another, as in the well-known examples of Paris, Moscow, and St. Petersburg. Ransel, *Mothers of Misery*, 37.

71. BOA, DH.MKT., 549/2, 4/Ca/1326 (04.06.1908).

72. BOA, DH.MKT., 2051/40, 24/B /1310 (11.02.1893).

73. BOA, DH.MKT., 2060/93, 20/Ş /1310 (09.03.1893).

74. The proper English translation of the word *ırzahane* would be "suckling house." The name of the department was changed to "crèche for nurslings" (*Darülaceze Süt Çocukları Yuvası*) after 1908.

75. For a coherent account on philanthropy and legitimacy see Özbek, "Philanthropic Activity," 59–81.

76. 1916 Regulation, Article 12. Yıldırım, *İstanbul Darülaceze Müessesesi Tarihi*, 411.

77. BOA, DH.UMVM., 114/44, 13/Ra/1340 (14.11.1921), "Darülaceze ırzahanesi'nin tarih-i tesisi olan 9 Nisan 319."

78. BOA, DH.MKT., 1162/17, 08/Ra/1325 (21.04.1907).

79. Yıldırım, *İstanbul Darülaceze Müessesesi Tarihi*, 145.

80. Arsen Yarman, *Osmanlı Sağlık Hizmetlerinde Ermeniler ve Surp Pırgiç Ermeni Hastanesi Tarihi* (Istanbul: Ermeni Hastanesi Vakfı, 2001), 364.

81. BOA, DH.MKT., 816/40, 14/Za/1321 (1.2.1904).

82. BOA, DH.UMVM., 166/70, 27/B/1340 (26.3.1922).

83. BOA, DH.UMVM., 166/70, 26/N/1340, (24.05.1922).

84. "Palestine, Lettre de Soeur Sion, supérieure des Filles de la charité, à Jérusalem," *Bulletin des Oeuvres des Écoles d'Orient*, no. 180 (September 1890): 341–47.

85. . Soeur Sion, "Les Filles de la Charité en Terre Saint (Suite)," *Les Missions catholiques: bulletin hebdomadaire de l'Oeuvre de la propagation de la foi* 33 (1901): 537–38.

86. BOA, Hariciye, Tercüme Odası (HR.TO.), 458/1, 7.7.1874.

87. Kechriotis, "The Greek Community in Izmir."

88. Alysa Levene, "The Mortality Penalty of Illegitimate Children: Foundlings and Poor Children in Eighteenth-Century England," in *Illegitimacy in Britain, 1700–1920*, ed. A. Levene, T. Nutt, and S. Williams (New York: Palgrave Macmillan, 2005); Fuchs, *Poor and Pregnant*, 196–99; Ransel, *Mothers of Misery*, 259.

89. Jacqueline H. Wolf, *Don't Kill Your Baby: Public Health and the Decline of Breast-feeding in the Nineteenth and Twentieth Centuries* (Columbus: Ohio State Univ. Press, 2001), 136.

90. Özbek, *Osmanlı İmparatorluğu'nda Sosyal Devlet*, 210.

91. BOA, DH. MKT., 727/40, 26/Ra/1321, (22.06.1903).

92. After the official opening of the department, some cows and donkeys were purchased for the institution (BOA, DH. MKT., 745/32, 05/Ca/1321, [30.07.1903]).

93. BOA, DH.MKT., 1079/59, 21/Ra/1324 (15.05.1906).

94. BOA, DH.MKT., 1061/6, 26/M /1324 (22.03.1906).

95. *Sabah*, no. 3315, 13 February 1899, in Özbek, *Osmanlı İmparatorluğu'nda Sosyal Devlet*, 210–12.

96. Ransel, *Mothers of Misery*, 166; John R. Gillis, "Servants, Sexual Relations, and the Risks of Illegitimacy in London, 1801–1900," *Feminist Studies* 5, no. 1 (Spring 1979): 142–73.

97. Yıldırım, *İstanbul Darülaceze Müessesesi Tarihi*, 162.

98. Ahmet Rasim, "Darülaceze," *Bab-ı Şefkat*, no. 2 (April 2013): 22–25.

99. BOA. Dahiliye Nezareti Muhaberat Ve Tensikat Müdüriyeti (DH.EUM.MTK.) 79/43, 3/Ra/1333 (19.1.1915).

100. BOA, DH.UMVM., 114/44, 23/Ra/1340 (24.11.1921).

101. BOA, DH.EUM.MTK., 79/43, 3/Ra/1333 (19.1.1915).

102. BOA, DH.UMVM., 114/44, 9/Te/1336 (9.10.1920).

103. BOA, DH.UMVM., 115/46, 11/Ca/1340 (10.1.1922).

104. BOA, DH.UMVM., 114/44, 1/M/1340 (4.9.1921).

105. Ibid. "itikadat ve adat-ı batıleye merbut."

106. BOA, DH.UMVM., 119/23, 12/Ca/1340 (11.1.1922). The Administrative Council (*Meclis-i İdare*) approved the recruitment of only two wet nurses (BOA, DH.UMVM., 115/53, 06/C /1340 [4.2.1922]).

107. Yıldırım, *İstanbul Darülaceze Müessesesi Tarihi*, 165.

108. *Akşam* [The Evening], no. 575, 25.04.1920; no. 2470, 29.08.1925; no. 2573, 11.12.1925.

109. Ann S. Blum, "Dying of Sadness: Hospitalism and Child Welfare in Mexico City, 1920–1940," in *Disease in the History of Modern Latin America: From Malaria to AIDS*, ed. Diego Armus (Durham: Duke Univ. Press, 2003), 209–36.

110. Julie Miller noted the same infection problem for asylums in New York. Julie Miller, *Abandoned: Foundlings in Nineteenth-Century New York City* (New York: New York Univ. Press, 2008), 164.

111. BOA, DH. MKT., 919/29, 24/L/1322 (31 December 1904).

112. D'Ohsson, *Tableau Général*, 119; Sujimon, "The Treatment of the Foundling," 360–62.

113. Engin Nomer, *Vatandaşlık Hukuku* (Istanbul: Filiz Kitabevi, 1989), 44.

114. Anastassiadou, "La protection de l'enfance abandonnée," 310.

115. Boswell, *Kindness of Strangers*, 174.

116. I thank Vağarşak Seropyan for information on the registers of the Church of Surp Krikor Lusavoriç of Kınalıada.

117. Krikor Zohrab, "Rahmetli," *Öyküler* (Istanbul: Aras Yayıncılık, 2001), 46–57.

118. Rachel Simon, *Change within Tradition among Jewish Women in Libya* (Seattle: Univ. of Washington Press, 1992), 70.

119. On 19 May 1903,the superior of the Greek parish of Beyoğlu complained that "babies born from orthodox Greek parents were taken by the police and placed in non-Greek homes for education." Anastassiadou, "La protection de l'enfance abandonnée," 302.

120. BOA, DH.MKT., 549/2, 20/R /1320 (26 July 1902). This document is a voluminous dossier, containing numerous complaints and correspondence regarding the dispute over the identity of the foundlings.

121. BOA, DH.MKT., 783/6, 15/Ş/1321 (5 November 1903).

122. BOA, DH.MKT., 549/2, 20/R/1322 (04 July 1904).

123. Anastassiadou, "La protection de l'enfance abandonnée," 302.

124. The registration of non-Muslim babies as Muslim has a number of parallels with the practice of assimilation of Armenian children in Ottoman orphanages after the Armenian Genocide of 1915. Research on the humanitarian efforts during World War I, including subjects like the traffic of Armenian women and orphans, suggest a curious similarity between what was going at the turn of the twentieth century and enslavement, servitude, and sexual violence accounts from the war years. Keith Watenpaugh, "'Are There Any Children for Sale?': Genocide and the Forced Transfer of Armenian Children (1915–1922)," *Journal of Human Rights* 12, no. 3 (2013): 283–95; "The League of Nations' Rescue of Armenian Genocide Survivors and the Making of Modern Humanitarianism (1920–1927)," *American Historical Review* 115, no. 5 (2010): 1315–39; Lerna Ekmekçioğlu, "A Climate for Abduction, A Climate for Redemption: The Politics of Inclusion during and after the Armenian Genocide," *Comparative Studies in Society and History* 55, no. 3 (2013): 522–53.

125. BOA, DH.MKT., 549/2, 29/R/1320 (05 August 1902).

126. BOA, DH.MKT., 549/2, 23/Ş/1320 (24 November 1902).

127. BOA, DH.MKT., 549/2, 17/R/1320 (22 July 1902).

128. "devletçe mültezim olan tahrir-i nüfus," BOA, DH.MKT., 549/2, 17/L/1321 (06.01.1904).

129. The same specification was repeated in the Law of Population Registration (*Sicill-i Nüfus Kanunu*) of 27 August 1914 (Art. 20–21).

130. BOA, DH. MKT., 1007/53, 19/B/1323 (19 September 1905).

131. Ibid., 5/Ş/1321 (27 October 1903).

132. Ibid., 27/Ş/1322 (5 November 1904).

133. Ibid., 30/Z/1322 (5 February 1905).

134. Ibid., 23/R/1323 (27 June 1905).

135. BOA, Meclis-i Vükela Mazbataları (MV), 113/119, 20/R/1324 (13 June 1906).

136. A similar form of charity for abandoned children was also provided by Egyptian rulers. Cairenes brought abandoned children to the *Zabtiye* of Cairo to have them admitted to the Madrasat-al-Wilada, the midwifery training school located in the Civilian Hospital of Azbakiyya, which contained a foundling home and an orphanage. Mine Ener, "Charity of the Khedive," in Ener, Singer, and Bonner, *Poverty and Charity*, 185–201.

2. Private Negotiation of Child Fosterage

1. "ırzına tasallut ve bikrini izale." BOA, DH.MKT., 948/93, 17/S/1323 (22.04.1905).

2. "cihaz vererek evlendireceğine dair birçok vaatlerde bulunmuş." BOA, DH.MKT., 948/93, 17/S/1323 (22.04.1905).

3. BOA, DH.MKT., 948/93, 17/S/1323 (22.04.1905).

4. Tuba Demirci and Selçuk Akşin Somel, "Women's Bodies, Demography, and Public Health: Abortion Policy and Perspectives in the Ottoman Empire of the Nineteenth Century," *Journal of the History of Sexuality* 17, no. 3 (2008): 377–420.

5. Ruth A. Miller, "Rights, Reproduction, Sexuality, and Citizenship in the Ottoman Empire and Turkey," *Signs: Journal of Women in Culture and Society* 32, no. 2 (2007): 347–73.

6. Gillis, "Servants, Sexual Relations, and the Risks of Illegitimacy in London, 1801–1900"; J. Boulton, "London Domestic Servants from Depositional Evidence, 1660–1750: Servant-Employer Sexuality in the Patriarchal Household," in *Chronicling Poverty: The Voices and Strategies of the English Poor, 1640–1840*, ed. Tim Hitchcock, Peter King, and Pamela Sharpe (New York: St. Martin's Press, 1997); Sarah C. Maza, *Servants and Masters in Eighteenth-Century France: The Uses of Loyalty* (Princeton: Princeton Univ. Press, 1983); Tim Meldrum, *Domestic Service and Gender, 1660–1750: Life and Work in the London Household* (New York: Pearson Education, 2000); Cissie Fairchilds, *Domestic Enemies: Servants and Their Masters in Old Regime France* (Baltimore: Johns Hopkins Univ. Press, 1984); Douglas Hay and Paul Craven, *Masters, Servants, and Magistrates in Britain and the Empire, 1562–1955* (Chapel Hill: Univ. of North Carolina Press, 2004); Leonore Davidoff, *Worlds Between: Historical Perspectives on Gender and Class* (New York: Routledge, 1995); and Tim Hitchcock, *English Sexualities, 1700–1800* (London: Macmillan, 1997).

7. Pathbreaking studies of Ferhunde Özbay are worth noting: *Turkish Female Child Domestic Workers* (Istanbul: Boğaziçi Üniversitesi Yayınevi 1999); *Türkiye'de Evlatlık Kurumu: Köle mi Evlat mı?* (Istanbul: Boğaziçi Üniversitesi Yayınevi, 1999); "Evlerde Elkızları: Cariyeler, Evlatlıklar, Gelinler," in *Feminist Tarihyazımında Sınıf ve Cinsiyet*, ed. Leonore Davidoff and Ayşe Durakbaşa (Istanbul: İletişim, 2002); "1911–1912 Yıllarında Kimsesiz Kız Çocukları," in *Savaş Çocukları: Öksüzler ve Yetimler*, ed. Emine Gürsoy Naskalı and Aylin Koç (Istanbul: n.p., 2003). My contribution to this body of work was to recover the agency of the girls: "Foster-Daughter or Servant, Charity or Abuse: *Besleme*s in the Late Ottoman Empire," *Journal of Historical Sociology* 21, no. 4 (2008): 488–512.

8. Michel Foucault, *History of Sexuality: An Introduction* (New York: Vintage Press, 1990), 47.

9. Ann Laura Stoler, *Race and the Education of Desire* (Durham: Duke Univ. Press, 1995), 137.

10. James W. Redhouse, *Redhouse's Turkish Dictionary, in two parts, English and Turkish, and Turkish and English* (London: B. Quaritch, 1880), 459.

11. BOA, Dahiliye, Emniyet-i Umumiye, Tahrirat Kalemi (DH.EUM.THR.), 29/1, 14/Ra/1328 (26.03.1910). Ahmet Muhtar Bey's *besleme*, maidservant from Adana (a city in southern Anatolia).

12. Kurt, *Bursa Sicillerine Göre Osmanlı Ailesi*, 77.

13. "peder ve mader ve 'amm ve birader gibi hiçbir kimsesi bulunmadığından," BOA, DH.MKT., 1018/43, 17/N/1323 (14.12.1905).

14. "Patriarcat Arménien Catholique, Lettre de S. B. Mgr Azarian, patriarche des Arméniens catholiques, à M. le directeur général de l'Oeuvre d'Orient, Constantinople, le 21 juin 1898," *Oeuvres des écoles d'orient*, no. 227, juillet 1898, 411–22.

15. Aron Rodrigue, *De l'Instruction à l'Emancipation: les Enseignants de l'Alliance Israélite Universelle et les Juifs d'Orient* (Paris: Calmann-Levy, 1989), 90.

16. "Mission Dominicaine de Mésopotamie, Kurdistan et Arménie, Rapport adressé par le R.P. Galland, supérieur de la Mission, à Mgr Charmetant, Directeur général des Oeuvres d'Orient," *Oeuvres des écoles d'orient*, no. 265, novembre 1904, 373.

17. "Report of Mardin Orphan Department for 1897," *ABC 16.5*, reel 512, nos. 202–30.

18. "Report and the Financial Statement of the West Broussa Orphanage [1902]," *ABC 16.9.3*, reel 617, nos. 512–14.

19. BOA, İrade, Şura-yı Devlet (İ. ŞD.), 2554/19, 8/Z/1303 (7.9.1886).

20. BOA, ZB, 329/106, 01/Ks/1324 (14.01.1909); BOA, DH.MKT., 2718/13, 02/M /1327 (25.01.1909).

21. BOA, DH.UMVM, 119/19, 18/R/1340 (18.12.1921).

22. BOA, DH.MKT., 2704/97, 19/Z/1326 (12.01.1909).

23. Vicdan was adopted from the Poorhouse as a *besleme* at the age of eleven, and had to suffer unbearable misery. Ethem İzzet Benice, *Yakılacak Kitap* (Istanbul: Tan Basımevi, 1942).

24. E. W. Lane, *The Manners and Customs of the Modern Egyptians* (London: E. P. Dutton, 1860), 130; Leslie Peirce, *Morality Tales: Law and Gender in the Ottoman Court of Aintab* (Berkeley: Univ. of California Press, 2003), 150-51.

BOA, İ. ŞD., 2554/19, 8/Z/1303 (7.9.1886). The Council of State ruled that orphaned and abandoned girls should be educated to serve as servants.

25. Anastassiadou, "La protection de l'enfance abandonnée," 313.

26. Suraiya Faroqhi, *Subjects of the Sultan: Culture and Daily Life in the Ottoman Empire* (New York: I. B. Tauris, 2005), 113.

In an Aintab court record from 1541, Fatma registered Kamer as her *besleme*; see Peirce, *Morality Tales*, 151.

27. Nimet Cemil, "Meclis-i Mebusan'ın Nazar-ı Dikkatine, Çocuklarımızı Hırpalamayalım," *Kadınlar Dünyası*, no. 144, 22 May 1330 (04.06.1914), 4–5.

28. Ginio, "Living on the Margins of Charity," 183.

29. Kurt, *Bursa Sicillerine Göre Osmanlı Ailesi*, 78.

30. "nafaka ve kisveye eşedd-i ihtiyaç ile muhtace," ibid., 172–73.

31. "4. Allah has not made for any man two hearts in his (one) body: nor has He made your wives whom you divorce by Zihar your mothers: nor has He made your adopted sons your sons. Such is (only) your (manner of) speech by your mouths. But Allah tells (you) the Truth, and He shows the (right) Way.

"5. Call them [the children you adopted] by (the names of) their fathers: that is juster in the sight of Allah. But if you know not their father's (names, call them) your Brothers in faith, or your mawlas. But there is no blame on you if you make a mistake therein: (what counts is) the intention of your hearts: and Allah is Oft-Returning, Most Merciful." Abdullah Yusuf Ali, *The Meaning of the Holy Qur'an* (Kuala Lumpur: Islamic Book Trust, 2007), 508.

32. Mustafa Yıldırım, *İslam Hukuku Açısından Evlat Edinme* (Izmir: İzmir İlahiyat Vakfı, 2005), 43–46.

33. La Baronne Durand De Fontmagne, *Un Séjour à l'Ambassade de France à Constantinople sous le Second Empire* (Paris: Plon-Nourrit, 1902), 285.

34. Ülker Gürkan, "Evlat Edinme ve Beslemelerin Hukuki Durumu," in *Türk Hukuku ve Toplumu Üzerine İncelemeler*, ed. Peter Benedict and Adnan Güriz (Ankara: Türk Kalkınma Vakfı Yayınları, 1974), 163–226.

35. BOA, DH.MKT., 1018/43, 17/N/1323 (14.12.1905).

36. Refi Cevat Ulunay, *Eski İstanbul Yosmaları* (Istanbul: Arba, 1995), 57–58.

37. Henry Otis Dwight, *Constantinople and Its Problems: Its Peoples, Customs, Religions and Progress* (New York: Young People's Missionary Movement, 1901), 97–98.

38. "ücret-i kavlinsiz makulesinden."

39. "hiçbir ücret vermeyerek ancak bir boğaz tokluğuna," BOA, Dahiliye, Emniyet-i Umumiye Müdüriyeti, Evrak Odası (DH.EUM.VRK.), 21/50, 07/Ca/1329 (06.05.1911).

40. Ginio, "Living on the Margins of Charity," 175. Demands of exoneration were quite common; *besleme*s were asked to sign a document (*ibrâ*) in which they testified

that their masters owed them nothing, Gürkan, "Evlat Edinme ve Beslemelerin Hukuki Durumu," 220.

41. Michael Ursinus, *Grievance Administration (Şikayet) in an Ottoman Province: The Kaymakam Of Rumelia's "Record Book of Complaints" of 1781–1783* (New York: Routledge Curzon, 2005), 163.

42. Mustafa Reşit Belgesay, "Evişleri Yapanların Ücret İddiaları," *İleri Hukuk Dergisi* 1, no. 13 (1946): 29.

43. Ginio, "Living on the Margins of Charity," 174.

44. *121 Numaralı Şer'iyye Sicili*, 70–71. "2 entari, 1 şali cübbe, 1 hırka ve 1 çuka ferace ve 2 yorgan ve çarşaf ve bir döşek ve bir baş yastığı ve 3 minder ve 8 beledi yastık ve 3 çaput makad ve bir sepet sandık."

45. Gürkan, "Evlat Edinme ve Beslemelerin Hukuki Durumu," 200.

46. Suraiya Faroqhi, *Towns and Townsmen of Ottoman Anatolia: Trade, Crafts and Food Production in an Urban Setting* (Cambridge: Cambridge Univ. Press, 1984), 279–80; Gürkan, "Evlat Edinme ve Beslemelerin Hukuki Durumu," 163–226.

47. Davidoff, *Worlds Between*, 20.

48. Given the contemporary definitions of childhood and womanhood, the same argument could be made even for a younger girl. BOA, DH.EUM.VRK., 21/50, 07/Ca/1329 (06.05.1911).

49. "sini izdivaca gayr-ı müsaid olduğu," BOA, DH.MKT., 1018/43, 17/N/1323 (14.12.1905).

50. Ibid., 10/C/1326 (09.06.1908).

51. BOA, Dahiliye, Emniyet-i Umumiye, Asayiş Kalemi (DH.EUM.AYŞ.), 13/27, 23/N/1337 (22.06.1919).

52. BOA, Dahiliye, Muhaberat-ı Umumiye İdaresi (DH.MUİ.), 41-2/20, 21/Ra/1328 (02.04.1910).

53. Faroqhi, *Towns and Townsmen*, 279–80.

54. Memduh Şevket Esendal, *Bizim Nesibe* (Ankara: Bilgi Yayınevi, 1985).

55. Toledano, *Slavery and Abolition*, 130.

56. Ahmet Midhat, *Müşahedat*, 138.

57. Ahmet Midhat Efendi, *Henüz Onyedi Yaşında* (Ankara: Türk Dil Kurumu, 2000), 122–23.

58. There was also a specific term in Greek for adopted girls: *psyhokores*, which actually meant the "child of soul," similar to the term in the Turkish language: *manevi evlat* or *evlad-ı maneviyye*. While such a formulation subtly indicates a higher value for these girls, the typical Turkish term, *besleme*, simply means "feeding" and carries serious negative connotations. There is need for ethnographic, historical, and anthropological studies to better grasp the similarities and differences between families and households from all communal backgrounds.

59. Kurt, *Bursa Sicillerine Göre Osmanlı Ailesi*, 174.

60. BOA, DH.MKT., 2107/141, 03/Ca/1316 (19.09.1898).

61. Ibid., "işar-ı islamiyeye gayr-ı layık"; "islamiyete münafî olan şu adat."

62. BOA, Sadaret Mektubi Kalemi Umum Vilayat Evrakı (A.MKT.UM.), 382/33, 5/ Ca/1276 (01.12.1859).

63. Tucker, *Women in Nineteenth-Century Egypt*, 92.

64. "Hanım İle Hizmetçinin Münasebeti," *Hanımlara Mahsus Gazete*, no. 19, 23 Teşrinievvel 1311 (04.11.1895), 1–2.

65. Mehmed Nureddin, "Hizmetçiler," *Kadın*, no. 8, 20 Haziran 1327 (3.7.1911), 1–2.

66. Anastassiadou, "La protection de l'enfance abandonnée," 313.

67. BOA, DH.MKT., 361/29, 14/L /1312 (10.4.1895).

68. BOA, DH.MKT., 386/20, 24/Z/1312 (18.06.1895).

69. BOA, İrade, Harbiye (İ.HB.), 175/1333-Za-083, 28/Za/1333 (09.10.1915).

70. BOA, DH.EUM.KADL., 3/13, 26/Z /1328 (29.12.1910).

71. BOA, DH.MKT., 224/79, 09/L/1311 (16.04.1894).

72. In a short story of Krikor Zohrab from 1901, it was difficult for the *tellal* to find the girl the mistress was looking for, since she was cautious not to hire an experienced servant who could be crafty enough to seduce her husband. She was looking for a "credulous and naïve girl, which can no longer be found in Istanbul." Krikor Zohrab, "Postal," *Öyküler* (Istanbul: Aras Yayıncılık, 2001), 32.

73. BOA, DH.MKT., 1785/68, 14/R /1308 (27.11.1890).

74. BOA, DH.EUM.KADL., 21/18, 10/Ş /1328 (17.08.1910).

75. Ömer Şen, "19. Yüzyılda Osmanlı Devleti'ndeki Köle Ticaretinde Kafkasya Göçmenlerinin Rolü," in *Dünü ve Bugünüyle Toplum ve Ekonomi* (Istanbul: Bağlam Yayınları, 1994), 171–92.

76. Bernard Lewis, *Race and Slavery in the Middle East: An Historical Enquiry* (Oxford: Oxford Univ. Press, 1990), 196–97.

77. Toledano, *Slavery and Abolition*, 10.

78. Duben, Behar, *Istanbul Households*, 67.

79. Özbay, *Türkiye'de Evlatlık Kurumu*, 16; Özbay, *Female Child Labor in Domestic Work*, 19.

80. Ipsen, *Italy in the Age of Pinocchio*, 188.

81. BOA, DH.MKT., 1417/14, 9/Ş/1304 (03.05.1887).

82. BOA, Yıldız Perakende Evrakı Askeri Maruzat (Y.PRK.ASK.), 154/70, 28/R/1317 (05.09.1899).

83. BOA, Yıldız Perakende Yaveran ve Maiyet-i Seniyye Erkan-ı Harbiye Dairesi (Y.PRK.MYD.), 23/2, 09/L/1317 (10.02.1900).

84. BOA, DH.MKT., 831/45, 01/M /1322 (18.03.1904).

85. Ibid., "gittikleri mahalde suret-i meşruda istihsal-i maişet eyleyecekleri."

The existence of an international market of prostitution was denounced as early as the 1860s. On the continent, organizations like the *Union Internationale des Amies de la Jeune Fille* turned their attention to "white slavery," which meant the inducement by force or subterfuge of girls to migrate for purpose of prostitution. Ipsen, *Italy in the Age of Pinocchio,* 70.

86. BOA, DH.MKT., 884/47, 17/C /1322 (29.08.1904).

87. Ibid., "fena yollara bırakmayacaklarına."

88. Judith Butler calls this the paradox of subjectivation; see her *The Psychic Life of Power: Theories in Subjection* (Stanford: Stanford Univ. Press, 1997).

89. Michel De Certeau, *The Practice of Everyday Life* (Berkeley: Univ. of California Press, 1984).

90. Saba Mahmood, "Feminist Theory, Embodiment, and the Docile Agent: Some Reflections on the Egyptian Islamic Revival," *Cultural Anthropology* 16, no. 2 (2001): 202–36.

91. Tucker, *In the House of the Law,* 134.

92. A.MKT.MVL., 84/82, 26/C /1273 (22.02.1857).

93. BOA, Rumeli Müfettişliği Kosova Evrakı (TFR.I.KV.), 59/5851, 16/S /1322 (02.05.1904).

94. Maza, *Servants and Masters in Eighteenth-Century France,* 70.

95. Meldrum, *Domestic Service and Gender,* 104.

96. In her study on twentieth-century Iran, Friedl points to similar strategies for young girls married off before menarche. Erika Friedl, "Tribal Enterprises and Marriage Issues in Twentieth Century Iran," in *Family History in the Middle East: Household, Property and Gender,* ed. Beshara Doumani (Albany: State Univ. of New York Press, 2003), 151–70.

97. BOA, DH.EUM.KADL., 13/3, 03/R/1329 (03.04.1911).

98. BOA, DH.EUM.THR., 29/1, 14/Ra/1328 (26.03.1910).

99. BOA, Hariciye, Mektubi Kalemi (HR.MKT.), 260/20, 02/Ra/1275 (10.10.1858).

100. BOA, DH.MKT., 221/34, 26.02.1894.

101. Ibid., 28/N /1311 (05.04.1894), "saika-yı aşk ve muhabbetle."

102. BOA, DH.EUM.THR., 28/65, 12/Ra/1328 (24.03.1910).

103. BOA, Yıldız Perakende Evrakı Şehremaneti Maruzatı (Y.PRK.ŞH.), 3/98, 14/S/1309 (19.09.1891).

104. "düçar olduğu cinnet," BOA, DH.EUM.KADL., 4/1, 05/M /1329 (6.1.1911).

105. BOA, DH.EUM.THR., 48/3, 24/Ş /1328 (29.08.1910).

106. Rudolph Peters, *Crime and Punishment in Islamic Law: Theory in Practice from the Sixteenth to the Twenty-First Century* (Cambridge: Cambridge Univ. Press, 2006), 59–62.

107. Elyse Semerdjian, *Off the Straight Path: Illicit Sex, Law, and Community in Ottoman Aleppo* (Syracuse: Syracuse Univ. Press, 2008), 33–47.

108. Joseph Schacht, *An Introduction to Islamic Law* (Oxford: Clarendon Press, 1982), 177.

109. Peirce, *Morality Tales,* 353.

110. Boğaç A. Ergene, "Why Did Ümmü Gülsüm Go to Court?: Ottoman Legal Practice between History and Anthropology," *Islamic Law and Society* 17, no. 2 (2010): 215–44, 239–40.

111. Schacht, *An Introduction to Islamic Law,* 178.

112. Najwa Al-Qattan, "Dhimmis in the Muslim Court: Legal Autonomy and Religious Discrimination," *IJMES* 31, no. 3 (1999): 429–44.

113. Dror Ze'evi, "Changes in Legal-Sexual Discourses: Sex Crimes in the Ottoman Empire," *Continuity and Change* 16, no. 2 (2001): 219–42; "Kanunname-i Ceza (1274/1858)," *Düstur*, Tertib 1, vol. 1 (Istanbul: Matbaa-i Amire, 1289 [1872]), 537.

114. Rudolph Peters, "Islamic and Secular Criminal Law in Nineteenth Century Egypt: The Role and Function of the Qadi," *Islamic Law and Society* 4, no. 1 (1997): 70–90, 82.

115. Farhat J. Ziadeh, "Criminal Law," in *The Oxford Encyclopedia of the Islamic World*, ed. John L. Esposito (New York: Oxford Univ. Press, 1995).

116. Zafer Toprak, "From Plurality to Unity: Codification and Jurisprudence in the Late Ottoman Empire," in *Ways to Modernity in Greece and Turkey: Encounters with Europe, 1850–1950*, ed. Anna Frangoudaki and Çaglar Keyder (London and New York: I. B. Tauris, 2007), 36; Avi Rubin, "Ottoman Modernity: The Nizamiye Courts in the Late Nineteenth Century," Ph.D. diss., Harvard Univ., 2006.

117. Ze'evi, "Changes in Legal-Sexual Discourses," 240.

118. Amira al-Azhary Sonbol, "Rape and Law in Ottoman and Modern Egypt," in *Women in the Ottoman Empire: Middle Eastern Women in the Early Modern Era*, ed. Madeline C. Zilfi (Leiden: Brill, 1997), 214–31, 222.

119. Peirce, *Morality Tales*, 354.

120. Tucker, *Women in Nineteenth-Century Egypt*, 93.

121. Rudolph Peters, *Crime and Punishment in Islamic Law* (Cambridge: Cambridge Univ. Press, 2006), 62.

122. Peirce, *Morality Tales*, 354.

123. Ergene, "Why Did Ümmü Gülsüm Go to Court?," 241.

3. State Orphanages (*Islahhanes*)

1. "Islahhanelere dair nizamname," *Vilayetlerin İdare-i Mahsusa ve Nizamatının Suver-i İcraiyesi Hakkında Talimat* (Istanbul: n.p., 1284 [1867]), 193–96.

2. "başıboş gezmekte olan yetim ve bikes çocuklar," ibid.

3. "Vilayat Islahhaneleri Nizamnamesi" (hereafter "Nizamname"), in *Düstur*, Tertib 1, vol. 2 (Istanbul: Matbaa-i Amire, 1289 [1872]), 277–95.

4. Osman Nuri Ergin, *Türkiye Maarif Tarihi*, vol. 3 (Istanbul: Eser Kültür Yayınları, 1977); Hans Jurgen Kornrumpf, "Islahhaneler," in *Colloques internationaux du CNRS, no. 601—Économie et Sociétés dans l'Empire Ottoman (fin du XVIIIe–début du XXe siècle)* (Paris: CNRS Editions, 1983), 149–56.

5. Midhat Paşa, *Midhat Paşa'nın Hatıraları: Hayatım İbret Olsun [Tabsıra-i ibret]*, ed. Osman Selim Kocahanoğlu (Istanbul: Temel Yayınları, 1997), 34–35.

6. İhsan Şerif, "Midhat Paşa, Sanayi Mektepleri," *Tedrisat Mecmuası: Nazariyat ve Malumat Kısmı* 5, no. 30 (1915): 65–68: "birer 'darüleytam' demek olan ıslahhaneler."

7. "yetime-yi şahanenin ıslah-ı ahvali ve terbiyeleri," BOA, İrade, Dahiliye (İ.DH.), 670/46687, 03.C.1290 (29.07.1873).

8. "Nizamname," Article 3. The criminal charge was expressed in the following formulation: "irtikab-ı töhmet ve cinayet."

9. "Nizamname," Article 3, 44 and 49.

10. Roderic Davison, *Reform in the Ottoman Empire: 1856–1876* (Princeton: Princeton Univ. Press, 1963), 406.

11. Maurus Reinkowski, "The State's Security and the Subjects' Prosperity: Notions of Order in Ottoman Bureaucratic Correspondence (19th Century)," in *Legitimizing the Order: The Ottoman Rhetoric of State Power*, ed. Hakan T. Karateke and Maurus Reinkowski (Leiden: Brill, 2005), 195–212.

12. For further information on urban reform policies see Murat Gül, and Richard Lamb, "Mapping, Regularizing and Modernizing Ottoman Istanbul: Aspects of the Genesis of the 1839 Development Policy," *Urban History* 31 (2004): 420–36.

13. For more information on the subject, see the excellent study of Milen V. Petrov, "Tanzimat for the Countryside: Midhat Paşa and the Vilayet of Danube, 1864–1868," Ph.D. diss., Princeton Univ., 2006.

14. Faik Reşit Unat, "Niş Islahhanesinin Kuruluş Tarihini Aydınlatan Bir Belge," *Mesleki ve Teknik Öğretim* 10, no. 114 (1962): 5-6.

15. Petrov, "Tanzimat for the Countryside," 147–49.

16. Anna Davin, *Growing Up Poor: Home, School, and Street in London* (London: Rivers Oram Press, 1996); Lydia Murdoch, *Imagined Orphans: Poor Families, Child Welfare, and Contested Citizenship in London* (Brunswick: Rutgers Univ. Press, 2006), 12–42.

17. For further information, see Şerif Mardin, *Türkiye'de Toplum ve Siyaset* (İstanbul: İletişim, 1990), 297–304; and Niyazi Berkes, *The Development of Secularism in Turkey* (London: Hurst & Co., 1998), 128–32.

18. Nazan Maksudyan, "Orphans, Cities, and the State: Vocational Orphanages (*Islahhanes*) and 'Reform' in the Late Ottoman Urban Space," *IJMES* 43, no. 3 (2011): 493–511.

19. Nora Lafi, "Mediterranean Connections: The Circulation of Municipal Knowledge and Practices during the Ottoman Reforms, c. 1830–1910," in *Another Global City: Historical Explorations into the Transnational Municipal Moment, 1850–2000*, ed. Pierre-Yves Saunier and Shane Ewen (New York: Palgrave MacMillan, 2008), 35–50.

20. Cem Emrence, "Imperial Paths, Big Comparisons: The Late Ottoman Empire," *Journal of Global History* 3, no. 3 (2008): 289–311, 301.

21. Zarinebaf argues that control of migration became an issue in the eighteenth century. The government was concerned especially about "the water and food shortages, overcrowding, fire hazards, rising cost of living, shrinking tax base in the countryside, vagrancy, crime, and urban violence that migration might entail." Fariba Zarinebaf, *Crime and Punishment in Istanbul, 1700–1800* (Berkeley: Univ. of California Press, 2010), 48.

22. Ferdan Ergut, "Policing the Poor in the Late Ottoman Empire," *Middle Eastern Studies* 38, no. 2 (2002): 149–64; Mark Mazower, *Salonica: The City of Ghosts* (New York: Alfred A. Knopf, 2005), 230–31; Timothy Mitchell, *Colonising Egypt* (Cambridge: Cambridge Univ. Press, 1988).

23. Midhat Paşa, *Midhat Paşa'nın Hatıraları*, 53.

24. BOA, İ.MVL., 584/26270, 26/L/1284, (20.2.1868).

25. BOA, DH.MKT., 2413/113, 16/C /1318 (11.10.1900).

26. BOA, Sadaret Mühimme Kalemi Evrakı (A.MKT.MHM.), 300/9, 5/Z/1280 (11.05.1864).

27. BOA, Yıldız Mütenevvi Maruzat Evrakı (Y.MTV.), 3/94, 05/C /1297 (14.05.1880).

28. "muharebede ve istilada ana ve babaları ölen kimsesiz çocuklar için açılmış olan ıslahhane": BOA, Yıldız Perakende Evrakı Başkitabet Dairesi (Y. PRK. BŞK.), 1/49, 20/ Za/1295 (15.11.1878). On the wave of refugees settled in Izmir, see Fikret Yılmaz, "Portrait d'une Communauté Méconnu: les Musulmans," in *Smyrne, la Ville Oubliée? 1830–1930*, ed. Marie-Carmen Smyrnelis (Paris: Autrement, 2006), 52–62. Also Gülnaz Koyuncu, "İzmir Sanayi Mektebi (1868–1923)," master's thesis, Dokuz Eylül Univ., 1993.

29. BOA, İ.MVL., 584/26270, 26/L/1284, (20.2.1868): "işbu ıslahhanelerin yapılmasından maksad-ı asli sokaklarda ve şurada burada zell-i sual ve su-i efali irtikab eden bir takım aceze-yi etfal ve eytamın bir mahall-i mahsusda ictima ettirilerek."

30. Zarinebaf, 45.

31. Other major regulations were "Serseri ve Mazannae-i Su-i Eşhas Hakkında Kanun, 9/R/1327 (10.5.1909)," *Düstur*, Tertib 2, vol. 1 (1908–1909) (Istanbul: Matbaa-i Osmaniye, 1329 [1911]), 169–72; and "Tese'ülün men'ine dair nizâmname, 13/Ş/1313 (29.01.1896)," *Düstur*, Tertib 1, vol. 7 (1895–1904) (Ankara: Başvekalet Devlet Matbaası, 1941), 48–49.

32. "hadd-i bülûğu tecavüz edenler adeta Haleb'in meşhur haşeratı cümlesine dahil olmakta," BOA, İ. ŞD., 13/610, 15/Z/1285 (29.3.1869).

33. BOA, Yıldız Esas Evrakı (Y. EE.), 44/138, 10/R/1298 (10.2.1881).

34. Ibid., "kâr ve zanaata süluk etmek."

35. *Tuna/Dunav*, vol. 2, no. 135, 18/30 December 1866: "Çocuklar mektep tatillerinde, cuma ve pazar ve yortu günlerinde muzır olmayan oyunlar oynamağa mezun olup, fakat zararlı oyunlar oynamak ve kızak kaymak ve gelip geçenlere ilişmek ve mektep ve sanat vakitlerinde sokaklarda oynamak yasak olduğundan öyle görülen çocuklar ve velileri iptida tekdir ve ikinci defa da hapis olup yine mütenebbih olmazlar ise o makule çocuklar ıslahhaneye konulacaktır."

36. *Tuna/Dunav*, vol. 1, no. 21, 21 July/2 August 1865; vol. 1, no. 42, 15/27 December 1865.

37. Rahikainen, *Centuries of Child Labor*, 49.

38. I discuss elsewhere that poor parents, including non-Muslims, benefited from the *ıslahhane*s and actively searched for assistance options. So, the Foucauldian social control model in the strict sense fails to recognize that the poor and needy could also assume

agency in deciding on their and their children's best interests among the viable options. Nazan Maksudyan, "State 'Parenthood' and Industrial Orphanages (*Islahhanes*): Transformation of Urbanity and Family Life," *History of the Family* 16, no. 2 (2011): 172–92.

39. BOA, Yıldız Perakende Evrakı Komisyonlar Maruzatı (Y.PRK.KOM.), 4/29, 29/Z/1300 (31.10.1883).

40. Ibid., "bir takım ef'al-i gayr-ı marziyat."

41. Ibid., "kızları bir takım halatdan muhafaza ile zabt u rabt."

42. Regulation of prostitution began in this period in Istanbul, especially in Pera and Galata, as part of a concern over both venereal diseases and the trafficking of women and girls, which was becoming an international issue at the end of the nineteenth century. Müge Özbek, "The Regulation of Prostitution in Beyoğlu (1875–1915)," *Middle Eastern Studies* 46 (2010): 555–68.

43. BOA, İ.MVL., 502/22735, 21/N/1280, (29.2.1864).

44. BOA, Cevdet Maarif (C.MF.), 131/6542, 3/N/1289 (4.11.1872).

45. BOA, Y.PRK.BŞK., 5/38, 16/M/1299 (8.12.1881); BOA, İ.DH., 841/67590, 21/M/1299 (13.12.1881).

46. BOA, Yıldız Sadaret Hususi Maruzat Evrakı (Y.A.HUS.), 169/30, 28/M/1299 (20.12.1881).

47. BOA, İ.HUS., 87/1318-Z-58, 1318/Z/29 (1901/04/19); BOA, A.MKT.MHM., 707/23, 1319/M/02 (1901/04/21); BOA, İ.HUS., 88/1318-M-29, 1319/M/09 (1901/04/28); BOA, Y.A.HUS., 415/35, 1319/M/12 (1901/05/01); BOA, ZB., 375/52, 1322/Ke/09 (1906/12/22).

48. The Imperial Arsenal was the largest of the Ottoman state factories, having the highest concentration of industrial workers in the Empire. For a detailed study, see İdris Bostan, *Osmanlı Bahriye Teşkilâtı: XVII. Yüzyılda Tersâne-i Âmire* (Ankara: Türk Tarih Kurumu, 1992).

49. Ergut, "Policing the Poor in the Late Ottoman Empire," 161.

50. Donald Quataert, *The Ottoman Empire, 1700–1922* (New York: Cambridge Univ. Press, 2000), 137.

51. Şevket Pamuk, *The Ottoman Empire and European Capitalism, 1820–1913* (New York: Cambridge Univ. Press, 1987), 18.

52. Pamuk, *The Ottoman Empire and European Capitalism*, 26–27.

53. Edhem Eldem, "Capitulations and Western Trade," in *The Cambridge History of Turkey: The Later Ottoman Empire, 1603–1839*, ed. Suraiya Faroqhi (Cambridge: Cambridge Univ. Press, 2006), 311.

54. Namık Kemal, *Hürriyet*, No. 7, 21 Rebiülahir 1285 (11.8.1868).

55. Osman Nuri Ergin, *Mecelle-i Umur-ı Belediye* (Istanbul: Matbaa-ı Osmaniye, 1338 [1922]), 738–44.

56. *Takvim-i Vekayi*, 9 Şaban 1285 (25.12.1868).

57. Adnan Giz, "1868 de İstanbul Sanayicilerinin Şirketler Halinde Birleştirilmesi Teşebbüsü," *İstanbul Sanayi Odası Dergisi* 34 (1968): 16–19; Ergin, *Mecelle-i Umur-ı Belediye*, 748.

58. Ömer Celal Sarc, "Tanzimat ve Sanayiimiz," in *Tanzimat: Yüzüncü Yıldönümü Münasebetiyle* (Istanbul: Maarif Matbaası, 1940), 423–40.

59. "aceze ve bikes eytamın muhafaza ve terbiyesi," Midhat Paşa, *Midhat Paşa'nın Hatıraları*, 81.

60. "dahili sanayiin ve ehl-i sanat ve hirfetin teksiri," Midhat Paşa, *Midhat Paşa'nın Hatıraları*, 81. Also check Adnan Giz, "İstanbul'da İlk Sanayi Mektebinin Kuruluşu," *İstanbul Sanayi Odası Dergisi* 3, no. 35 (1969): 20–22.

61. "Avrupa ehl-i sanatına kıyasen gerek usul ve gerek masnuatca geride kalmakta olduğu meşhud olan hirfet ve sanatların ilmi," BOA, İ.DH., 583/40618, 4/Ş/1285 (19.11.1868).

62. "sanayice memalik-i mahruse-yi şahanenin ekserisine faik ve çıkan emtiası her yerde medh ve senaya layık," BOA, İ.ŞD., 13/610, 15/Z/1285 (29.3.1869).

63. "sanayi-i müteaddidenin ihyası," BOA, Dahiliye, Teşri-i Muamelat ve Islahat Komisyonu (DH.TMIK.S.), 39/19, 18/R/1320 (24.07.1902).

64. "Diyarbekir vilayetinde mahsur kalmayarak vilayat-ı mütecavire dahi şümulü," BOA, DH.TMIK.S., 39/19, 18/R/1320 (24.07.1902).

65. BOA, A.MKT.MHM., 302/67, 1/M/1281 (6.6.1864), "hirfet ve sanayii devama alışdırılarak."

66. BOA, İ.MVL., 502/22735, 21/N/1280, (29.2.1864).

67. "müktesib-i ilm ve marifet," "fail-i refah ve servet," BOA, İ.DH., 604/42096, 21/Ş/1286 (26.11.1869).

68. BOA, Y.MTV., 38/46, 13/S/1306 (19.10.1888).

69. "Nizamname," Article 8.

70. "Nizamname," Article 9.

71. BOA, İ.DH., 591/41114, 20.M.1286 (2.5.1869).

72. *Tuna/Dunav*, vol. 1, no. 17, 23 June/5 July 1865.

73. "Nizamname," Article 10.

74. "Nizamname," Article 36.

75. BOA, Maarif, Mektubi Kalemi (MF.MKT.),15/104, 25/L/1290 (16.12.1873).

76. "meleke peyda eden," BOA, MF.MKT., 26/133, 21/S/1292 (29.03.1875). In the end, İbrahim Efendi, who was competent in shoemaking (*kunduracılıkta liyakatli*), and Hıristo Efendi, competent in tailoring (*terzilikte liyakatli*), were sent to Izmir. BOA, MF.MKT., 31/21, 06/Ş/1292 (06.09.1875).

77. BOA, İ.DH., 591/41114, 20.M.1286 (2.5.1869).

78. BOA, İ.DH., 604/42096, 21/Ş/1286 (26.11.1869).

79. BOA, İ.ŞD., 13/610, 15/Z/1285 (29.3.1869).

80. For further information on this institution, see Yaşar Semiz and Recai Kuş, "Osmanlıda Mesleki Teknik Eğitim: İstanbul Sanayi Mektebi (1869–1930)," *Selçuk Üniversitesi Türkiyat Araştırmaları Dergisi* 15 (2004): 275–95.

81. Midhat Paşa, *Midhat Paşa'nın Hatıraları*, 81.

82. BOA, İ.DH., 591/41114, 20.M.1286 (2.5.1869).

83. İsmail Eren, "Kosova Sanayi Mektebi," *Belgelerle Türk Tarihi Dergisi* 3, no. 18 (1969): 34–38.

84. Aydın Talay, *Eserleri ve Hizmetleriyle Sultan Abdülhamid* (Istanbul: Risale, 1991), 117, 139–40.

85. BOA, İ.ŞD., 13/610, 15/Z/1285 (29.3.1869).

86. Halil İnalcık and Donald Quataert, eds., *An Economic and Social History of the Ottoman Empire, vol. 2 (1600–1914)* (Cambridge: Cambridge Univ. Press, 1997), 900.

87. Donald Quataert, *Ottoman Manufacturing in the Age of the Industrial Revolution* (Cambridge: Cambridge Univ. Press, 1993), 47, 175.

88. Midhat Paşa, *Midhat Paşa'nın Hatıraları*, 52–53.

89. Sakaoğlu, *Osmanlı'dan Günümüze Eğitim Tarihi*, 79; *Salname 1295* (Dersaadet: Rıza Efendi Matbaası, 1878), 256.

90. BOA, İ.DH., 604/42092, 22/N /1286 (26.12.1869).

91. Adnan Şişman, *Tanzimat Döneminde Fransa'ya Gönderilen Osmanlı Öğrencileri (1839–1876)* (Ankara: Türk Tarih Kurumu, 2004), 74–75.

92. BOA, İ.HR., 228/13360, 22/C /1284 (20.10.1867).

93. Şişman, *Tanzimat Döneminde Fransa'ya Gönderilen Osmanlı Öğrencileri*, 93–158.

94. Ibid., 77; BOA, A.MKT.MHM., 12/39, 28/Ca/1290 (24.07.1873).

95. BOA, A.MKT.MHM., 446/32, 28/Za/1289 (28.01.1873).

96. BOA, İ.HR., 267/16059, 16/Ca/1292 (20.06.1875).

97. Rıfat Önsoy, "Tanzimat Dönemi Sanayileşme Politikası, 1839–1876," *Hacettepe Üniversitesi Edebiyat Fakültesi Dergisi* 2, no. 2 (1984): 5–12.

98. Since Ruse no longer belonged to the Ottoman lands, former inhabitants of the city were concerned about their acquired legitimate rights.

99. BOA, DH.MKT., 2346/12, 17/M /1318 (16.05.1900). Also the father of three girls, Lütfiye, Şemsiye, and Münire, demanded the money his daughters earned during their stay in the orphanage. BOA, DH.MKT., 2413/113, 16/C /1318 (11.10.1900).

100. BOA, DH.MKT., 1635/33, 08/Za/1306 (06.07.1889).

101. "Nizamname," Article 52.

102. *Salname-yi Vilayet-i Aydın* ([Izmir]: Vilayet Matbaası, 1319), 88–89.

103. BOA, Y.MTV., 206/83, 16/Ca/1318 (11.09.1900).

104. "Nizamname," Article 31.

105. Mahmud Cevad İbnü'ş-Şeyh Nafî, *Maarif-i Umûmiye Nezâreti Târihçe-i Teşkilat ve İcrââtı: XIX. Asır Osmanlı Maarif Tarihi* (Ankara: Yeni Türkiye Yayınları, 2001).

106. The first school of forestry followed the first school of agriculture in 1857. For clerks of justice or scribes, a three-year middle school was opened in 1862–1863 along with the first school of translators of modern languages. For training foremen or technicians, a school of mining was opened in 1874.

107. "sanayi-i mebhusenin itibar-ı alisinin iadesiyle servet-i millet ve memleketin ikmali," BOA, İ.ŞD., 13/610, 1285/Z/15 (1869/03/29).

108. Niyazi Berkes, *The Development of Secularism in Turkey* (New York: Routledge, 1998), 189.

109. "Maarif-i Umûmiyye Nizamnamesi," *Düstur*, Tertib 1, vol. 2 (Istanbul: Matbaa-i Amire, 1289 [1872]), 184–219.

110. Bekir Koç, "Osmanlı Islahhanelerinin İşlevlerine İlişkin Bazı Görüşler," *Gaziantep Üniversitesi Sosyal Bilimler Dergisi* 6, no. 2 (2007): 113–27.

111. "yerli ve yabancı ve İslam ve hıristiyan her ne olur ise müsavaten," "Nizamname," Article 1.

112. "islam ve hıristiyan etfalinden her ferdini bilistisna kendi evladı hükmünde tutarak."

113. "hıristiyan çocukları dahi ayin ve mezhebleri üzere ibadet edecektir."

114. BOA, A.MKT.MHM., 302/67, 1/M/1281 (6.6.1864).

115. BOA, MF.MKT., 44/42, 15/L/1293 (03.11.1876).

116. *Salname-yi Vilayet-i Aydın*, 1319, 88.

117. BOA, MF.MKT., 24/94, 29/Z/1291 (06.02.1875).

118. BOA, İ.DH., 604/42096, 21/Ş/1286 (26.11.1869).

119. BOA, A.MKT.MHM., 329/9, 14/Za/1281 (10.4.1865).

120. BOA, A.MKT.MHM., 302/67, 1/M/1281 (6.6.1864).

121. BOA, İ.DH., 591/41114, 20.M.1286 (2.5.1869).

122. BOA, C.MF., 131/6542, 3/N/1289 (4.11.1872).

123. For instance, in 1901, there were 257 Muslims as opposed to 17 Greeks, 1 Armenian, and 1 Jew. *Salname-yi Vilayet-i Aydın* (Izmir: Vilayet Matbaası, 1318), 490.

124. Midhat Paşa, *Midhat Paşa'nın Hatıraları*, 233.

125. "milletler beynlerinde cari taassubata münafi," BOA, İ.ŞD., 13/610, 15/Z/1285 (29.3.1869).

126. "rüesa-yı ruhaniye dürlü davalar çıkaracak," ibid.

127. "edyandan bahs açtırmamak."

128. "haset ve zıddiyetleri zail [olacağı]."

129. "birbirlerine ülfetleri hasıl olacağı."

130. For example, a complete set of uniforms was sent from Istanbul to Trabzon to be used as an example for the orphanage there. BOA, MF.MKT., 440/22, 16/Z /1285 (30.03.1869).

131. Books, booklets (*risale*), and tracts (*cüz*) were sent from Istanbul to various places such as Erzurum, Janina, Ruse, Izmir, and Ankara. BOA, MF.MKT., 27/78, 09/Ra/1292 (15.04.1875); 33/82, 25/Z/1292 (22.01.1876); 25/98, 11/M/1292 (17.02.1875); 36/32, 12/R/1293 (06.05.1876).

132. Students were sent to Salonika and Izmir. BOA, MF.MKT.,15/104, 25/L/1290 (16.12.1873); BOA, MF.MKT., 26/133, 21/S/1292 (29.03.1875).

133. BOA, MF.MKT., 12/109, 17/Ca/1290 (13.07.1873).

134. "ezcümle sanayiice olan terakkiyat-ı asriyyenin bu taraflarda intişarı," BOA, MF.MKT., 12/59, 17/Ca/1290 (13.07.1873).

135. BOA, MF.MKT., 12/109, 26/Ca/1290 (22.07.1873).

136. BOA, MF.MKT., 15/62, 18/L/1290 (09.12.1873).

137. "vilayet-i celilenin taht-ı nezaret ve idaresinde," BOA, MF.MKT., 26/133, 21/S/1292 (29.03.1875).

138. "Islahhaneler vilayetler tarafından idare edildiği için," BOA, MF.MKT., 596/22, 20/N /1319 (31.12.1901).

139. BOA, DH.MKT., 586/63, 28/C/1320 (01.10.1902).

140. Kemâl Kutgün Eyüpgiller, "Kastamonu Kent Tarihi," *Electronic Journal of Oriental Studies* 1 (1998): 1–149, 106.

141. BOA, A.MKT.MHM., 302/67, 1/M/1281 (6.6.1864); BOA, İ.ŞD., 8/142, 2/R/1285 (22.7.1868); BOA, İ.ŞD., 13/610, 15/Z/1285 (29.3.1869); BOA, İ.DH., 591/41114, 20.M.1286 (2.5.1869); BOA, DH.MKT., 1376/85, 9/S/1304 (7.11.1886); BOA, İ.ŞD., 14/629, 16/M/1286 (28.4.1869).

142. BOA, İ.DH., 591/41114, 20.M.1286 (2.5.1869).

143. *Zevra* 128 (28/Z/1287), 255. Midhat Paşa, *Midhat Paşa'nın Hatıraları*, 113. The construction expenses of the Harput orphanage, opened in 1873, were also met with the benevolent contributions of the locals. BOA, A.MKT.MHM., 446/17, 26/Za/1289 (25.1.1873).

144. An extraordinary tax that was collected for several purposes.

145. For instance, to generate income for the orphanage in Adana, real estate was constructed, both with benevolent contributions (*iane*) and extraordinary tax revenues (*avarız varidatı*). BOA, MF.MKT., 550/9, 16/Z /1318 (06.04.1901).

146. BOA, İ.ŞD., 8/142, 2/R/1285 (22.7.1868). In order to reward her generosity, the Education Department of the Council of State (*Şura-yı Devlet Maarif Dairesi*) decided to honor her with an *atiyye-i seniyye* (gift from the sultan), a bracelet worth 20,000 kuruş.

147. "kimsesizlerin iaşesinin temininin sekteye uğramaması," BOA, DH.MKT., 2026/13, 09/Ca/1310 (29.11.1892).

148. BOA, DH.MKT., 2335/118, 23/Z /1317 (23.04.1900); BOA, Yıldız Sadaret Resmi Maruzat Evrakı (Y.A.RES.), 116/26, 10/S/1320 (18.05.1902); BOA, İrade, Maliye (İ.ML.), 52/1320-B-08, 18/B /1320 (20.10.1902); BOA, MF.MKT., 729/73, 29/Ca/1321 (23.08.1903).

149. Eyüpgiller, "Kastamonu Kent Tarihi," 106.

150. *Aydın Salnamesi*, 1312, 151; Abdullah Martal, *Değişim Sürecinde İzmir'de Sanayileşme, 19. Yüzyıl* (İzmir: Dokuz Eylül Yayınları, 1999), 41.

151. BOA, İ.DH., 1312/1311-Za-19, 15/Za/1311, (21.05.1894). The buildings were quite spacious and large (see Figure 8).

152. *Selanik Vilayeti Salnamesi*, 1311, 139–40.

153. "Islahhanelere dair nizamname," 193–96.

154. BOA, İ.ŞD., 2433/27, 11/Ş /1297 (19.07.1880); BOA, DH.MKT., 397/20, 21/M/1313 (14.07.1895).

155. Midhat Paşa, *Midhat Paşa'nın Hatıraları*, 52–53; BOA, A.MKT.MHM., 329/9, 14/Za/1281 (10.4.1865).

156. Midhat Paşa, *Midhat Paşa'nın Hatıraları*, 113.

157. Eyüpgiller, "Kastamonu Kent Tarihi," 109–10.

158. *1311 Sene-yi Hicrisine Mahsus Selanik Vilayeti Salnamesi* (Salonika: Mekteb-i Sanayi Matbaası, 1311). The title page of the yearbook reads: "Hamidiye Mekteb-i Sanayi Matbaasında tab ve temsil edilmiştir."

159. BOA, İ.DH., 604/42096, 21/Ş/1286 (26.11.1869).

160. *Yeni Mektep Dergisi* 8 (Kanunuevvel 1327 [1911]): 245.

161. "heves ve istidadı olan," *1311 Selanik Vilayeti Salnamesi*, 142.

162. *1311 Selanik Vilayeti Salnamesi*, 142, 144.

163. Interview with Yaşar Ürük, former director of the Izmir State Theater, conducted in 5.6.2007 by Orhan Beşikçi, http://www.kentyasam.com/ilk-izmir-bandosu-elemanlar -inin-hepsi-kunduraciydi-ksdty-5.html, accessed 2 June 2014.

164. *Aydın Salnamesi*, 1894–95, 147–53.

165. *Salname-yi Vilayet-i Aydın*, 1319, 88.

166. Olga Demetriou, "Streets Not Named: Discursive Dead Ends and the Politics of Orientation in Intercommunal Spatial Relations in Northern Greece," *Cultural Anthropology* 21, no. 2 (2006): 295–321.

167. The house of Mustafa Kemal was also situated on this street. Carole L. Crumley, "Exploring Venues of Social Memory: Social Memory and Environmental Change," in *Social Memory and History: Anthropological Perspectives*, ed. Jacob Climo and Maria G. Cattell (California: AltaMira Press, 2002), 39–51.

168. The park appears in a poem of Necati Zekeriya (Skopje, 11.11.1928–Novi Sad, 10.06.1988), "Üsküp'e Yeşili Ozanlar Vermiş." Nevzat Kösoğlu, ed., *Türkiye Dışındaki Türk Edebiyatları Antolojisi, vol. 7: Makedonya, Yugoslavya (Kosova) Türk Edebiyatı* (Ankara: T.C. Kültür Bakanlığı Yayınları, 2002).

169. Researching more than 6,000 slave narratives, Powell underlined the difficulty of hearing the real voices of the slaves. Eve M. Troutt Powel, "Will that Subaltern Ever Speak?: Finding African Slaves in the Historiography of the Middle East," in *Middle East Historiographies: Narrating the Twentieth-Century*, ed. Israel Gershoni, Amy Singer, and Hakan Erdem (Seattle: Univ. of Washington Press, 2006), 242–61.

170. BOA, DH.MKT., 312/39, 1312/Ca/29 (1894/11/27); BOA, MF.MKT., 522/44, 1318/ Ca/01 (1900/08/27); BOA, DH.MKT., 1367/69, 1303/Z/24 (1886/09/22).

171. BOA, İ.DH., 604/42096, 21/Ş/1286 (26.11.1869): "bizler daha evvelleri anasız babasız çıplak olarak sokaklarda ve çamurlar içinde sürünürken yardım eden ve elimizden tutan ve terbiye edüb selamete çıkaracak kimsemiz yoktu. Çok şükürler olsun ki şimdi o sefaletten kurtulup bu saadete nail olduk."

172. Hakan Y. Erdem, "Kırım Savaşı'nda Karadeniz Beyaz Köle Ticareti," in *Savaştan Barışa: 150. Yıldönümünde Kırım Savaşı ve Paris Antlaşması (1853–1856), Bildiriler* (Istanbul: İstanbul Üniversitesi Edebiyat Fakültesi Tarih Araştırma Merkezi, 2007), 108–11.

173. Natalie Zemon Davis, *Fiction in the Archives: Pardon Tales and Their Tellers in Six-teenth-Century France* (Stanford: Stanford Univ. Press, 1987), 5.

174. BOA, DH.İD., 190/37, 15/C/1332 (11.5.1914).

4. The Internationalization of Orphans

1. Adam Sabra, *Poverty and Charity in Medieval Islam: Mamluk Egypt, 1250–1517* (New York: Cambridge Univ. Press, 2000); Amy Singer, *Constructing Ottoman Beneficence: An Imperial Soup Kitchen in Jerusalem* (Albany: State Univ. of New York Press, 2002); Michael Bonner, "Definition of Poverty and the Rise of the Muslim Poor," *Journal of the Royal Asiatic Society* 6, no. 3 (1996): 335–44; Ener, Singer, and Bonner, *Poverty and Charity*; Özbek, "Osmanlı İmparatorluğu'nda 'Sosyal Yardım' Uygulamaları"; Özbek, "Philanthropic Activity," 59–81; Özbek, "The Politics of Poor Relief," 1–33; Oded Peri, "Waqf and Ottoman Welfare Policy: The Poor Kitchen of Hasseki Sultan in Eighteenth Century Jerusalem," *Journal of Economic and Social History of the Orient* 35 (1992): 167–86.

2. Amy Singer, "Serving Up Charity: The Ottoman Public Kitchen," *Journal of Interdisciplinary History* 35, no. 3 (2005): 481–500.

3. Marco Van Leeuwen, "Logic of Charity: Poor Relief in Preindustrial Europe," *Journal of Interdisciplinary History* 24 (1994): 589–613.

4. Michel Foucault, *Histoire de la folie à l'âge classique: folie et déraison* (Paris: Plon, 1961).

5. Anne C. McCants, *Civic Charity in a Golden Age: Orphan Care in Early Modern Amsterdam* (Urbana: Univ. of Illinois Press, 1997), 3–15.

6. Timothy S. Miller, *The Orphans of Byzantium: Child Welfare in the Christian Empire* (Washington, D.C.: Catholic Univ. of America Press, 2003).

7. Terrible massacres took place at Trabzon, Erzurum, Erzincan, Sivas, Merzifon, Kayseri, Harput, Diyarbakır, Maraş, and Antep. As discussed by the missionaries, "these massacres were not isolated outbreaks, but were conducted according to a definite plan. They were conducted in a uniform way, reached one class of people, and they ceased the moment authorities intervened. These authorities did not interfere, but, on the other hand, aided in the carnage till the works of destruction had gone far enough." "The Massacres in Turkey," *Missionary Herald*, vol. 92, February 1896, 54–57.

8. The ABCFM was established in 1810 and the mission for the Ottoman Empire was established in 1819. Continuously expanding its activities in the areas of education and health, missionaries had a significant presence in especially remote provinces of the Empire. Uygur Kocabaşoğlu, *Anadolu'daki Amerika: Kendi Belgeleriyle 19. Yüzyılda Osmanlı İmparatorluğu'ndaki Amerikan Misyoner Okulları* (Ankara: İmge Kitabevi Yayınları, 2000); Hans Lukas Kieser, *Iskalanmış Barış: Doğu Vilayetlerinde Misyonerlik, Etnik Kimlik ve Devlet 1839–1938*, trans. Atilla Dirim (Istanbul: İletişim, 2005).

9. As an exception, a refugee house was opened in Istanbul for some of the neediest. Dr. Wood, "Constantinople Station Report," *Missionary Herald*, vol. 74, October 1878, 328–29.

10. In earlier accounts, the number was usually stated as 50,000. Rev. Edwin Munsell Bliss, *Turkey and the Armenian Atrocities* (Philadelphia: J. H. Moore, 1896), 544. Johannes Lepsius's *Armenia and Europe: An Indictment* (London: Hodder & Stoughton, 1897) gives an 88,000-plus figure (330–31) taken from earlier figures compiled a year before the massacres ended. He adds subsequent deaths in his preface for a total of ca. 100,000. These did not include those who died later from wounds, exposure, or loss of breadwinner. Later, higher numbers (between 100,000 and 300,000) were provided. By 1903, French and Italian commentators were putting the number of victims at 300,000. *Pour l'Arménie et la Macédoine* (Paris: n.p., 1904), vii, 64, 142, 184–85, 250–53. Hovannisian suggests that the number may vary between 100,000 and 200,000. Richard G. Hovannisian, *Armenia on the Road to Independence* (Berkeley: Univ. of California Press, 1967), 28. Some researchers suggested 300,000; see Arman J. Kirakossian, ed., *The Armenian Massacres, 1894–1896: U.S. Media Testimony* (Detroit: Wayne State Univ. Press, 2004), 29.

11. "Orphans in Turkey," *Missionary Herald*, vol. 94, May 1898, 204–8. "Editorial Paragraphs," *Missionary Herald*, vol. 95, October 1899, 396: "No special object is of more pressing importance than this effort to rescue some of 50,000 Armenian orphans scattered over Turkey." The *New York Times* used the number as well: "Fifty Thousand Orphans Made So by the Turkish Massacres of Armenians," *New York Times*, December 18, 1896.

12. Margaret Lavinia Anderson, "'Down in Turkey, Far Away': Human Rights, the Armenian Massacres, and Orientalism in Wilhelmine Germany," *Journal of Modern History* 79 (2007): 80–111, 92.

13. Rev. George F. Herrick, "Canon Taylor on Missionary Methods," *Missionary Herald*, January 1889, vol. 85, 13–16.

14. "Orphans in Turkey," *Missionary Herald*, vol. 94, May 1898, 204–8.

15. Western Turkey Mission of the ABCFM, in its annual report to the head office, defined the orphanages as "emergency work." *Summary of the Reports of Stations of the Mission of the A.B.C.F.M. to Western Turkey Presented at The Annual Meeting, May, 1901, with Map, Statistical Tables and a List of Names of Missionaries* (Gloucester: John Bellows, 1901), 20.

16. Mr. Sanders, "In the Interior," *Missionary Herald*, vol. 92, August 1896, 333–34.

17. "Editorial Paragraphs," *Missionary Herald*, vol. 98, May 1902, 184–85 (italics mine).

18. "Central Turkey Mission—Marash—Orphanage Work, 1911," ABC 16.9.5, reel 667, no. 378–83.

19. The society, *Filles de la Charité* or *Soeurs de St. Vincent de Paul*, was founded by Saint Vincent de Paul (1581–1660) in 1633 to work among the poor. The Soeurs were seriously involved in hospitals, prisons, and care for abandoned children. Georges Goyau, *La Congrégation de la Mission des Lazaristes* (Paris: Grasset, 1938).

20. *Congrégation de la Mission [lazaristes]; répertoire historique et table générale des annales de la congrégation de la Mission depuis leur origine jusqu'à la fin de l'année 1899* (Paris: à la procure de la congrégation de la mission, 1900), 208–17.

21. "Patriarcat Arménien Catholique, Lettre de S. B. Mgr Azarian, patriarche des Arméniens catholiques, à M. le directeur général de l'Oeuvre d'Orient, Constantinople, le 21 juin 1898," *Oeuvres des écoles d'orient*, no. 227, juillet 1898, 411–22.

22. For more information on French educational establishments in the Empire, see Max Roche, *Education, Assistance et Culture Française dans l'Empire Ottoman, 1748–1868* (Istanbul: Les Edition Isis, 1989).

23. Mr. Dwight, "Opposition from Romanism and Moslems," *Missionary Herald*, vol. 78, July 1882, 266.

24. Mr. Walker, "Diarbekir: Letter from Mr. Walker, April 2, 1857," *Missionary Herald*, vol. 53, August 1857, 271–74.

25. Dr. Goodale, "Marash: Letter from Dr. Goodale, September 18 1860," *Missionary Herald*, vol. 57, January 1861, 17–18.

26. "Mission Dominicaine de Mésopotamie, Kurdistan et Arménie, Rapport adressé par le R.P. Galland, supérieur de la Mission, à Mgr Charmetant, Directeur général des Oeuvres d'Orient," *Oeuvres des écoles d'orient*, no. 265, novembre 1904, 366–75.

27. John P. Spagnolo, "The Definition of a Style of Imperialism: The Internal Politics of the French Educational Investment in Ottoman Beirut," *French Historical Studies* 8, no. 4 (1974): 563–84; Richard Drevet, "Laïques de France et missions catholiques au XIXe siècle: l'OEuvre de la Propagation de la Foi, origines et développement lyonnais (1822–1922)," Ph.D. diss., Université Lyon 2, 2002.

28. Dr. Raynolds, "Relief at Sassoun," *Missionary Herald*, vol. 91, October 1895, 403–4.

29. "Editorial Paragraphs," *Missionary Herald*, vol. 94, April 1898, 129 (italics mine).

30. American Board missionaries adopted a discourse of civility equating their particular Puritan Christianity with civilization. Makdisi underlines that "their routine denigration of foreign cultures and their determination to restructure them" made them particularly vulnerable to the accusation of cultural imperialism. Ussama Makdisi, *Artillery of Heaven: American Missionaries and the Failed Conversion of the Middle East* (Ithaca: Cornell University Press, 2008), 9.

31. Clarence D. Ussher and Grace H. Knapp, *An American Physician in Turkey: A Narrative of Adventures in Peace and War* (Astoria, N.Y.: J.C. & A.L. Fawcett, 1917), 331–32 (italics mine).

32. Nazan Maksudyan, "'Being Saved to Serve': Armenian Orphans of 1894–96 and Interested Relief in Missionary Orphanages," *Turcica* 42 (2010): 47–88.

33. "Editorial Paragraphs," *Missionary Herald*, vol. 93, March 1897, 90 (italics mine).

34. Dr. Raynolds, "Relief and Orphanage Work at Van," *Missionary Herald*, vol. 93, July 1897, 277–78.

35. Mr. Hubbard, "Orphanage Work at Sivas," *Missionary Herald*, vol. 94, January 1898, 23–24 (italics mine).

36. "Mardin Orphanage, Reports for 1897–1899," ABC 16.5, reel 512, no. 201–30 (italics mine).

37. G. C. Raynolds, "Report of Relief and Orphanage Work at Van, July to December, 1898," ABC 16.9.7, reel 694, no. 1122 (italics mine).

38. Kieser, *Iskalanmış Barış*, 258.

39. "Adoption d'orphelins Arméniens en France," *Oeuvres des écoles d'orient*, no. 216, octobre 1896, 449–52.

40. "Patriarcat Arménien Catholique, Lettre de S. B. Mgr Azarian, patriarche des Arméniens catholiques, à M. le directeur général de l'Oeuvre d'Orient, Constantinople, le 21 juin 1898," *Oeuvres des écoles d'orient*, no. 227, juillet 1898, 411–22.

41. Selim Deringil, "Redefining Identities in the Late Ottoman Empire: Policies of Conversion and Apostasy," in *Imperial Rule,* ed. Alexei Miller, and Alfred J. Rieber (Budapest: Central European Univ. Press, 2004), 107–30; Selim Deringil, "'The Armenian Question Is Finally Closed': Mass Conversions of Armenians in Anatolia during the Hamidian Massacres of 1895–1897," *Comparative Studies in Society and History* 51, no. 2 (2009): 344–71.

42. "Editorial Paragraphs," *Missionary Herald*, vol. 92, August 1896, 308.

43. BOA, Y.A.HUS., 358/2, 15/Ra/1314 (24.8.1896).

44. "Mésopotamie et Kurdistan, Rapport du R.P. Galland, supérieur de la Mission dominicaine de Mossoul, à M. le directeur de l'Oeuvre d'Orient," *Oeuvres des écoles d'orient*, no. 222, septembre 1897, 204–17.

45. "Editorial Paragraphs," *Missionary Herald*, vol. 95, June 1899, 221.

46. "Editorial Paragraphs," *Missionary Herald*, vol. 93, July 1897, 264.

47. Ephraim K. Jernazian, *Judgment Unto Truth: Witnessing the Armenian Genocide* (Edison, N.J.: Transaction Publishers, 1990), 20.

48. Malte Fuhrmann, *Der Traum vom deutschen Orient. Zwei deutsche Kolonien im Osmanischen Reich 1851–1918* (Frankfurt: Campus, 2006), 109–256.

49. BOA, Y.MTV., 177/67, 03/M /1316 (24.5.1898).

50. BOA, A.MKT.MHM., 702/21, 25/Ra/1314 (3.9.1896).

51. BOA, A.MKT.MHM., 640/39, 8/B/1314 (14.12.1896).

52. Bardezag Orphanage for Boys housed a smaller number of orphans from eastern villages and towns. "The Bardezag Orphanage for Boys, February 12th 1897–February 12th 1898," ABC 16.9.3, reel 606, no. 787–8. West Bursa Orphanage also received about 45 girls from Arabkir and Erzincan in 1897. "Report and the Financial Statement of the West Broussa Orphanage," ABC 16.9.3, reel 617, no. 512–14.

53. Ibid., 873–74.

54. Mr. Baldwin, "The Orphanages," *Missionary Herald*, vol. 95, March 1899, 111 (italics mine).

55. "Eastern Turkey Mission Report, 1904," ABC 16.5, reel 505, no. 222–27 (italics mine).

56. "Patriarcat Arménien Catholique, Lettre de S. B. Mgr Azarian, patriarche des Arméniens catholiques, à M. le directeur général de l'Oeuvre d'Orient, Constantinople, le 21 juin 1898," *Oeuvres des écoles d'orient*, no. 227, juillet 1898, 411–22 (italics mine)

57. "Adoption d'orphelins Arméniens en France," *Oeuvres des écoles d'orient*, no. 216, octobre 1896, 449–52.

58. "Lettre du R. P. Raphael, supérieur de la Mission des Capucins à Mezre (Mamo-uret-ul-Aziz) à M. le Directeur sur la fondation d'un orphelinat pour les enfants arméniens, Mezre, le 20 janvier 1898," *Oeuvres des écoles d'orient*, no. 225, mars 1898, 342–43.

59. BOA Y.MTV, 188/118, 22.Za.1316 (3.4.1899).

60. *El Tiyempo*, Istanbul, 25 March 1897, no. 54, 1.

61. BOA Y.MTV, 188/118, 22.Za.1316 (3.4.1899).

62. *El Tiyempo*, Istanbul, 1 April 1897, no. 56, 2.

63. Trabzon (20), Malatya (15), Sis (5), Bitlis (5), Diyarbekir (25), Sasun (10), Eğin (25), Aintab (5), Palu (20), Bayburd (25), Gürün (20), Van (10), Urfa (25) Mamüretülaziz (40), Sivas (20), Arabkir (35), Hısnımansur (5), Çüngüş (10), Erzincan (15), Kilis (10).

64. BOA, A.MKT.MHM., 702/22, 1/R/1315 (29.8.1897).

65. BOA, A.MKT.MHM., 702/22, 2/R/1315 (30.8.1897).

66. BOA, A.MKT.MHM., 702/22, 2/Ra/1315 (1.8.1897).

67. BOA, A.MKT.MHM., 702/22, 20/Za/1317 (22.3.1900).

68. "Editorial Paragraphs," *Missionary Herald*, vol. 92, July 1896, 265.

69. "Mésopotamie et Kurdistan, Rapport du R.P. Galland, supérieur de la Mission dominicaine de Mossoul, à M. le directeur de l'Oeuvre d'Orient," *Oeuvres des écoles d'orient*, no. 222, septembre 1897, 204–17.

70. "The Bardezag Orphanage," *Missionary Herald*, vol. 95, November 1899, 482–83.

71. Mr. Baldwin, "The Orphanages," *Missionary Herald*, vol. 95, March 1899, 111 (italics mine).

72. Florence A. Fensham, Mary I. Lyman, and H. B. Humphrey, *A Modern Crusade in the Turkish Empire* (Chicago: Women's Board of Missions of the Interior, 1908), 48.

73. "Mésopotamie et Kurdistan, Rapport du R.P. Galland, supérieur de la Mission dominicaine de Mossoul, à M. le directeur de l'Oeuvre d'Orient," *Oeuvres des écoles d'orient*, no. 222, septembre 1897, 204–17.

74. "The Summary of Armenian Patriarch's Complaint to the British Embassy, 1897," ABC 16.9.7, reel 694, no. 706-9.

75. Dr. Chambers, "The Annual Meeting," *Missionary Herald*, vol. 93, October 1897, 396–97.

76. Edwin W. Martin, *Hubbards of Sivas: A Chronicle of Love and Faith* (Santa Barbara: Fithian Press, 1991), 280.

77. "Concerning Work for Orphans, June 10 1897," ABC 16.9.3, reel 607, no. 610 (italics mine).

78. "Work for Orphans in the Harput Field, July 28, 1897," ABC 16.9.7, reel 694, no. 1093-94 (italics mine).

79. Dr. Raynolds, "Relations with the Gregorian Church," *Missionary Herald*, vol. 95, October 1899, 418–19 (italics mine).

80. BOA, A.MKT.MHM., 702/29, 14/Ş/1317 (18.12.1899): "cerad-ı münteşir gibi bu havaliye dağılan misyonerler."

81. Selim Deringil, *The Well-Protected Domains: Ideology and the Legitimation of Power in the Ottoman Empire, 1876–1909* (London: I. B. Tauris, 1998).

82. "Haçin'de hiçbir olayın meydana gelmediği, dolayısıyla ebeveynini iğtişaşta kaybeden yetim bulunmadığı halde, Amerika ve Avrupa kamuoyunu iğfal amacıyla kasıtlı, hilâf-ı hakikat yayınlar yapıldığı," BOA, Hariciye, Siyasi (HR.SYS.), 2792/69, 21.12.1897.

83. Bliss wrote that the commission was composed of five members, two of them Christians. They stayed in the area for three months, yet did not work much, distributing less than £400 of the reported £2,000 ($8,800) in its hands. Rev. Edwin Munsell Bliss, *Turkey and the Armenian Atrocities* (Philadelphia: J. H. Moore, 1896), 506. The Ottoman documents call this body an "Aid Commission" (*İane Komisyonu*). BOA, İ.HUS. 66/1316-Ra043, 10/Ra/1316 (29.7.1898).

84. "Editorial Paragraphs," *Missionary Herald*, vol. 91, December 1895, 485.

85. Clarissa Harlowe Barton, 1821–1912, philanthropist, founder of the American Red Cross Society. During the Armenian massacres of 1894–1896 she came to the Ottoman Empire to take part in the relief effort. Elizabeth Brown Pryor, *Clara Barton: Professional Angel* (Philadelphia: Univ. of Pennsylvania Press, 1987).

86. Bliss, *Turkey and the Armenian Atrocities*, 513.

87. BOA, İ.HUS., 56/1315-R/78, 18/R/1315 (16.9.1897).

88. Ibid., "ecnebilerin bu suretle hareketlerinin muzırratı derkar olduğundan ve ahaliye olunacak iane bir muavenet-i insaniye ise hükümet memurlarının marifetiyle cereyanı lazım geleceğinden ahval-i mümessilenin adem-i tekrarı."

89. BOA, İ.HUS. 66/1316-Ra043, (14.6.1897).

90. BOA, İ.HUS. 66/1316-Ra043, (17.5.1898). "iğtişaşın hasarı yalnız Ermenilere münhasır olmayub az çok İslamın cevami ve mekatibince dahi hasarat vaki olmasıyla."

91. BOA, İ.HUS. 66/1316-Ra043, (14.6.1897).

92. BOA, İ.HUS. 123, 3/R/1315 (1.9.1897).

93. BOA, Yıldız Perakende Evrakı Umum Vilayetler Tahriratı (Y.PRK.UM.), 46/63, 28/M/1317 (8.6.1899) (italics mine).

94. "Protestan mezhebinin tevsine malen ve bedenen çalışmakta," BOA, Y.PRK.UM., 51/38, 11/R/1318 (7.8.1900).

95. In mid-1900, the governorships of Adana, Aleppo, and Diyarbekir reported that there were no cases of conversion and only a few children were registered to the American or Latin schools. BOA, Y.PRK.UM., 51/38, 11/R/1318 (7.8.1900).

96. "ahali-yi mahalliyenin ahlak ve efkarı fesad-pezir olunarak bilahare milliyetlerini dahi gaib edecekleri," BOA, İ.HUS., 74/1316-Z/59, 19/Z/1316 (30.4.1899).

97. BOA, DH.TMIK.S., 11/13, 25/M /1315 (25.06.1897); BOA, Y.PRK.UM., 39/6, 04/S /1315 (04.07.1897); BOA, DH.TMIK.S., 12/37, 25/S /1315 (25.07.1897); BOA, DH.TMIK.S.,12/72, 03/Ra/1315 (02.08.1897).

98. BOA, A.MKT.MHM., 702/29, 21/N/1316 (2.2.1899).

99. "lisan-ı maderzadları muhafaza," BOA, A.MKT.MHM., 702/24, 2/C/1315 (28.10.1897).

100. "temin-i maişet," BOA, A.MKT.MHM., 702/24, 13/L/1314 (17.3.1897).

101. BOA, A.MKT.MHM., 702/24, 21/Şb/1313 (5.3.1898).

102. BOA, A.MKT.MHM., 702/24, 15/M/1316 (4.6.1898).

103. BOA, A.MKT.MHM., 702/24, 12/C/1315 (8.11.1897).

104. BOA, A.MKT.MHM., 702/29, 21/N/1316 (2.2.1899).

105. The Ambassador claimed that there were only 15 orphans in Diyarbekir orphanages. Yet, the ABCFM documents verify that there were around 100 children in Diyarbekir: "Harput Orphanage, Jan. 5 1898," ABC 16.9.7, reel 694, no. 1112-3. Later reports written by Lepsius to reopen the orphanage also provide a figure of 94: BOA, A.MKT.MHM., 702/29, 28/Ca/1317 (4.10.1899).

106. BOA, A.MKT.MHM., 702/29, 21/N/1316 (2.2.1899).

107. "işbu müessesat-ı hayriye mekteb ittihaz edilmediği," ibid.

108. "bikes ve bivaye bazı etfalin sefaletten tahlisi maksad-ı insaniyetkaranesiyle," ibid.

109. "Amerikalılar'ın harekat ve ifalarının muzırratını," ibid.

110. BOA, A.MKT.MHM., 702/29, 26/N/1316 (7.2.1899).

111. "bunları açlıktan helak olmaktan muhafaza eden Protestanlar," BOA, A.MKT. MHM, 702/24, 21.03.1899.

112. BOA, HR.SYS, 2793/2, 18/2/1899.

113. BOA, A.MKT.MHM., 702/29,18/Ra/1317 (26.08.1899).

114. "Editorial Paragraphs," *Missionary Herald*, vol. 95, June 1899, 221.

115. "hafiyen aşırmağa," BOA, A.MKT.MHM., 702/30, 12/Hz/1315 (24.6.1899).

116. "gönderilen polisi tard ve tahkir etmek gibi ahval-i serkeşane," ibid.

117. "Editorial Paragraphs," *Missionary Herald*, vol. 95, June 1899, 221. *Daily Telegraph* of 8 April 1899 wrote that three orphanages in Diyarbekir, which were being run by British charitable donations, were closed and that immediate orders were given to the Ottoman government to open them. BOA, Yıldız Perakende Evrakı Tahrirat-ı Ecnebiye ve Mabeyn Mütercimliği (Y.PRK.TKM.), 41/91, 28/Za/1316 (9.4.1899).

118. BOA, A.MKT.MHM., 702/29, 9/R/1317 (17.8.1899).

119. "Editorial Paragraphs," *Missionary Herald*, vol. 91, July 1895, 267.

120. BOA, A.MKT.MHM., 702/29, 9/R/1317 (17.8.1899), "Vakıa her ne kadar müessesat-ı mezkureye eytamhane namı verilmekde ise de hakikat-ı halde derununda ikame ettirilen çocukların orada yalnız geceleri beytutetle infak ve iaşe olunmakta olduklarına ve talim ve tedrisatı mahalli mekteblerinde görmekte olduklarına nazaran bunlara eytamhaneden ise mesken denilmesi daha münasib olur."

121. BOA, Y.A.HUS., 399/51, 22/R/1317 (29.8.1899).

122. BOA, A.MKT.MHM., 702/29, 28/Ca/1317 (04.10.1899).

123. BOA, Y.PRK.UM., 49/38, 25/Ş/1317 (28.12.1899).

124. BOA, A.MKT.MHM., 702/29, 12/Ş/1317 (16.12.1899),"ruhsat verilecek olursa teba-yı devlet-i aliyyeden bir müdür-ü mesul tayiniyle idarelerinin hükümetçe taht-ı nezaret-i mütemadiyede bulundurulması suretinin şart ittihaz edilmesi."

125. BOA, Y.A.HUS., 396/12, 2/M/1317, (13.5.1899), "öteden beri mevcud olan mekatib-i ecnebiyyenin tedrisattan meni maddesi cay-ı nazar olarak çünkü bunlar memalik-i şahanenin ekser tarafında ve katbekat bir takrib açılarak yerleşmiş ve gerçi bir çoğu ruhsatsız ise de bir takımı da ruhsata merbut bulunmuş olmağla şimdi tatilleri pek müşgül ve belki gayr-ı kabil olduğu."

126. Kieser, *Iskalanmış Barış*, 250.

127. BOA, A.MKT.MHM., 702/30, 24 April 1315, (6.5.1899).

128. BOA Y.MTV., 188/118, 22.Za.1316 (3.4.1899).

129. "memalik-i şahanenin bazı mahallerinde bulunan etfal-i yetimenin devletce yapılacak mekteblerde terbiyelereine ecanibin bir şey demeğe bir güna hak ve salahiyetleri olamayacağına," BOA, Y.A.RES., 101/39, 19/S/1317 (29.6.1899).

130. BOA, A.MKT.MHM., 702/30, 24 April 1315, (6.5.1899).

131. "muhtelit ve meccani darüttalimler," BOA, Y.A.HUS., 396/12, 2/M/1317, (13.5.1899). In many of these documents, the Ottoman term for orphanage took a number of forms: *eytamhane, yetimhane, darütterbiye, darüttalim.*

132. BOA, Y.A.HUS., 396/12, 2/M/1317, (13.5.1899); BOA, Y.PRK.BŞK., 59/62, 3/M/1317 (14.5.1899).

133. BOA, Y.A.RES., 101/39, 19/S/1317 (29.6.1899): "mekteblerin tesisi halinde bir veche maruz-ı müessesat-ı ecnebiyyenin muzırratına karşı oldukça müdafaatta bulunulmuş olacağı gibi."

134. Ibid., "memalik-i şahane ahalisinin ahlak ve lisanını muhafaza."

135. BOA, Y.A.RES., 101/39, 19/S/1317 (29.6.1899).

136. BOA, A.MKT.MHM., 702/29, 14 August 1315 (26.8.1899).

137. BOA, A. MKT.MHM., 702/30, 12/Hz/1315 (24.6.1899).

138. BOA, Y.MTV., 202/18, 03/M /1318 (2.5.1900); BOA, A.MKT.MHM., 702/30, 29/ Ns/1316 (12.5.1900).

139. BOA, Y.MTV., 202/18, 03/M /1318 (2.5.1900).

140. BOA, Y.MTV., 206/83, 16/Ca/1318 (11.9.1900).

141. "sanayi-i müteaddidenin ihyası," BOA, DH.TMIK.S., 39/19, 18/R/1320 (25.07.1902).

142. BOA, İ.HUS., 74/1316-Z/59, 19/Z/1316 (30.4.1899), "Anadolu'nun münasib bir mahallinde hükümetçe bir eytamhane inşasıyla oraya her sunuf tebaa-yı şahane eyta-mının kabulü ve bunların milletlerini muhafazaya ve ahlakını tehzibe kafil olmak üzere tedrisine."

143. BOA, Y.MTV., 193/44, 7.R.1317 (15.8.1899).

144. Ibid.

145. "ahali-yi müslime evladının bikes kalan sıbyanına mahsus," BOA, Y.A.RES., 104/34, 25/B/1317 (29.11.1899).

146. For further information, Nadir Özbek, "II. Abdülhamid ve Kimsesiz Çocuklar: Darülhayr-ı Âlî," *Tarih ve Toplum* 31, no. 182 (1999): 11–21.

147. BOA, ZB, 320/123, 18/Şu/1322 (3.3.1907).

148. Michael Ignatieff, *Human Rights as Politics and Idolatry*, ed. Amy Gutman (Princeton: Princeton Univ. Press, 2001), 9.

149. Ignatieff, *Human Rights as Politics and Idolatry*, 20.

150. Dr. Raynolds of Van wrote: "To what extent the jealousy of Armenian patriarch in Constantinople, of Protestant influence may have had to do with this [closure of orphanages] I cannot say." "Women's Armenian Relief Fund: Extracts from Dr. Raynolds' Letters (March–April 1899)," ABC 16.9.7, reel 694, no. 1162–3.

151. "Editorial Paragraphs," *Missionary Herald*, vol. 92, March 1896, 90.

152. "Editorial Paragraphs," *Missionary Herald*, vol. 93, June 1897, 217.

153. Fifteen years later, when faced with a similar situation in Adana, Zabel Esayan interpreted the events as the destruction of two generations with only one blow. Zabel Esayan, "Giligio Vorpanotsnerı [Orphanages of Cilicia]," *Arakadz* 1, no. 13 (17 August 1911): 196–97.

Conclusion: Ottoman Children as Historical Actors

1. The word is a neologism originating from the 2013 protests in Turkey, coined from Prime Minister Erdoğan's use of the term *çapulcu* (roughly translated as "looter") to describe the protesters.

2. Haydar Darıcı, "Politics of Privacy: Forced Migration and the Spatial Struggle of the Kurdish Youth," *Journal of Balkan and Near Eastern Studies* 13 (2011): 457–74.

3. Schull's designation "laboratories of modernity," which he uses for prisons of the Second Constitutional Period, perfectly captures the idea of *experiment* regarding *ıslahhane*s. These institutional structures were really microcosms with the potential to reveal the larger picture of the Ottoman modernization. Kent Schull, "Tutuklu Sayımı: Jön Türklerin Sistematik Bir Şekilde Hapishane İstatistikleri Toplama Çalışmaları ve Bunların 1911–1918 Hapishane Reformu Üzerine Etkileri," in *Osmanlı'da Asayiş, Suç ve Ceza: 18.–20. Yüzyıllar*, ed. Noémi Lévy and Alexandre Toumarkine (Istanbul: Tarih Vakfı, Yurt Yayınları, 2007), 212–38.

4. Rogan, *Frontiers of the State*; Yonca Köksal, "Coercion and Mediation: Centralization and Sedentarization of Tribes in the Ottoman Empire," *Middle Eastern Studies* 42, no. 3 (2006): 469–91; Nadir Özbek, "Policing the Countryside."

5. Jernazian, *Judgment Unto Truth*, 17–25.

6. Nissim M. Benezra, *Une Enfance Juive à Istanbul, 1911–1929* (Istanbul: Isis, 1996).

Bibliography

Published Official Documents

1311 Sene-yi Hicrisine Mahsus Selanik Vilayeti Salnamesi. Salonika: Mekteb-i Sanayi Matbaası, 1311 [1893].

Hüdavendigar Vilayeti Salname-yi Resmiyyesi. Bursa: Vilayet Matbaası, 1324 [1906–1907].

İstanbul Mahkemesi 121 Numaralı Şer'iyye Sicili. Istanbul: Sabancı Üniversitesi, 2006.

"Kanunname-i Ceza (1274/1858)." In *Düstur,* Tertib 1, vol. 1, 537. Istanbul: Matbaa-i Amire, 1289 [1872].

"Maarif-i Umûmiyye Nizamnamesi." In *Düstur,* Tertib 1, vol. 2, 184–219. Istanbul: Matbaa-i Amire, 1289 [1872].

Salname 1295. Dersaadet: Rıza Efendi Matbaası, 1295 [1878].

Salname-i Nezaret-i Maarif-i Umumiye, 6. Sene, 1321 Sene-i Hicriyyesine Mahsustur. Istanbul: Asır Matbaası [1903].

Salname-i Vilayet-i Aydın (1314–1319). Izmir: Vilayet Matbaası, 1314–1319 [1896–1902].

"Serseri ve Mazannae-i Su-i Eşhas Hakkında Kanun, 9/R/1327 (10.5.1909)." In *Düstur,* Tertib 2, vol. 1 (1908–1909), 169–72. Istanbul: Matbaa-i Osmaniye, 1329 [1911].

Sivas Vilayeti Salnamesi. Sivas: Sivas Vilayeti Matbaası, 1325 [1907].

"Tese'ülün men'ine dair nizâmname, 13/Ş/1313 (29.01.1896)." In *Düstur,* Tertib 1, vol. 7 (1895–1904), 48–49. Ankara: Başvekalet Devlet Matbaası, 1941.

"Vilayat Islahhaneleri Nizamnamesi." In *Düstur,* Tertib 1, vol. 2, 277–95. Istanbul, Matbaa-i Amire, 1289 [1872].

Books, Articles, Periodicals, Dissertations, and Papers

Adair, Richard. *Courtship, Illegitimacy, and Marriage in Early Modern England.* New York: Manchester Univ. Press, 1996.

205

Agmon, Iris. *Family and Court: Legal Culture and Modernity in Late Ottoman Palestine*. Syracuse: Syracuse Univ. Press, 2006.

Ahmet Midhat Efendi. *Acayib-i Alem*. 1882. Reprint, Ankara: Türk Dil Kurumu, 2000.

———. *Dürdane Hanım*. Ankara: Türk Dil Kurumu, 2000 [1882].

———. *Henüz Onyedi Yaşında*. Ankara: Türk Dil Kurumu, 2000 [1882].

———. *Müşahedat*. Ankara: Türk Dil Kurumu, 2000 [1891].

Akın, Yiğit. *Gürbüz ve Yavuz Evlatlar: Erken Cumhuriyet'te Beden Terbiyesi ve Spor*. Istanbul: İletişim, 2004.

Altınbaş, Ayten, and Oğuz Ceylan."Viladethane." *Tombak* 17 (1997): 26–32.

Anastassiadou, Méropi. "Médecine hygiéniste et pédagogie sociale à Istanbul à la fin du XIXe siècle: Le cas du docteur Spyridon Zavitziano." In *Médecins et ingénieurs ottomans à l'âge des nationalismes*, ed. Méropi Anastassiadou, 63–99. Paris and Istanbul: Maisonneuve & Larose et IFEA, 2003.

———. "La protection de l'enfance abandonnée dans l'Empire ottoman au XIXe siècle. Le cas de la communauté grecque orthodoxe de Beyoğlu (Istanbul)." *Südost-Forschungen* 59–60 (2000–2001): 272–322.

Anderson, Margaret Lavinia. "'Down in Turkey, Far Away': Human Rights, the Armenian Massacres, and Orientalism in Wilhelmine Germany." *Journal of Modern History* 79 (2007): 80–111.

Ariès, Philippe. *Centuries of Childhood: A Social History of Family Life*. New York: Vintage, 1962.

Bargach, Jamila. *Orphans of Islam: Family, Abandonment, and Secret Adoption in Morocco*. Lanham: Rowman & Littlefield, 2002.

Baron, Beth. *Egypt as a Woman: Nationalism, Gender, and Politics*. Berkeley: Univ. of California Press, 2005.

———. "Nile Mother: Lillian Trasher and Egypt's Orphans." In *Competing Kingdoms: Women, Mission, Nation, and American Empire, 1776–1960*, ed. Barbara Reeves Ellington et al., 240–68. Durham: Duke Univ. Press, 2010.

———. "Orphans and Abandoned Children in Modern Egypt." In *Interpreting Welfare and Relief in the Middle East*, ed. Nefissa Neguib and Inger Marie Okkenhaug, 12–34. Leiden: Brill, 2008.

Bayle, St. John. *The Turks in Europe: A Sketch of Manners and Politics in the Ottoman Empire*. London: Chapman & Hall, 1853.

Belgesay, Mustafa Reşit."Ev İşleri Yapanların Ücret İddiaları." *İleri Hukuk Dergisi* 1, no. 13 (1946): 129–31.

Benezra, Nissim M. *Une Enfance Juive à Istanbul, 1911–1929*. Istanbul: Isis, 1996.

Benice, Ethem İzzet. *Yakılacak Kitap*. Istanbul: Tan Basımevi, 1942.

Berelowitch, Wladimir. "Les Hospices des Enfants Trouvés en Russie (1763–1914)." In *Enfance abandonnée et société en Europe: XIVe–XXe siècle: actes du colloque international, Rome, 30 et 31 janvier 1987*, 167–217. Paris: De Boccard, 1991.

Berkes, Niyazi. *The Development of Secularism in Turkey*. New York: Routledge, 1998.

Bliss, Rev. Edwin Munsell. *Turkey and the Armenian Atrocities*. Philadelphia: J. H. Moore, 1896.

Blum, Ann S. "Dying of Sadness: Hospitalism and Child Welfare in Mexico City, 1920–1940." In *Disease in the History of Modern Latin America: From Malaria to AIDS*, ed. Diego Armus, 209–36. Durham: Duke Univ. Press, 2003.

Bonner, Michael. "Definition of the Poverty and the Rise of the Muslim Poor." *Journal of the Royal Asiatic Society* 6, no. 3 (1996): 335–44.

————, Mine Ener, and Amy Singer, eds. *Poverty and Charity in Middle Eastern Contexts*. Albany: State Univ. of New York Press, 2003.

Boswell, John. *The Kindness of Strangers: The Abandonment of Children in Western Europe from Late Antiquity to the Renaissance*. Chicago: Univ. of Chicago Press, 1998.

Boulton, J. "London Domestic Servants from Depositional Evidence, 1660–1750: Servant-Employer Sexuality in the Patriarchal Household." In *Chronicling Poverty: The Voices and Strategies of the English Poor, 1660–1840*, ed. Tim Hitchcock, Peter King, and Pamela Sharpe, 47–69. New York: St. Martin's Press, 1997.

Butler, Judith. *The Psychic Life of Power: Theories in Subjection*. Stanford: Stanford Univ. Press, 1997.

————. *Undoing Gender*. London: Routledge, 2004.

de Certeau, Michel. *The Practice of Everyday Life*. Berkeley: Univ. of California Press, 1984.

Çiftçi, Cafer. *Bursa'da Vakıfların Sosyo-Ekonomik İşlevleri*. Bursa: Gaye Kitabevi, 2004.

Congrégation de la Mission [lazaristes]. *Répertoire historique et table générale des Annales de la Congrégation de la Mission depuis leur origine jusqu'à la fin de l'année 1899*. Paris: à la procure de la congrégation de la mission, 1900.

Crumley, Carole L. "Exploring Venues of Social Memory: Social Memory and Environmental Change." In *Social Memory and History: Anthropological Perspectives*, ed. Jacob Climo and Maria G. Cattell, 39–51. California: AltaMira Press, 2002.

Cunningham, Hugh. *Children and Childhood in Western Society since 1500*. London: Longman, 1995.

Daniluk, Judith C. *Women's Sexuality across the Life Span: Challenging Myths, Creating Meanings.* New York: Guilford Press, 2003.

Davidoff, Leonore. *Worlds Between: Historical Perspectives on Gender and Class.* New York: Routledge, 1995.

Davin, Anna. *Growing up Poor: Home, School, and Street in London.* London: Rivers Oram Press, 1996.

Davis, Natalie Zemon. *Fiction in the Archives: Pardon Tales and Their Tellers in Sixteenth-Century France.* Stanford: Stanford Univ. Press, 1987.

Davison, Roderic. *Reform in the Ottoman Empire: 1856–1876.* Princeton: Princeton Univ. Press, 1963.

Deans, William. *History of the Ottoman Empire: From the Earliest Period to the Present Time.* Edinburgh: A. Fullarton, 1854.

Demetriou, Olga. "Streets Not Named: Discursive Dead Ends and the Politics of Orientation in Intercommunal Spatial Relations in Northern Greece." *Cultural Anthropology* 21, no. 2 (2006): 295–321.

Demos, John. *Family Life in a Plymouth Colony.* Oxford: Oxford Univ. Press, 1970.

Deringil, Selim. "'The Armenian Question Is Finally Closed': Mass Conversions of Armenians in Anatolia during the Hamidian Massacres of 1895–1897." *Comparative Studies in Society and History* 51, no. 2 (2009): 344–71.

———. "Redefining Identities in the Late Ottoman Empire: Policies of Conversion and Apostasy." In *Imperial Rule,* edited by Alexei Miller, Alfred J. Rieber, 107–30. Budapest: Central European Univ. Press, 2004.

———. "'They Live in a State of Nomadism and Savagery': The Late Ottoman Empire and the Post-Colonial Debate." *Comparative Studies in Society and History* 45, no. 2 (2003): 311–42.

———. *The Well-Protected Domains: Ideology and Legitimation of Power in the Ottoman Empire 1876–1909.* London: I. B. Tauris, 1998.

Dirks, Nicholas B., Geoff Eley, and Sherry B. Ortner, eds. *Culture/Power/History: A Reader in Contemporary Social Theory.* Princeton: Princeton Univ. Press, 1994.

Donzelot, Jacques. *The Policing of Families.* Translated by Robert Hurley. New York: Pantheon Book, 1979.

Drevet, Richard. "Laïques de France et missions catholiques au XIXe siècle: l'OEuvre de la Propagation de la Foi, origines et développement lyonnais (1822–1922)." Ph.D. diss., Université Lyon 2, 2002.

Duben, Alan, and Cem Behar. *Istanbul Households: Marriage, Family and Fertility, 1880–1940.* Cambridge: Cambridge Univ. Press, 1991.

Dwight, Henry Otis. *Constantinople and Its Problems: Its Peoples, Customs, Religions and Progress.* New York: Young People's Missionary Movement, 1901.

Ekmekçioğlu, Lerna. "A Climate for Abduction, A Climate for Redemption: The Politics of Inclusion during and after the Armenian Genocide." *Comparative Studies in Society and History* 55, no. 3 (2013): 522–53.

Eldem, Edhem. "Capitulations and Western Trade." In *The Cambridge History of Turkey: The Later Ottoman Empire, 1603–1839,* edited by Suraiya Faroqhi, 283–335. Cambridge: Cambridge Univ. Press, 2006.

Elshakry, Marwa. "The Gospel of Science and American Evangelism in Late Ottoman Beirut." *Past and Present* 196, no. 1 (2007): 173–214.

Emrence, Cem. "Imperial Paths, Big Comparisons: The Late Ottoman Empire." *Journal of Global History* 3, no. 3 (2008): 289–311.

Ener, Mine. "Charity of the Khedive." In *Poverty and Charity in the Middle Eastern Contexts,* edited by Mine Ener, Amy Singer, and Michael Bonner, 185–201. New York: State Univ. of New York Press, 2003.

———. *Managing Egypt's Poor and the Politics of Benevolence, 1800–1952.* Princeton: Princeton Univ. Press, 2004.

Erdem, Hakan Y. "Kırım Savaşı'nda Karadeniz Beyaz Köle Ticareti." In *Savaştan Barışa: 150. Yıldönümünde Kırım Savaşı ve Paris Antlaşması (1853–1856), 22–23 Mayıs 2006, Bildiriler,* 85–118. Istanbul: İstanbul Üniversitesi Edebiyat Fakültesi Tarih Araştırma Merkezi, 2007.

———. *Slavery in the Ottoman Empire and Its Demise, 1800–1909.* Houndmills: Macmillan, 1996.

Eren, İsmail. "Kosova Sanayi Mektebi." *Belgelerle Türk Tarihi Dergisi* 3, no. 18 (1969): 34–38.

Ergin, Osman Nuri. *Mecelle-i Umur-ı Belediye.* Istanbul: Matbaa-ı Osmaniye, 1338 [1922].

———. *Türkiye Maarif Tarihi,* Istanbul: Eser Kültür Yayınları, 1977.

Ergut, Ferdan. "Policing the Poor in the Late Ottoman Empire." *Middle Eastern Studies* 38, no. 2 (2002): 149–64.

Erten, Hayri. *Konya Şeriyye Sicilleri Işığında Ailenin Sosyo-Ekonomik ve Kültürel Yapısı (XVIII. yy'in İlk Yarısı).* Ankara: Kültür Başkanlığı Kültür Eserleri, 2001.

Esayan, Zabel. "Giligio Vorpanotsnerı [Orphanages of Cilicia]." *Arakadz* 1, no. 13 (1911): 196–97.

Esendal, Memduh Şevket. *Bizim Nesibe.* Ankara: Bilgi Yayınevi, 1985.

Eyüpgiller, Kemâl Kutgün. "Kastamonu Kent Tarihi." *Electronic Journal of Oriental Studies* 1 (1998): 1–149.

Fahmy, Khaled. *All the Pasha's Men: Mehmed Ali, His Army and the Making of Modern Egypt*. Cambridge: Cambridge Univ. Press, 1997.

———. "Modernizing Cairo: A Revisionist Narrative." In *Making Cairo Medieval*, edited by Nasser O. Rabbat, Irene A. Bierman, and Nezar Alsayyad, 173–200. Lanham: Lexington Books, 2005.

———. "Women, Medicine, and Power in Nineteenth-Century Egypt." In *Remaking Women: Feminism and Modernity in the Middle East*, edited by Lila Abu-Lughod, 35–72. Princeton: Princeton Univ. Press, 1998.

Fairchilds, Cissie. *Domestic Enemies: Servants and Their Masters in Old Regime France*. Baltimore: Johns Hopkins Univ. Press, 1984.

Fargues, Philippe. "Family and the Household in Mid-Nineteenth Century Cairo." In *Family History in the Middle East: Household, Property and Gender*, edited by Beshara Doumani, 23–50. Albany: State Univ. of New York Press, 2003.

Faroqhi, Suraiya. "Bosnian Merchants in the Adriatic." In *Ottoman Bosnia: A History in Peril*, edited by Markus Koller and Kemal Karpat, 225–39. Madison: Univ. of Wisconsin Press, 2004.

———. *Subjects of the Sultan: Culture and Daily Life in the Ottoman Empire*. New York: I. B. Tauris, 2005.

———. *Towns and Townsmen of Ottoman Anatolia: Trade, Crafts and Food Production in an Urban Setting*. Cambridge: Cambridge Univ. Press, 1984.

Fensham, Florence A., Mary I. Lyman, and H. B. Humphrey. *A Modern Crusade in the Turkish Empire*. Chicago: Women's Board of Missions of the Interior, 1908.

Fernea, Elizabeth W., ed. *Children in the Muslim Middle East*. Austin: Univ. of Texas Press, 1996.

———. *Remembering Childhood in the Middle East: Memoirs from a Century of Change*. Austin: Univ. of Texas Press, 2003.

Finzsch, Norbert, and Robert Jutte. *Institutions of Confinement: Hospitals, Asylums, and Prisons in Western Europe and North America, 1500–1950*. New York: Cambridge Univ. Press, 1996.

Flueh-Lobban, Carolyn. *Islamic Society in Practice*. Talahassee: Univ. Press of Florida, 1994.

de Fontmagne, La Baronne Durand. *Un séjour à l'ambassade de France à Constantinople sous le second Empire*. Paris: Plon-Nourrit, 1902.

Fortna, Benjamin C. *The Imperial Classroom: Islam, the State, and Education in the Late Ottoman Empire*. Oxford: Oxford Univ. Press, 2002.

————. "Kindergartens in the Ottoman Empire and the Turkish Republic." In *Kindergartens and Cultures: The Global Diffusion of an Idea*, edited by Roberta Wollons, 252–73. New Haven: Yale Univ. Press, 2000.

————. *Learning to Read in the Late Ottoman Empire and the Early Turkish Republic*. New York: Palgrave Macmillan, 2011.

Foucault, Michel. *Histoire de la folie à l'âge classique: folie et déraison*. Paris: Plon, 1961.

————. *History of Sexuality: An Introduction*. New York: Vintage, 1990.

Friedl, Erika. "Tribal Enterprises and Marriage Issues in Twentieth Century Iran." In *Family History in the Middle East: Household, Property and Gender*, edited by Beshara Doumani, 151–70. Albany: State Univ. of New York Press, 2003.

Fuchs, Rachel G. *Abandoned Children: Foundlings and Child Welfare in Nineteenth Century France*. Albany: State Univ. of New York Press, 1984.

————. *Poor and Pregnant in Paris: Strategies for Survival in the Nineteenth Century*. New Brunswick: Rutgers Univ. Press, 1992.

Fuhrmann, Malte. "Cosmopolitan Imperialists and the Ottoman Port Cities: Conflicting Logics in the Urban Social Fabric." *Cahiers de la Méditerranée* 67 (2003): http://cdlm.revues.org/document128.html.

————. *Der Traum vom deutschen Orient. Zwei deutsche Kolonien im Osmanischen Reich 1851–1918* (Imagining a German Orient: Two German Colonies in the Ottoman Empire 1851–1918). Frankfurt: Campus 2006.

Gallant, Thomas W. "Agency, Structure, and Explanation in Social History: The Case of the Foundling Home on Kephallenia, Greece, during the 1830s." *Social Science History* 15, no. 4 (1991): 479–508.

Georgelin, Hervé. *La fin de Smyrne: Du Cosmopolitisme aux Nationalismes*. Paris: CNRS, 2005.

Georgeon, François, and Klaus Kreiser, eds. *Enfance et Jeunesse dans le Monde Musulman/Childhood and Youth in the Muslim World*. Paris: Maisonneuve & Larose, 2007.

Gerber, Haim. "Anthropology and Family History: The Ottoman and Turkish Families." *Journal of Family History* 14, no. 4 (1989): 409–21.

Gershoni, Israel, Hakan Y. Erdem, and Ursula Woköck, eds. *Histories of the Modern Middle East: New Directions*. London: Lynne Rienner, 2002.

————, Amy Singer, and Hakan Y. Erdem, eds. *Middle East Historiographies: Narrating the Twentieth-Century*. Seattle: Univ. of Washington Press, 2006.

Giladi, Avner. *Children of Islam: Concepts of Childhood in Medieval Muslim Society*. New York: St. Martin's Press, 1992.

————. "History of Childhood in Premodern Muslim Societies." In *Individu et Société dans le Monde Méditerranéen Musulman: Questions et Sources*, edited by Robert Ilbert and Randi Deguilhem, 57–68. Strasbourg: European Science Foundation, 1998.

————. *Infants, Parents, and Wet Nurses: Medieval Islamic Views on Breast-Feeding and Their Social Implications*. Leiden: Brill, 1999.

Gillis, John R. "Servants, Sexual Relations, and the Risks of Illegitimacy in London, 1801–1900." *Feminist Studies* 5, no. 1 (1979): 142–73.

Ginio, Eyal. "18. Yüzyıl Selanikinde Yoksul Kadınlar." *Toplum ve Bilim* 89 (2001): 190–204.

————. "Living on the Margins of Charity." In *Poverty and Charity in the Middle Eastern Contexts*, edited by Mine Ener, Amy Singer, and Michael Bonner, 165–84. New York: State Univ. of New York Press, 2003.

Giz, Adnan. "1868'de İstanbul Sanayicilerinin Şirketler Halinde Birleştirilmesi Teşebbüsü." *İstanbul Sanayi Odası Dergisi* 34 (1968): 16–19.

————. "İstanbul'da İlk Sanayi Mektebinin Kuruluşu." *İstanbul Sanayi Odası Dergisi* 3, no. 35 (1969): 20–22.

Goffman, Erving. *Asylums: Essays of the Social Situation of Mental Patients and Other Inmates*. Garden City: Anchor Books, 1961.

Goitein, S. D. *A Mediterranean Society*. Vol. 3, *The Jewish Communities of the Arab World as Portrayed in the Documents of the Cairo Geniza, The Family*. Berkeley: Univ. of California Press, 1978.

Gök, Fatma. "The Girls' Institutes in the Early Period of the Turkish Republic." In *Education in "Multicultural" Societies Turkish and Swedish Perspectives*, edited by Marie Carlson, Annika Rabo, and Fatma Gök, 95–107. Stockholm: Swedish Research Institute in Istanbul, 2007.

Goyau, Georges. *La Congrégation de la Mission des Lazaristes*. Paris: Grasset, 1938.

Gül, Murat, and Richard Lamb. "Mapping, Regularizing and Modernizing Ottoman Istanbul: Aspects of the Genesis of the 1839 Development Policy." *Urban History* 31 (2004): 420–36.

Gürkan, Ülker. "Evlat Edinme ve Beslemelerin Hukuki Durumu." In *Türk Hukuku ve Toplumu Üzerine İncelemeler*, edited by Peter Benedict and Adnan Güriz, 163–226. Ankara: Türk Kalkınma Vakfı Yayınları, 1974.

Hamzah, Dyala. *The Making of the Arab Intellectual: Empire, Public Sphere and the Colonial Coordinates of Selfhood*. London: Routledge, 2010.

Hay, Douglas, and Paul Craven, eds. *Masters, Servants, and Magistrates in Britain and the Empire, 1562–1955*. Chapel Hill: Univ. of North Carolina Press, 2004.

Hayrullah Efendi. *Avrupa Seyahatnamesi.* Edited by Belkıs Altuniş-Gürsoy. Ankara: T. C. Kültür Bakanlığı, 2002.

Hendrick, Harry. "The Child as a Social Actor in Historical Sources: Problems of Identification and Interpretation." In *Research with Children: Perspectives and Practices,* edited by Pia Christensen and Allison James, 40–63. New York: Routledge, 2008.

Heywood, Colin. *Children and Childhood in the West from Medieval to Modern Times.* Cambridge: Polity Press, 2002.

Hitchcock, Tim. *English Sexualities, 1700–1800.* London: Macmillan, 1997.

Hovannisian, Richard G. *Armenia on the Road to Independence.* Berkeley: Univ. of California Press, 1967.

Hoyles, Martin, ed. *Changing Childhood.* London: Writers' and Readers' Co-operative, 1979.

Hufton, Olwen. "Women, Work, and Family." In *A History of Women in the West.* Vol. 3, *Renaissance and Enlightenment Paradoxes,* edited by Natalie Zemon Davis and Arlette Farge, 26–45. Cambridge: Belknap Press of Harvard Univ. Press, 1994.

Hunt, David. *Parents and Children in History.* New York: Harper & Row, 1972.

Hyamson, Albert M. *The Sephardim of England: A History of Spanish and Portuguese Jewish Community 1492–1951.* London: Methuen, 1951.

Ignatieff, Michael. *Human Rights as Politics and Idolatry.* Edited by Amy Gutman. Princeton: Princeton Univ. Press, 2001.

Ipsen, Carl. *Italy in the Age of Pinocchio: Children and Danger in the Liberal Era.* New York: Palgrave Macmillan, 2006.

İhsan Şerif. "Midhat Paşa, Sanayi Mektepleri." *Tedrisat Mecmuası: Nazariyat ve Malumat Kısmı* 5, no. 30 (1915): 65–68.

İnalcık, Halil, and Donald Quataert, eds. *An Economic and Social History of the Ottoman Empire.* Vol. 2, *(1600–1914).* Cambridge: Cambridge Univ. Press, 1997.

Issawi, Charles. *The Fertile Crescent, 1800–1914: A Documentary Economic History.* New York: Oxford Univ. Press, 1988.

Jernazian, Ephraim K. *Judgment unto Truth: Witnessing the Armenian Genocide.* Edison, N.J.: Transaction Publishers, 1990.

Kabadayı, Erdem M. "Working for the State in a Factory in Istanbul: The Role of Factory Workers' Ethno-Religious and Gender Characteristics in State-Subject Interaction in the Late Ottoman Empire." Ph.D. diss., Ludwig-Maximilian Univ., 2008.

Káldy-Nagy, Gyula. *Kanuni Devri Budin Tahrir Defteri (1546–1562).* Ankara: Ankara Üniversitesi Basımevi, 1971.

Kancı, Tuba. "Imagining the Turkish Men and Women: Nationalism, Modernism and Militarism in Primary School Textbooks, 1928–2000." Ph.D. diss., Sabancı Univ., 2008.

———, and Ayşe Gül Altınay. "Educating Little Soldiers and Little Ayşes: Militarised and Gendered Citizenship in Turkish Textbooks." In *Education in "Multicultural" Societies: Turkish and Swedish Perspectives*, edited by Marie Carlson, Annika Rabo, and Fatma Gök, 51–71. Stockholm: Swedish Research Institute in Istanbul, 2007.

Kechriotis, Vangelis. "The Greek Community in Izmir, 1897–1914." Ph.D. diss., Leiden Univ., 2005.

Kerman, Zeynep. *1862–1910 Yılları Arasında Victor Hugo'dan Türçeye Yapılan Tercümeler Üzerinde Bir Araştırma*. Istanbul: İstanbul Üniversitesi Edebiyat Fakültesi Yayınları, 1978.

Kertzer, David I. *Sacrificed for Honor: Italian Infant Abandonment and the Politics of Reproductive Control*. Boston: Beacon Press, 1993.

Kieser, Hans-Lukas. *Iskalanmış Barış: Doğu Vilayetlerinde Misyonerlik, Etnik Kimlik ve Devlet 1839–1938*. Translated by Atilla Dirim. Istanbul: İletişim, 2005.

———. "Die Schweiz des Fin de Siècle und 'Armenien': Patriotische Identifikation, Weltbürgertum und Protestantismus in der Schweizerischen Philarmenischen Bewegung." In *Die Armenische Frage und die Schweiz, 1896–1923*, edited by Hans-Lukas Kieser, 133–57. Zurich: Chronos, 1999.

Kirakossian, Arman J., ed. *The Armenian Massacres, 1894–1896: U.S. Media Testimony*. Detroit: Wayne State Univ. Press, 2004.

Kocabaşoğlu, Uygur. *Anadolu'daki Amerika: Kendi Belgeleriyle 19. Yüzyılda Osmanlı İmparatorluğu'ndaki Amerikan Misyoner Okulları*. Ankara: İmge Kitabevi Yayınları, 2000.

Köksal, Duygu. "İsmayıl Hakkı Baltacıoğlu, İnkilap ve Terbiye: Ulusun 'Çocukluğu.'" *Toplumsal Tarih* 7, no. 40 (1997): 7–12.

Köksal, Yonca. "Coercion and Mediation: Centralization and Sedentarization of Tribes in the Ottoman Empire." *Middle Eastern Studies* 42, no. 3 (2006): 469–91.

Kösoğlu, Nevzat, ed. *Türkiye Dışındaki Türk Edebiyatları Antolojisi, vol. 7: Makedonya, Yugoslavya (Kosova) Türk Edebiyatı*. Ankara: T. C. Kültür Bakanlığı Yayınları, 2002.

Köstüklü, Nuri. *Sosyal Tarih Perspektifinden Yalvaç'ta Aile (1892–1908): Bir Osmanlı Kazası Örneğinde Türk Ailesinin Temel Bazı Özellikleri*. Konya: Günay Ofset, 1996.

Koyuncu, Gülnaz. "İzmir Sanayi Mektebi Piyangosu." *Tarih ve Toplum* 18, no. 107 (1992): 22–27.

———. "İzmir Sanayi Mektebi (1868–1923)." Master's thesis, Dokuz Eylül Univ., 1993.

Kuban, Doğan. *İzmir ve Ege'den Mimari İzlenimler: Kaybolan bir Geçmişten Görüntüler (Mimari Çizimler)*. İzmir: Çimentaş Vakfı Yayınları, 1994.

Kurt, Abdurrahman. *Bursa Sicillerine Göre Osmanlı Ailesi (1839–1876)*. Bursa: Uludağ Üniversitesi Yayınları, 1998.

Kuyulu, İnci Ersoy. "Orientalist Buildings in Izmir: The Case of the Kemeraltı, Çorakkapı, Keçeciler and Kemer Police Stations." *Electronic Journal of Oriental Studies* 4, no. 29 (2001): 1–24.

Lafi, Nora. "Mediterranean Connections: The Circulation of Municipal Knowledge and Practices during the Ottoman Reforms, c. 1830–1910." In *Another Global City: Historical Explorations into the Transnational Municipal Moment, 1850–2000*, edited by Pierre-Yves Saunier and Shane Ewen, 35–50. New York: Palgrave Macmillan, 2008.

Lane, E. W. *The Manners and Customs of the Modern Egyptians*. London: E. P. Dutton, 1860.

Laslett, Peter, Karla Oosterveen, and Richard M. Smith, eds. *Bastardy and Its Comparative History: Studies in the History of Illegitimacy and Marital Nonconformism in Britain, France, Germany, Sweden, North America, Jamaica, and Japan*. Cambridge: Harvard Univ. Press, 1980.

van Leeuwen, Marco. "Logic of Charity: Poor Relief in Preindustrial Europe." *Journal of Interdisciplinary History* 24 (1994): 589–613.

Lepsius, Johannes. *Armenia and Europe: An Indictment*. London: Hodder & Stoughton, 1897.

Levy, Avigdor. "The Officer Corps in Sultan Mahmud's New Army 1826–1839." *IJMES* 2 (1971): 21–39.

Lewis, Bernard. *Race and Slavery in the Middle East: An Historical Enquiry*. Oxford: Oxford University Press, 1990.

Libal, Kathryn R. "'The Child Question': The Politics of Child Welfare in Early Republican Turkey." In *Poverty and Charity in Middle Eastern Contexts*, edited by Mine Ener, Michael Bonner, and Amy Singer, 255–72. Binghamton: State Univ. of New York Press, 2003.

———. "The Children's Protection Society: Nationalizing Child Welfare in Early Republican Turkey." *New Perspectives on Turkey* 23 (2000): 53–78.

———. "Realizing Modernity Through the Robust Turkish Child, 1923–1938." In *Symbolic Childhood*, edited by Daniel Cook, 109–30. New York: Peter Lang, 2002.

Lowry, Heath W. *Trabzon Şehrinin İslâmlaşma ve Türkleşmesi, 1461–1583 Trabzon Örneğinde Osmanlı Tahrir Defterinin Şehirleşme Demoğrafik Tarihi için Kaynak Olarak Kullanılması*. Istanbul: Boğaziçi Üniversitesi Yayınları, 1998.

Macura, Vladimir. "Culture as Translation." In *Translation, History and Culture*, edited by Susan Bassnett and André Lefevere, 64–70. London: Cassell, 1990.

Mahmood, Saba. "Feminist Theory, Embodiment, and the Docile Agent: Some Reflections on the Egyptian Islamic Revival." *Cultural Anthropology* 16, no. 2 (2001): 202–36.

Makdisi, Ussama. *Artillery of Heaven: American Missionaries and the Failed Conversion of the Middle East*. Ithaca: Cornell University Press, 2008.

Maksudyan, Nazan. "'Being Saved to Serve': Armenian Orphans of 1894–96 and Interested Relief in Missionary Orphanages." *Turcica* 42 (2010): 47–88.

———. "Fight over 'Nobody's Children': Religion, Nationality, and Citizenship of Foundlings in Nineteenth-Century Ottoman Empire." *New Perspectives on Turkey* 41, no. 2 (2009): 151–80.

———. "Foster-Daughter or Servant, Charity or Abuse: *Besleme*s in the Late Ottoman Empire," *Journal of Historical Sociology* 21, no. 4 (2008): 488–512.

———. "Modernization of Welfare or Further Deprivation? State Provisions for Foundlings in the Late Ottoman Empire." *Journal of History of Childhood and Youth* 2, no. 3 (2009): 361–92.

———. "Orphans, Cities, and the State: Vocational Orphanages (*Islahhane*s) and 'Reform' in the Late Ottoman Urban Space." *IJMES* 43, no. 3 (2011): 493–511.

———. "State 'Parenthood' and Industrial Orphanages (*Islahhane*s): Transformation of Urbanity and Family Life." *History of the Family* 16, no. 2 (2011): 172–92.

———. "Street Children as a Transgression in the New Bourgeois Urban Space: Expertise on Juvenile Delinquency, Public Order and Philanthropy in the Late Ottoman Empire." In *Expertise and Juvenile Violence, 19th–21st century*, edited by Aurore François, Veerle Massin, and David Niget, 21–39. Louvain: Presses Universitaires de Louvain, 2011.

Malečková, Jitka. "Ludwig Büchner versus Nat Pinkerton: Turkish Translations from Western Languages, 1880–1914." *Mediterranean Historical Review* 9, no. 1 (1994): 73–99.

Marcus, Abraham. "Privacy in Eighteenth-Century Aleppo: The Limits of Cultural Ideals." *IJMES* 18 (1986): 165–83.

Martal, Abdullah. *Değişim Sürecinde İzmir'de Sanayileşme, 19. Yüzyıl*. Izmir: Dokuz Eylül Yayınları, 1999.

Martin, Edwin W. *Hubbards of Sivas: A Chronicle of Love and Faith*. Santa Barbara: Fithian Press, 1991.

de Mause, Lloyd, ed. *The History of Childhood*. London: Souvenir Press, 1976.

Maza, Sarah C. *Servants and Masters in Eighteenth-Century France: the Uses of Loyalty*. Princeton: Princeton Univ. Press, 1983.

Mazower, Mark. *Salonica: The City of Ghosts*. New York: Alfred A. Knopf, 2005.

McCants, Anne C. *Civic Charity in a Golden Age: Orphan Care in Early Modern Amsterdam*. Urbana: Univ. of Illinois Press, 1997.

Meldrum, Tim. *Domestic Service and Gender, 1660–1750: Life and Work in the London Household*. New York: Pearson, 2000.

———. "'Unlawfully Begotten on Her Body': Illegitimacy and the Parish Poor in St Luke's, Chelsea." In *Chronicling Poverty: The Voices and Strategies of the English Poor, 1640–1840*, edited by Tim Hitchcock, Peter King, and Pamela Sharpe, 70–86. New York: St. Martin's Press, 1997.

Meriwether, Margaret L. *The Kin Who Count: Family and Society in Ottoman Aleppo, 1770–1840*. Austin: Univ. of Texas Press, 1999.

———. "The Rights of Children and the Responsibilities of Women: Women as Wasis in Ottoman Aleppo, 1770–1840." In *Women, the Family, and Divorce Laws in Islamic History*, edited by Amira al-Azhary Sonbol, 219–35. Syracuse: Syracuse Univ. Press, 1996.

———, and Judith E. Tucker, eds. *Social History of Women and Gender in the Modern Middle East*. Boulder: Westview Press, 1999.

Meyer, Jean. "Illegitimates and Foundlings in Pre-Industrial France." In *Bastardy and Its Comparative History: Studies in the History of Illegitimacy and Marital Nonconformism in Britain, France, Germany, Sweden, North America, Jamaica, and Japan*, edited by Peter Laslett, Karla Oosterveen, and Richard M. Smith, 249–63. Cambridge: Harvard Univ. Press, 1980.

Midhat Paşa. *Midhat Paşa'nın Hatıraları: Hayatım İbret Olsun [Tabsıra-i ibret]*. Edited by Osman Selim Kocahanoğlu. Istanbul: Temel Yayınları, 1997.

Milanich, Nara. "The *Casa de Huerfanos* and Child Circulation in Late-Nineteenth-Century Chile." *Journal of Social History* 38, no. 2 (2004): 311–40.

Miller, Ruth A. "The Ottoman and Islamic Substratum of Turkey's Swiss Civil Code." *Journal of Islamic Studies* 11, no. 3 (2000): 335–61.

Miller, Timothy S. *The Orphans of Byzantium: Child Welfare in the Christian Empire*. Washington, D.C.: Catholic Univ. of America Press, 2003.

Mitchell, Timothy. *Colonising Egypt*. Cambridge: Cambridge Univ. Press, 1988.

————. *Rule of Experts: Egypt, Techno-Politics, Modernity.* Berkeley: Univ. of California Press, 2002.

Motzki, Harald. "Child Marriage in Seventeenth-Century Palestine." In *Islamic Legal Interpretation: Muftis and Their Fatwas,* edited by Muhammad Khalid Masud, Brinkley Messick, and David S. Powers, 129–40. Cambridge: Harvard Univ. Press, 1996.

Moutassem-Mimouni, Badra. *Naissances et abandons en Algérie.* Paris: Éd. Karthala, 2001.

Murdoch, Lydia. *Imagined Orphans: Poor Families, Child Welfare, and Contested Citizenship in London.* New Brunswick: Rutgers Univ. Press, 2006.

Murray, John (Firm), and Charles William Wilson. *Handbook for Travellers in Asia Minor, Transcaucasia, Persia, Etc.* London: J. Murray, 1895.

Naumović, Slobodan, and Miroslav Jovanović, eds. *Childhood in South East Europe: Historical Perspectives on Growing Up in the 19th and 20th Century.* Belgrade: Graz, 2001.

Nesin, Aziz. *Böyle Gelmiş Böyle Gitmez 1: Yol.* Istanbul: Adam, 1996.

Nomer, Engin. *Vatandaşlık Hukuku.* Istanbul: Filiz Kitabevi, 1989.

d'Ohsson, Mouradgea. *Tableau Général de l'Empire Othoman: Divisé en Deux Parties, dont l'une Comprend la Législation Mahométane; l'Autre, l'Histoire de l'Empire Othoman,* vols. 1–5. Istanbul: Les Editions ISIS, 2001.

Okay, Cüneyd. *Belgelerle Himaye-i Etfal Cemiyeti 1917–1923.* Istanbul: Şule Yayınları 1999.

————. *Eski Harfli Çocuk Dergileri.* Istanbul: Kitabevi Yayınevi, 1999.

————. "İki Çocuk Dergisinin Rekabeti ve Müslüman Boykotajı." *Toplumsal Tarih* 44 (1997): 42–45.

————. *Meşrutiyet Çocukları.* Istanbul: Bordo Yayınları, 2000.

————. *Meşrutiyet Dönemi Çocuk Edebiyatı.* Istanbul: Medyatek Yayınları, 2002.

————. *Osmanlı Çocuk Hayatında Yenileşmeler 1850–1900.* Istanbul: Kırkambar Yayınları 1998.

————. "Politics and Children's Literature in the Late Ottoman Empire 1908–1918 Using Children's Poetry to Create a Nationalistic/Patriotic Generation." *Journal of Turkish Studies* 28, no. 3 (2004): 177–90.

————. "Tedrisat-i İbtidaiyye Mecmuası." *Müteferrika* 19 (2001): 131–42.

————. "Türkiye'de Çocuk Tarihi: Tespitler—Öneriler." *Kebikeç* 19 (2005): 121–27.

Okkenhaug, Inger Marie. *The Quality of Heroic Living, of High Endeavour and Adventure: Anglican Mission, Women and Education in Palestine, 1888–1948.* Leiden: Brill, 2002.

————, and Nefissa Neguib, eds. *Interpreting Welfare and Relief in the Middle East.* Leiden: Brill, 2008.

Önsoy, Rıfat. "Tanzimat Dönemi Sanayileşme Politikası, 1839–1876." *Hacettepe Üniversitesi Edebiyat Fakültesi Dergisi* 2, no. 2 (1984): 5–12.

Onur, Bekir, ed. *Anılardaki Aşklar: Çocukluğun ve Gençliğin Psikoseksüel Tarihi.* Istanbul: Kitap Yayınevi, 2005.

————. *Çocuk Kültürü.* Ankara: Ankara Üniversitesi Çocuk Kültürü Araştırma ve Uygulama Merkezi Yayınları, 1997.

————. *Çocuk Tarih ve Toplum.* Ankara: İmge, 2007.

————. *Cumhuriyet ve Çocuk.* Ankara: Ankara Üniversitesi Çocuk Kültürü Araştırma ve Uygulama Merkezi Yayınları, 1999.

————. *Dünyada ve Türkiye'de Değişen Çocukluk.* Ankara: Ankara Üniversitesi Çocuk Kültürü Araştırma ve Uygulama Merkezi Yayınları, 2001.

————. *Oyuncaklı Dünya: Toplumsal Tarih Üzerine Eğlenceli Bir Deneme.* Ankara: Dost Kitabevi, 2002.

————. *Toplumsal Tarihte Çocuk: Sempozyum, 23–24 Nisan 1993.* Istanbul: Tarih Vakfı Yurt Yayınları, 1994.

————. *Türkiye'de Çocukluğun Tarihi.* Ankara: İmge, 2005.

Orme, Nicholas. *Medieval Children.* New Haven: Yale Univ. Press, 2001.

Ortaylı, İlber. "Midhat Paşa'nın Vilayet Yönetimindeki Kadroları ve Politikası." In *Uluslararası Midhat Paşa Semineri, Bildiriler ve Tartışmalar. Edirne, 8–10 Mayıs 1984,* 227–33. Ankara: Türk Tarih Kurumu Basımevi, 1986.

Özbay, Ferhunde. "1911–1912 Yıllarında Kimsesiz Kız Çocukları." In *Savaş Çocukları: Öksüzler ve Yetimler,* edited by Emine Gürsoy Naskalı and Aylin Koç, 111–22. Istanbul: s.n., 2003.

————. "Evlerde Elkızları: Cariyeler, Evlatlıklar, Gelinler." In *Feminist Tarihyazımında Sınıf ve Cinsiyet,* edited by Leonore Davidoff and Ayşe Durakbaşa, 13–48. Istanbul: İletişim, 2002.

————. "Gendered Space: A New Look at Turkish Modernization." *Gender and History* 11, no. 3 (November 1999): 555–68.

————. *Turkish Female Child Domestic Workers.* Istanbul: Boğaziçi Üniversitesi Yayınevi,1999.

————. *Türkiye'de Evlatlık Kurumu: Köle mi Evlat mı?.* Istanbul: Boğaziçi Üniversitesi Yayınevi, 1999.

————. "Türkiye'de Evlatlık Kurumu: Köle mi Evlat mı?" In *International Conference on History of Turkish Republic: A Reassessment, Volume II, Economy, Society and Environment,* 277–88. Istanbul: Tarih Vakfı Yurt Yayınları, 1998.

————. "Türkiye'de Kadın ve Çocuk Emeği." *Toplum ve Bilim* 53 (1991): 41–54.

Özbek, Nadir. "II. Abdülhamid ve Kimsesiz Çocuklar: Darülhayr-ı Âlî." *Tarih ve Toplum* 31, no. 182 (1999): 11–21.

————. "II. Meşrutiyet İstanbul'unda Dilenciler ve Serseriler." *Toplumsal Tarih* 64 (1999): 34–43.

————. *Osmanlı İmparatorluğu'nda Sosyal Devlet: Siyaset, İktidar ve Meşruiyet 1876–1914*. Istanbul: İletişim Yayınları, 2002.

————. "Osmanlı İmparatorluğu'nda 'Sosyal Yardım' Uygulamaları, 1839–1918." *Toplum ve Bilim* 83 (2000): 111–32.

————. "Philanthropic Activity, Ottoman Patriotism, and The Hamidian Regime, 1876–1909." *IJMES* 37, no. 1 (2005): 59–81.

————. "Policing the Countryside: Gendarmes of the Late-Nineteenth-Century Ottoman Empire (1876–1908)." *IJMES* 40, no. 1(2008): 47–67.

————. "The Politics of Poor Relief in the Late Ottoman Empire: 1876–1914." *New Perspectives on Turkey* 21 (1999): 1–33.

Pamuk, Şevket. *The Ottoman Empire and European Capitalism, 1820–1913*. New York: Cambridge Univ. Press, 1987.

Peirce, Leslie. *Morality Tales: Law and Gender in the Ottoman Court of Aintab*. Berkeley: Univ. of California Press, 2003.

Peri, Oded. "Waqf and Ottoman Welfare Policy: the Poor Kitchen of Hasseki Sultan in Eighteenth Century Jerusalem." *Journal of Economic and Social History of the Orient* 35 (1992): 167–86.

Peters, Rudolph. *Crime and Punishment in Islamic Law: Theory in Practice from the Sixteenth to the Twenty-First Century*. Cambridge: Cambridge University Press, 2006.

————. "Islamic and Secular Criminal Law in Nineteenth Century Egypt: The Role and Function of the Qadi." *Islamic Law and Society* 4, no. 1 (1997): 70–90.

Petrov, Milen V. "Everyday Forms of Compliance: Subaltern Commentaries on Ottoman Reform, 1864–1868." *Comparative Studies in Society and History* 46, no. 4 (2004): 730–59.

————. "Tanzimat for the Countryside: Midhat Paşa and the Vilayet of Danube, 1864–1868." Ph.D. diss., Princeton Univ., 2006.

Piolet, Père J. B. *La France au Dehors Les Missions Catholiques Françaises au XIXe Siècle, Tome Premier, Missions d'Orient*. Paris: Librairie Armand Colin, 1900.

Pollock, Linda A. *Forgotten Children: Parent-Child Relations from 1500 to 1900*. Cambridge: Cambridge Univ. Press, 1983.

Pour l'Arménie et la Macédoine. Paris, 1904.

Powell, Eve M. Troutt. "Slaves or Siblings? Abdallah al-Nadim's Dialogues About the Family." In *Histories of the Modern Middle East: New Directions,* edited by Israel Gershoni, Hakan Erdem, and Ursula Woköck, 155–65. London: Lynne Rienner, 2002.

———. "Will That Subaltern Ever Speak?: Finding African Slaves in the Historiography of the Middle East." In *Middle East Historiographies: Narrating the Twentieth-Century,* edited by Israel Gershoni, Amy Singer, and Hakan Erdem, 242–61. Seattle: Univ. of Washington Press, 2006.

Pryor, Elizabeth Brown. *Clara Barton: Professional Angel.* Philadelphia: Univ. of Pennsylvania Press, 1987.

Al-Qattan, Najwa. "Dhimmis in the Muslim Court: Legal Autonomy and Religious Discrimination." *IJMES* 31, no. 3 (1999): 429–44.

Quataert, Donald, ed. *Manufacturing in the Ottoman Empire and Turkey, 1500–1950.* Albany: State Univ. of New York Press, 1994.

———. *Miners and the State in the Ottoman Empire: The Zonguldak Coalfield.* New York: Berghahn, 2006.

———. *The Ottoman Empire, 1700–1922.* New York: Cambridge Univ. Press, 2000.

———. *Ottoman Manufacturing in the Age of the Industrial Revolution.* Cambridge: Cambridge Univ. Press, 1993.

Rahikainen, Marjatta. *Centuries of Child Labor: European Experiences from the Seventeenth to the Twentieth Century.* Hampshire: Ashgate, 2004.

Ransel, David. *Mothers of Misery: Child Abandonment in Russia.* Princeton: Princeton Univ. Press, 1988.

Redhouse, James William. *Redhouse's Turkish Dictionary, in two parts, English and Turkish, and Turkish and English.* London: B. Quaritch, 1880.

Roche, Max. *Education, Assistance et Culture Française dans l'Empire Ottoman, 1748–1868.* Istanbul: Les Edition Isis, 1989.

Rodrigue, Aron. *De l'Instruction à l'Emancipation: les Enseignants de l'Alliance Israélite Universelle et les Juifs d'Orient.* Paris: Calmann-Levy, 1989.

Rogan, Eugene L. *Frontiers of the State in the Late Ottoman Empire: Transjordan, 1850–1921.* Cambridge: Cambridge Univ. Press, 1999.

Rothman, David J. *The Discovery of the Asylum: Social Order and Disorder in the New Republic.* New York: Aldine de Gruyter, 2002.

Rubin, Avi. "Ottoman Modernity: The Nizamiye Courts in the Late Nineteenth Century." Ph.D. diss., Harvard Univ., 2006.

Rugh, Andrea B. "Orphanages in Egypt: Contradiction or Affirmation in a Family-Oriented Society." In *Children in the Muslim Middle East*, edited by Elizabeth Warnock Fernea, 124–41. Austin: Univ. of Texas Press, 1995.

Sablayrolles, Élisabeth. *L'Enfance abandonnée à Strasbourg au XVIIIe siècle et la fondation de la Maison des enfants-trouvés*. Strasbourg: Librairie ISTRA, 1976.

Sabra, Adam. *Poverty and Charity in Medieval Islam: Mamluk Egypt, 1250–1517*. New York: Cambridge Univ. Press, 2000.

Safford, Philip L., and Elizabeth J. Safford. *Children with Disabilities in America: A Historical Handbook and Guide*. Westport: Greenwood Press, 2006.

Sakaoğlu, Necdet. *Osmanlı'dan Günümüze Eğitim Tarihi*. Istanbul: Bilgi Üniversitesi Yayınları, 2003.

Sanchez-Eppler, Karen. *Dependent States: The Child's Part in Nineteenth-Century American Culture*. Chicago: Univ. of Chicago Press, 2005.

Sarc, Ömer Celal. "Tanzimat ve Sanayiimiz." In *Tanzimat: Yüzüncü Yıldönümü Münasebetiyle*, 423–40. Istanbul: Maarif Matbaası, 1940.

Schacht, Joseph. *An Introduction to Islamic Law*. Oxford: Clarendon Press, 1982.

Schull, Kent F. *Prisons in the Late Ottoman Empire: Microcosms of Modernity*. Edinburgh: Edinburgh University Press, 2014.

———. "Tutuklu Sayımı: Jön Türklerin Sistematik Bir Şekilde Hapishane İstatistikleri Toplama Çalışmaları ve Bunların 1911–1918 Hapishane Reformu Üzerine Etkileri." In *Osmanlı'da Asayiş, Suç ve Ceza: 18.–20. Yüzyıllar*, edited by Noémi Lévy and Alexandre Toumarkine, 212–38. Istanbul: Tarih Vakfı, Yurt Yayınları, 2007.

Scott, Joan Wallach. *Gender and the Politics of History*. New York: Columbia University Press, 1988.

Semiz, Yaşar, and Recai Kuş. "Osmanlıda Mesleki Teknik Eğitim: İstanbul Sanayi Mektebi (1869–1930)." *Selçuk Üniversitesi Türkiyat Araştırmaları Dergisi* 15 (2004): 275–95.

Şen, Ömer. "19. Yüzyılda Osmanlı Devleti'ndeki Köle Ticaretinde Kafkasya Göçmenlerinin Rolü." In *Dünü ve Bugünüyle Toplum ve Ekonomi*, 171–92. Bağlam Yayınları: Istanbul, 1994.

Sherwood, Joan. *Poverty in Eighteenth-Century Spain: The Women and Children of the Inclusa*. Toronto: Univ. of Toronto Press, 1988.

Shorter, Edward. *The Making of the Modern Family*. London: William Collins, 1976.

Simon, Rachel. *Change within Tradition among Jewish Women in Libya*. Seattle: Univ. of Washington Press, 1992.

Singer, Amy. *Constructing Ottoman Beneficence: An Imperial Soup Kitchen in Jerusalem*. Albany: State Univ. of New York Press, 2002.

———. "Serving Up Charity: The Ottoman Public Kitchen." *Journal of Interdisciplinary History* 35, no. 3 (2005): 481–500.

Şişman, Adnan. *Tanzimat Döneminde Fransa'ya Gönderilen Osmanlı Öğrencileri (1839–1876)*. Ankara: Türk Tarih Kurumu, 2004.

Somel, Selçuk Akşin. *The Modernization of Public Education in the Ottoman Empire, 1839–1908: Islamization, Autocracy and Discipline*. Leiden: Brill, 2001.

———. "Regulations for Raising Children during the Hamidian Period." In *Enfance et Jeunesse dans le Monde Musulman/Childhood and Youth in the Muslim World*, edited by François Georgeon and Klaus Kreiser, 211–17. Paris: Maisonneuve & Larose, 2007.

Sonbol, Amira al-Azhary. "Adoption in Islamic Society: A Historical Survey." In *Children in the Muslim Middle East*, edited by Elizabeth Warnock Fernea, 45–67. Austin: Univ. of Texas Press, 1995.

———. "Rape and Law in Ottoman and Modern Egypt." In *Women in the Ottoman Empire: Middle Eastern Women in the Early Modern Era*, edited by Madeline C. Zilfi, 214–31. Leiden: Brill, 1997.

Spagnolo, John P. "The Definition of a Style of Imperialism: The Internal Politics of the French Educational Investment in Ottoman Beirut." *French Historical Studies* 8, no. 4 (1974): 563–84.

Stoler, Ann Laura. *Race and the Education of Desire*. Durham: Duke Univ. Press, 1995.

Stone, Lawrence. *The Family, Sex, and Marriage in England 1500–1800*. London: Wiedenfield & Nicolson, 1977.

Strauss, Johann. "Who Read What in the Ottoman Empire (19th–20th Centuries)?" *Middle Eastern Literatures* 6, no. 1 (2003): 39–76.

Sujimon, M. S. "The Treatment of the Foundling (al-laqit) according to the Hanafis." *Islamic Law and Society* 9, no. 3 (2002): 358–85.

Summary of the Reports of Stations of the Mission of the A.B.C.F.M. to Western Turkey Presented at The Annual Meeting, May, 1901, with Map, Statistical Tables and a List of Names of Missionaries. Gloucester: John Bellows, 1901.

Talay, Aydın. *Eserleri ve Hizmetleriyle Sultan Abdülhamid*. Istanbul: Risale, 1991.

Tan, Mine Göğüş. "Bir Genç Kız Yetişiyor: Düriye Köprülü'nün Çocukluğu." *Tarih ve Toplum* 207 (2001): 39–46.

———. "Çağlar Boyunca Çocukluk." *Ankara Üniversitesi Eğitim Bilimleri Fakültesi Dergisi* 22, no. 1 (1990): 71–88.

———. "Cumhuriyet'te Çocuktular: Bir Sözlü Tarih Projesinden İki Çocuk/İki Kadın." In *Aydınlanmanın Kadınları*, edited by Necla Arat, 144–57. Istanbul: Cumhuriyet Kitapları, 1998.

———. "Erken Cumhuriyet'in Çocuklarıyla Bir Sözlü Tarih Çalışması." In *Cumhuriyet ve Çocuk*, edited by Bekir Onur, 25–33. Ankara: Ankara Üniversitesi Çocuk Kültürü Araştırma ve Uygulama Merkezi Yayınları, 1999.

———. "An Oral History Project with the Children of the Republic." In *XIth International Oral History Conference, vol. 1: Crossroads of History: Experience, Memory, Orality*, 346–55. Istanbul: Boğaziçi Üniversitesi Yayınevi, 2000.

———, Özlem Şahin, Mustafa Sever, and Aksu Bora, eds. *Cumhuriyet'te Çocuktular*. Istanbul: Boğaziçi Üniversitesi Yayınevi, 2007.

Toledano, Ehud R. *As If Silent and Absent: Bonds of Enslavement in the Islamic Middle East*. New Haven: Yale Univ. Press, 2007.

———. *Slavery and Abolition in the Ottoman Middle East*, Seattle: Univ. of Washington Press, 1998.

Tolman, Deborah L. "Doing Desire: Adolescent Girls' Struggles for/with Sexuality." *Gender and Society* 8, no. 3 (1994): 324–42.

Toprak, Zafer. "II. Meşrutiyet Döneminde Paramiliter Gençlik Örgütleri." In *Tanzimattan Cumhuriyet'e Türkiye Ansiklopedisi*, 531–36. Istanbul: İletişim Yayınları, 1985.

———. "İttihat ve Terakki'nin Paramiliter Gençlik Örgütleri." *Boğaziçi Üniversitesi Dergisi—Beşeri Bilimler* 7 (1979): 95–112.

———. "Meşrutiyet ve Mütareke Yıllarında İzcilik." *Toplumsal Tarih* 52 (1998): 13–20.

———. "Taksim Stadında Mini-Olimpiyat 1922." *Toplumsal Tarih* 4 (1994): 15–18.

———. "Vay Em Si Ey (YMCA) Jimnastikhaneleri." *Toplumsal Tarih* 2 (1994): 8–12.

Tucker, Judith E. *In the House of the Law: Gender and Islamic Law in Ottoman Syria and Palestine*. Berkeley: Univ. of California Press, 1998.

———. *Women in Nineteenth-Century Egypt*. Cambridge: Cambridge Univ. Press, 1985.

Ülman, Yeşim Işıl. "Besim Ömer Akalın (1862–1940): ange gardien des femmes et des enfants; L'acclimatation d'un savoir veni d'ailleurs." In *Médecins et ingénieurs ottomans à l'âge des nationalismes*, edited by Méropi Anastassiadou, 101–21. Paris: Maisonneuve & Larose, 2003.

Ulunay, Refi Cevat. *Eski İstanbul Yosmaları*. Istanbul: Arba, 1995.

Unat, Faik Reşit. "Niş Islahhanesinin Kuruluş Tarihini Aydınlatan Bir Belge." *Mesleki ve Teknik Öğretim* 10, no. 114 (1962): 5–6.

Ursinus, Michael. *Grievance Administration (Şikayet) in an Ottoman Province: The Kaymakam Of Rumelia's "Record Book of Complaints" of 1781–1783*. New York: Routledge Curzon, 2005.

Ussher, Clarence D., and Grace H. Knapp. *An American Physician in Turkey: a Narrative of Adventures in Peace and War*. Astoria, N.Y.: J. C. & A. L. Fawcett, 1917.

van de Walle, Etienne. "Illegitimacy in France during the Nineteenth Century." In *Bastardy and Its Comparative History: Studies in the History of Illegitimacy and Marital Nonconformism in Britain, France, Germany, Sweden, North America, Jamaica, and Japan*, edited by Peter Laslett, Karla Oosterveen, and Richard M. Smith, 264–77. Cambridge: Harvard Univ. Press, 1980.

Watenpaugh, Keith. "'Are There Any Children for Sale?': Genocide and the Forced Transfer of Armenian Children (1915–1922)." *Journal of Human Rights* 12, no.3 (2013): 283–95.

———. "The League of Nations' Rescue of Armenian Genocide Survivors and the Making of Modern Humanitarianism (1920–1927)." *American Historical Review* 115, no. 5 (2010): 1315–39.

Wilson, Adrian. "Illegitimacy and Its Implications in Mid-Eighteenth-Century London: The Evidence of the Foundling Hospital." *Continuity and Change* 4 (1989): 103–64.

Wolf, Jacqueline H. *Don't Kill Your Baby: Public Health and the Decline of Breastfeeding in the Nineteenth and Twentieth Centuries*. Columbus: Ohio State Univ. Press, 2001.

Yarman, Arsen. *Osmanlı Sağlık Hizmetlerinde Ermeniler ve Surp Pırgiç Ermeni Hastanesi Tarihi*. Istanbul: Ermeni Hastanesi Vakfı, 2001.

Yazbak, Mahmoud. "Minor Marriages and Khiyar al-Bulugh in Ottoman Palestine: A Note on Women's Strategies in a Patriarchal Society." *Islamic Law and Society* 9, no. 3 (2002): 386–409.

———. "Muslim Orphans and the Sharia in Ottoman Palestine According to Sijill Records." *Journal of Economic and Social History of the Orient* 44 (2001): 123–40.

Yerasimos, Marianna. "16.–19. Yüzyılda Batı Kaynaklı Gravürlerde Osmanlı Çocuk Figürleri." In *Toplumsal Tarihte Çocuk: Sempozyum, 23–24 Nisan 1993*, edited by Bekir Onur, 65–75. Istanbul: Tarih Vakfı Yurt Yayınları, 1994.

Yıldırım, Mustafa. *İslam Hukuku Açısından Evlat Edinme*. Izmir: İzmir İlahiyat Vakfı, 2005.

Yıldırım, Nuran. "İstanbul'un İlk Doğumevi Viladethane." *Hastane Hospital News* 7 (2000): 26–27.

———. *İstanbul Darülaceze Müessesesi Tarihi*. Istanbul: Darülaceze Vakfı, 1997.

―――. "Viladethane." In *İstanbul Ansiklopedisi* 7 (1994): 388–89.

Yılmaz, Fikret. "Portrait d'une Communauté Méconnu: les Musulmans." In *Smyrne, la Ville Oubliée? 1830–1930*, edited by Marie-Carmen Smyrnelis, 52–62. Paris: Autrement, 2006.

Ze'evi, Dror. "Changes in Legal-Sexual Discourses: Sex Crimes in the Ottoman Empire." *Continuity and Change* 16, no. 2 (2001): 219–42.

―――. *Producing Desire: Changing Sexual Discourse in the Ottoman Middle East, 1500–1900*. Berkeley: Univ. of California Press, 2006.

―――. "Women in 17th-Century Jerusalem: Western and Indigenous Perspectives." *IJMES* 27, no. 2 (1995): 157–73.

Ziadeh, Farhat J. "Criminal Law." In *The Oxford Encyclopedia of the Islamic World*, edited by John L. Esposito. New York: Oxford Univ. Press, 1995.

Zilfi, Madeline C. *Women in the Ottoman Empire: Middle Eastern Women in the Early Modern Era*. Leiden: Brill, 1997.

Zohrab, Krikor. *Öyküler*. Translated by Hermon Araks. Istanbul: Aras Yayıncılık, 2001.

Index